THE RAF IN 100 OBJECTS

THE RAF IN 100 OBJECTS

PETER JACOBS

To all those who serve, or have served, in the Royal Air Force.

First published 2017

The History Press
The Mill, Brimscombe Port
Stroud, Gloucestershire, GL5 2QG
www.thehistorypress.co.uk

British Library Cataloguing in Publication Data.
A catalogue record for this book is available from the British Library.

ISBN 978 0 7509 6536 1

Typesetting and origination by The History Press
Printed in Turkey by Imak

Contents

Foreword
by Air Vice-Marshal
Nigel Baldwin CB CBE

SINCE THE THEN director of the British Museum, Neil MacGregor, published his *A History of the World in 100 Objects* to much acclaim in 2011, the idea has caught on. Waterloo in 1815, a history of birdwatching, American sports, the First World War, the history of Norfolk and a wide range of other subjects have been covered so it should come as no surprise that, approaching the Royal Air Force's centenary in 2018, one of the most active of modern RAF historians should take on another '100 Objects' task. He has produced a page-turner.

The author, Wing Commander Peter Jacobs, is widely published on RAF matters. I met him in 1996 when he had just researched the Roll of Honour 1939–45 of the nearly 2,000, mostly aircrew, of 50 and 61 Squadrons who lost their lives in the Second World War strategic bombing campaign. The great majority of them were, but not exclusively, Lancaster aircrew. Every year since then, on a June Sunday, Peter and I have stood together at the Squadrons' memorials at Birchwood near Lincoln (on the site of the Second World War airfield at RAF Skellingthorpe) and in the neighbouring village of Skellingthorpe and joined the villagers and local community leaders to salute the memory of those extraordinary men but also to comfort the small number of survivors – now in their nineties – as they too, with their families, make their annual pilgrimage.

I approached the book with trepidation and soon with a feeling of some shame and inadequacy. I have been fascinated by the RAF's history, achievements and people since a small boy. With the advantage of the RAF College, Cranwell, the RAF Staff College, Bracknell, and service as a pilot on three of the RAF's oldest and most distinguished squadrons (IX, 35 and 50 Squadrons) and having been chairman of the RAF Historical Society for over twenty years behind me, I thought I knew a thing or two about our history. Not a bit of it: for example, Object 3 with its story about the RAF roundel was almost brand new to me – certainly the detail was. As I turned the pages, more and more 'new' things emerged. A photograph of a SE5a windscreen (Object 7) rapidly leads us into the story of Major James McCudden VC, DSO and Bar, MC and Bar, MM who, at 23 years old and after fifty-seven aerial victories, crashed and was killed on take-off while on a simple delivery flight.

Presenting the 100 objects broadly chronologically, the author captures the reader by using an eye-catching title and photograph to move quickly into telling sometimes a complex story with much clarity in only a couple of pages or so. Wing Commander Guy Gibson's office, for example, now restored and back in place at RAF Scampton (Object 39), introduces the reader to the 617 Squadron attack in May 1943 on the German dams. Object 44, a humble aircrew scarf, draws the reader into the Lancaster bomb aimer Les Bartlett's experiences in that awful winter of 1943–44. Les Bartlett was in Flight Lieutenant Mike Beetham's crew. The latter, eventually the longest-serving Chief of the Air Staff after Hugh Trenchard (see Object 2), is introduced by his forage cap – Object 86. Peter Jacobs knew Sir Michael well and published his biography in 2013. Sir Michael was President of the 50/61 Squadrons' Association until the day he died in 2015.

In the latter part of the book, the reader is brought up to date with a fine description of the genesis of and the successful build of the RAF Bomber Command Memorial in London's Green Park which was unveiled by HM the Queen in June 2012 (Object 97) and this story is followed by those of the Red Arrows (Object 98) and that of today's front-line fighter and multi-role aircraft, the Typhoon (Object 99). Peter Jacobs' 100-year summary concludes with the story of the Reaper MQ9A Remotely Piloted Air System (Object 100). When our successors continue this venture in 100 years' time, will that be Object 1 I wonder?

The reader will be struck by the extraordinary advances in aircraft, engines and associated technologies in these 100 years – probably one of the most rapid series of advances in human history. But the reader will also be struck by something that has not changed: the bravery, spirit, determination, and enthusiasm of those who have 'reached for the sky' in defence of their homeland.

This book is a culmination of much study and imaginative enquiry. I defy any reader to 'know it all'. Most will be amazed by the detail and the colour of so many aspects of the RAF's relatively short life. It is a fine product to help mark the centenary on 1 April 2018 and, in addition, will be a splendid way of introducing a new generation to Her Majesty's youngest service.

Air Vice-Marshal Nigel Baldwin CB CBE
Chairman Royal Air Force Historical Society

Introduction

ASK PEOPLE TO name their best ten films, or ten favourite pieces of music, and you will get a different selection of answers from every person you ask. The same would also be true if you asked someone to select 100 objects that told the history of the RAF through its 100 years. And so, that was the position I found myself in more than two years ago, when first asked to write this book. I felt privileged, of course, to be given the opportunity to do so, but just where should I start and what should I include?

As I thought more about it, I became increasingly convinced that while individual lists might differ several of the objects would at least be common in theme. For example, I would be surprised if an aircraft such as the Spitfire or Lancaster was missing, or if the Battle of Britain or Dambusters were not included, or if the Red Arrows were not mentioned, or if some of the RAF's great names from the past were not represented in some way: leaders like Hugh Trenchard, often referred to as the founder of the RAF, Hugh Dowding and Arthur Harris, who had respectively ensured Britain's survival and then paved the way to victory during the Second World War, and legendary wartime pilots such as Douglas Bader and Guy Gibson. There were always going to be certain parts of the RAF's long and distinguished history that I felt needed to be included in the book, but would I be able to find suitable objects? This, I felt, would be the biggest challenge of all. And I was right.

There is so much to tell and, for a start, the RAF is not all about aircraft. Indeed, I did not want the 100 Objects to become a book of aircraft – it could so easily have become that – and so I wanted to find many different types of objects that would collectively allow me to tell the story – for example, buildings, vehicles, publications, weapons, uniforms, specialist clothing and equipment, to name but a few. Furthermore, the RAF is a way of life and so I wanted to include objects that helped me cover the ethos and culture of the service, such as music, sport and faith. And, of course, the RAF has always been about its people and so I wanted to find objects that helped me tell the occasional personal story along the way. Because an important part of service life is remembering the past, I wanted to include objects of remembrance and reunion. I also wanted to cover the many different capabilities of the RAF and include other important aspects of the service, such as the role played by women over the years, the value of the reserves and the importance of cadets. I was also mindful from the outset that the book had to be balanced and so the 100 objects would have to be spread across 100 years. For example, I did not want a disproportionate number of personal items from the Second World War at the expense of other significant periods of the RAF's history – such as the immediate aftermath of the First World War, when the newly formed RAF had to fight for its survival, the policing of the Empire and the development of high-speed flight during the interwar years, and the Berlin airlift, the dawn of the jet age and the Cold War in the difficult years following the Second World War. I could go on but I am sure you get the idea.

The challenge of trying to achieve all of this is obvious, but it was then a matter of going around the country to look for suitable objects. I wanted them to come from as many different places as I could to show just how the RAF's legacy is being preserved. What I found, in general terms, was that objects tend to be in one of four different types of place. Firstly, they are in museums. The most obvious, of course, are the large national museums, such as the RAF Museums at Hendon and Cosford, the Imperial War Museums (London, Duxford and Manchester), the Science Museum in London and the National Museum of Flight in Scotland. But I also knew there to be many other small museums and collections across the country, usually run by volunteers, where visitors can go to learn about the past. These might only be open at specific times of the year or on certain days of the week, but the Internet is a marvellous tool to seek them out and plan a visit. And so, I went to as many of these as I could in search of finding something that might be different or could not be seen elsewhere. I felt that if I could include just one object from as many of these locations as possible, it would help raise the profile of these marvellous places. The second place to look for objects is on RAF stations. This was particularly rewarding for me. There was more to be found than I expected and it was pleasing to see heritage centres and memorial rooms established on so many bases. These can usually be made accessible to the public with prior arrangement. The third category of where to look is in public places (other than museums), such as in parks. Admittedly, finding objects in this category is not easy and they tend to be memorials, with the focal point often being in London, but they do exist. The final category, and this applies mostly to personal items of interest, is in family or private collections. I wanted to make sure that as few objects as possible fell into this category because I wanted most of the 100 objects included in the story to be accessible to the public.

Having finally found plenty of wonderful objects, far more than are included here, it was then a case of deciding what should be included and what, sadly, would have to be missed. After all, the book is titled *The RAF in 100 Objects* and so 100 objects it had to be. Decisions had to be made and they were not easy. But having eventually decided on the final 100, I then had to decide how best to present them. There were at least a couple of ways this could have been done, but in the end I felt the story simply had to be told broadly chronologically – from the birth of the RAF to what it has become today. This is done in sections, starting in the latter stages of the First World War when German attacks on London ultimately led to the formation of the RAF. The sections then follow the fledgling new service through the interwar years as it built solid foundations for the future. By the Second World War it was fully established alongside its Royal Navy and army counterparts, and if anyone needed reminding of just how vital the RAF was for the nation's security then the Battle of Britain surely provided that defining moment. Then, with the country at peace once more, the RAF entered a new and exciting period of the jet age, but peace was not guaranteed for long and soon came the Cold War. The years that followed proved to be tense and uncertain, with the RAF at the centre of the nation's nuclear deterrent, before the Iron Curtain finally came down. Since then, the RAF has been involved in campaigns and conflicts across the world, either when the UK has operated alone or as part of a coalition force or alliance. The contrast between the first object and the last gives a good indication of just how far the RAF has come.

As its centenary, 2018 marks a significant year for the RAF. It is a milestone that many a century ago could never have foreseen. I feel immensely proud to have served through thirty-seven of those years – more than one-third of the RAF's history – during which I got to know the service very well. As I said at the start, we will all have our own ideas about what should be included in the 100 objects and what should be left out. These are my 100 objects of choice. Each helps tell a small part of what is a massive story to tell. Collectively, I believe they do. Enjoy the book!

Peter Jacobs

2017

Part 1
The First Year

REPORT BY GENERAL SMUTS ON AIR ORGANISATION

AND THE DIRECTION OF AERIAL OPERATIONS

August, 1917.

        Our first report dealt with the defence of the
London area against air raids.

        We proceed to deal in this report with the second
term of reference: the Air organisation generally and
the Direction of Air Operations. For the considerations
which will appear in the course of this report we consider
the early settlement of this matter of vital importance
to the successful prosecution of the war. The three most
important questions which press for an early answer are:-

1.   Shall there be instituted a real Air Ministry
      responsible for all Air Organisation and
      operations.

2.   Shall there be constituted a unified Air
      Service embracing both the present R.N.A.S.
      and R F.C? And if this second question is
      answered in the affirmative, the third
      question arises:-

3.   How shall the relations of the new Air
      Service to the Navy and the Army be
      determined so that the functions at present
      discharged for them by the R.N.A.S. and
      R.F.C. respectively shall continue to be
      efficiently performed by the new Air Service?

1

The Smuts Report

DECIDING WHAT SHOULD be object number one, and, therefore, what should start the story of the Royal Air Force's 100 years, was never going to be easy. People will have their own ideas but I have decided to go for a simple document, known as the Smuts Report, as it was this report that was instrumental in leading to the formation of the Royal Air Force.

With German bombing of London during 1917 causing public outrage, the British Prime Minister, David Lloyd George, commissioned a report for the Imperial War Cabinet – comprising the prime ministers and other senior officials of the Commonwealth nations – to co-ordinate military policy. The report was to be prepared by the prominent South African military leader, General Jan Smuts, and was to report on two key issues: firstly, to address the arrangements for Home Defence against the increasing number of enemy bombing raids on Britain and, secondly, to address the air organisation in general and the direction of aerial operations.

In response to the latter, Smuts recommended the establishment of a separate air service. It was a recommendation that was to be accepted by the War Cabinet, with Smuts then asked to lead an Air Organisation Committee to put the recommendation into effect. Much of the detailed work was led by Lieutenant General Sir David Henderson, a senior leader of British military aviation during the First World War, and in early 1918 Lord Rothermere was appointed as the first Secretary of State for Air, with the establishment of an Air Council. And so, it was the Smuts Report, which had recommended the creation of a single air force to hit back at Germany, that led to the amalgamation of the Royal Flying Corps (RFC)

Country of Origin:
UK
Date:
August 1917
Location:
RAF Museum
Hendon, London
(© RAF Museum)

and the Royal Naval Air Service (RNAS) on 1 April 1918 to become the Royal Air Force (RAF) under the newly created Air Ministry.

The RAF was the world's first independent air force (i.e., it was independent of army or navy control) and by the end of the First World War it had become the most powerful air force in the world with some 22,000 aircraft and more than 313,000 personnel (there had been just over 2,000 serving with the RFC and RNAS at the outbreak of war). However, the RAF had only been considered a temporary organisation on its formation, and for the next few months its future was uncertain. It would not be until the dust had settled long after the First World War was over that the cabinet decided to retain the country's third service – although the RAF was to be reduced in strength to 35,000. The rest, as they say, is history.

2

Trenchard's Boots

AT FIRST GLANCE, a pair of boots might not seem particularly interesting or historic but in this case the boots belonged to Marshal of the Royal Air Force Hugh Montague Trenchard, 1st Viscount Trenchard GCB OM GCVO DSO, a man often remembered as the Father of the Royal Air Force and a name that has become synonymous with the RAF and its strategic use of air power. If it was the Smuts Report that was instrumental in leading to the formation of the RAF, then it was the vision of Trenchard that made it work.

Trenchard was a former army officer. Born in Taunton in 1873, he had served as a young man in India and the Boer War, as well as West Africa where he commanded the Southern Nigeria Regiment. Encouraged by a colleague, he learned to fly in 1912 at the age of 39. Although he was no youngster, Trenchard quickly gained his aviator's certificate with just a couple of weeks of tuition and not much more than an hour spent in the air. At the outbreak of the First World War he was given command of the Military Wing with responsibility for the RFC at home, specifically for the training of replacement personnel and the raising of new squadrons for service overseas. But Trenchard was disappointed to have been left at home. He was keen to get to the front line and finally got his chance when he was given command of the RFC's First Wing in France. Then, in 1915, he was promoted to brigadier to command the RFC in the field, an appointment he held for more than two years and during which he was further promoted to the rank of major general.

When the decision was made to form the RAF, Trenchard was the man chosen to lead it. With his background, it can clearly be seen why. He understood the

Country of Origin: UK
Date: 1918
Location: RAF College Cranwell, Lincolnshire (By kind permission of the Commandant RAF College Cranwell)

importance of co-ordination between land and air assets, particularly when carrying out offensive air operations, and he also realised the importance of morale; not only the morale of those under his command but the effect that air power could have on the morale of his enemy.

In January 1918, Trenchard was summoned back from France, knighted and appointed Chief of the Air Staff (CAS) on the newly formed Air Council. The days leading up to the official formation of the RAF were never going to be easy but following weeks of disagreements with Lord Rothermere, Trenchard resigned and returned to France. For the final few months of the war he commanded the newly formed Independent Force, a strategic bomber force made up of day and night squadrons that were tasked with striking at key targets without co-ordination with the other services.

Trenchard had been replaced as CAS by Major General Frederick Sykes but when Winston Churchill became Secretary of State for War and Air in 1919 he was reinstated as CAS. It was an appointment Trenchard would hold for the next eleven years. He worked tirelessly in the immediate aftermath of war to establish the RAF in time of peace and to secure its future by finding a permanent role for his new service. It was a sizeable task. The RAF was only budgeted to around 10 per cent of its wartime establishment, both in terms of squadrons and manpower, and so he had to fend off the other services to prevent the RAF from being absorbed back into the army and the Royal Navy.

With a new rank structure in place, Trenchard first became an air vice-marshal and then an air marshal, and in 1920 an opportunity came along for him to show the value of air power when he successfully argued that the RAF should take the lead to restore peace in Somaliland. Although a small air

Marshal of the Royal Air Force Hugh Montague Trenchard, 1st Viscount Trenchard. (AHB)

operation, its success allowed Trenchard to put forward his case for the RAF to police the British Empire and, soon after, the RAF was given control of British forces in Iraq while also policing India's North-West Frontier.

Meanwhile back home, Trenchard's long-term vision for the RAF included the creation of its own institutions to develop an air force for the future and to engender an *esprit de corps*, and amongst his early successes were the founding of the RAF Cadet College at Cranwell, the Aircraft Apprentice scheme at Halton and the RAF Staff College at Andover. He was also quick to expand the RAF's strength with the creation of the Auxiliary Air Force (a reserve force) and he also instigated the University Air Squadron (UAS) scheme with the first three UAS squadrons formed at Oxford, Cambridge and London.

Trenchard had succeeded in securing the RAF's future. He became the first person to hold the rank of marshal of the Royal Air Force and continued as CAS until replaced by Sir John Salmond at the beginning of 1930. Trenchard was then created Baron of Wolfeton, entering the House of Lords as the RAF's first peer. He always maintained a keen interest in military affairs and remained a strong supporter of the RAF for the rest of his life. Trenchard died in 1956 at the age of 83, but he had never forgotten the importance of Cranwell and so his family gave some of his personal belongings, including these boots, to the RAF College.

So much is owed to Trenchard's vision and strength of character. Almost single-handedly he successfully fought off the seemingly endless attacks by the other services in order to keep the RAF in existence and to give it an enduring sense of pride that has lasted to this day.

3

RAF Roundel

THE RAF ROUNDEL is iconic and is known today all over the world. Essentially, the roundel has remained unchanged from its origins dating back to the early days of the First World War when the need to identify the nationality of an aircraft had first become apparent.

Early ideas of marking the nationality of an aircraft included painting the union flag but this proved unsatisfactory and so the RAF adopted a similar idea to the concentric circles used by the French. Although the colours of the union flag were maintained, the red, white and blue of the French markings were reversed so that the outer circle of the British marking was blue and its inner circle red. Initially the blue, white and red concentric circles of the British roundel were painted on the side of the fuselage, aft of the cockpit, and on the underside of the aircraft – as can clearly be seen on Object 4 – so that ground forces could clearly identify the aircraft's nationality. But as the war progressed the circles were also painted on the upper surface of the top wing so that they could be seen during aerial engagements or if the aircraft was manoeuvring when close to the ground.

Affectionately known during its early days as 'the target', the RAF roundel has been modified over the years with several variations seen. For example, during the interwar years the inner circle was reduced to not much more than a red dot whereas after the Second World War its diameter was increased so much that the white circle could barely be seen at all. There were also many variations of the roundel during the Second World War. One used an outer yellow ring of variable thickness, outside of the blue, to make the roundel even more visible against the various camouflage schemes of aircraft, while another variation was in the Far East where RAF aircraft carried just two colours: a blue

outer circle and a grey-blue inner. This was a different colour scheme altogether and used to differentiate between RAF aircraft and those of the Japanese, which wore the markings of a red circle.

In more recent years the RAF roundel has appeared in three main formats: a dark blue outer circle and a red inner (i.e., with no white circle at all) as seen on camouflaged aircraft and helicopters; a toned down pale blue outer and red inner circle for reduced visibility, such as on aircraft camouflaged in air defence grey; and the traditional blue, white and red roundel as seen on some transport and all training aircraft – an example of which is shown here on the fuselage of a Jet Provost trainer at RAF Cranwell.

Country of Origin: UK
Date: 1918
Location: RAF College Cranwell, Lincolnshire

4

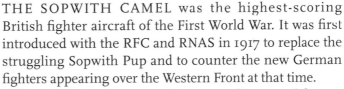

Sopwith Camel

THE SOPWITH CAMEL was the highest-scoring British fighter aircraft of the First World War. It was first introduced with the RFC and RNAS in 1917 to replace the struggling Sopwith Pup and to counter the new German fighters appearing over the Western Front at that time.

The Camel was so named because of the metal fairing 'hump' over the breeches of its twin machine guns. The design was intended to protect the guns from freezing at altitude and for the first time on a British fighter the machine guns were mounted directly in front of the cockpit and synchronised to fire through the propeller disc. Otherwise, the Camel's design, with its wooden and quite bulky box-style fuselage, was conventional for its time, although the aircraft was reportedly difficult to fly. This was because of the close placement of the engine, pilot, guns and fuel, as well as the power of its 9-cylinder rotary engine, which gave the aircraft a top speed of 115mph (185km/h) and an operating altitude up to 21,000ft (6,400m). Nonetheless, in the right hands, the Camel was highly manoeuvrable and proved to be an excellent fighter, and by the end of the war nearly 1,300 enemy aircraft had fallen to its guns – more than to any other Allied aircraft.

The Camel was not only a very good day fighter but it proved versatile enough to be used for night fighting, as well as supporting the army on the ground. Indeed, during the latter period of the war the RAF operated the Camel as a ground-attack aircraft, mainly because newer and better performing German fighters were arriving in great numbers over the Western Front.

By the time production came to an end, nearly 5,500 Camels of all types had been built. Its replacement, the

Country of Origin: UK
Date: 1917
Location: RAF Museum Hendon, London
(© RAF Museum)

Royal Flying Corps
Sopwith F1 Camel

Sopwith Snipe, entered operational service during the final weeks of the war and would remain the RAF's standard post-war single-seat fighter until the mid-1920s.

The Sopwith F1 Camel shown in the main image was probably built by Boulton & Paul at Norwich and sold as war surplus during the early 1920s. It was part of the renowned Nash Collection from 1936 and later restored at Heathrow airport between 1958 and 1962. It is now on display in the Grahame-White Factory at the RAF Museum Hendon.

5

Hythe MkIII Camera Gun

A RATHER UNUSUAL and rare object is this Hythe MkIII camera gun, which was used to train pilots and rear gunners in air-to-air fighting.

Designed in 1916 at the RFC's gunnery school at Hythe in Kent, and produced by Thornton-Pickard of Altrincham, this MkIII was the main production version. It was based on the chassis of the Lewis gun, and of the same weight, and could either be mounted on the top wing of single-seat fighters and operated by the pilot using Bowden cables or, in the case of two-seat aircraft, could be mounted on the rear gunner's Scarff ring (a type of machine gun mounting developed by Warrant Officer F.W. Scarff).

The mechanism can be divided into three parts: the barrel containing the lens and shutter; the middle section containing the film and film-advance mechanism; and the rear section containing the release. The shutter is connected to the release mechanism by a wire and coiled springs. When the release is operated, the wire is pulled to open the shutter; another spring closes the shutter.

Country of Origin: UK
Date: 1916
Location: RAF Waddington Heritage Centre, Lincolnshire (By kind permission of the Station Commander RAF Waddington)

The camera gun was fitted with the same round drum magazine as the Lewis gun, which could be changed after each firing, as per the original gun, so that operation was as close to the real thing as possible. To operate the camera was simple. Cocking the gun wound the film and operating the trigger took a photo, and so the camera gun could be 'fired' at other aircraft and targets without using ammunition; instead, the photos would later be assessed to judge the operator's aim.

The Hythe MkIII remained in service until 1934 when replaced by the Williamson camera gun, although some are known to have still been in use during the early days of the Second World War. How many homes the example

The camera gun shown
mounted on the rear
gunner's Scarff ring.
(RAF Waddington
Heritage Centre)

shown here had is unknown, but it is believed to have
been used to train air gunnery on 503 (County of Lincoln)
Squadron at RAF Waddington between the wars.

6

First Edition of the Air Force List

THE AIR FORCE List is an important publication for many reasons, not least for historical purposes because it provides us with a record of all officers serving with the RAF at specific times, and the branch structure under which they served, and helps us trace information about individual officers when researching their career.

Shown here is the historic first edition of the Air Force List as published by the newly created Air Ministry in April 1918 (corrected to 1 February 1918). The first paragraph of the opening notes page, written by the secretary at the Air Ministry, is interesting:

> The rules adopted for drawing up the Air Force List are arbitrary and only for the purpose of amalgamating the two Flying Services, and will not necessarily be followed after the Air Force has been formed.

The notes go on to state:

> It is realised that in the case of certain officers who hold temporary rank only, their grading, although in the correct rank, gives them an incorrect position in the list of that rank. In order that the publication of the Air Force List may not be delayed, these errors are left for future adjustment. Further, owing to errors, it may be found necessary to alter the ranks and positions in which officers are shown on the Gradation List, and the Air Council reserve to themselves the right to do so, should occasion arise.

Country of Origin: UK
Date: April 1918
Location: RAF College Cranwell, Lincolnshire (By kind permission of the Commandant RAF College Cranwell)

Notwithstanding the notes above, this first edition of the Air Force List is historically important as it records the

LISTS

OF

OFFICERS

OF THE

ROYAL AIR FORCE

Corrected to 1st FEBRUARY, 1918.

Air Ministry.
April, 1918.

names and ranks of those serving on the formation of the RAF having transferred from the RFC or RNAS. Under the Gradation Lists, HM King George V is shown as the General-in-Chief, after which the most senior officer listed is Lieutenant General Sir David Henderson. After Henderson there are five officers listed in the rank of major general: Mark Kerr; Sir Hugh Trenchard; Godfrey Paine; Sefton Brancker; and Richard Munday. There are just nine colonels listed with all other officers being of lower rank. All officers are listed under a branch. The branches are: Staff officers; aeroplane and seaplane officers (by far the biggest section); dirigible officers; kite balloon officers; observer officers; administrative officers; technical officers: and unclassified officers. The seniority for all officers is shown as 1 April 1918. Those demobilised are also listed under the heading 'Technical Reserve'. However, the full list of officers serving under the Ministry of Munitions was not available in time for insertion in the first issue of the Air Force List and so their names would appear in the next edition the following month.

The Air Force List continued to be produced monthly during the interwar years and included details of the officer's units and locations, as well as details of any decorations or awards. It was produced every two months during the Second World War until October 1944, after which it was issued quarterly, then annually and eventually biennially. From 1939 until 1954 there was also a Confidential Air Force List and from 1949 there has been a Retired List, providing key information about an officer, such as date of birth, date commissioned, and the rank and date of retirement. The Royal Navy and army have their own published lists (the Navy List and the Army List respectively).

The Air Force List can now be viewed online and downloaded from the government website, while past editions can be found at The National Archives and at other specialist libraries and archives across the country.

7

SE5a Windscreen

ON 9 JULY 1918, the First World War flying ace Major James McCudden VC DSO & Bar MC & Bar MM was killed – not by enemy air action but in a tragic flying accident – and shown here is the shattered glass windscreen of his SE5a fighter.

Born in Gillingham, Kent, Jimmy McCudden joined the Royal Engineers in 1910. At the outbreak of the First World War he was an aircraft mechanic and immediately went to France with the RFC. By the following year, he was a sergeant but his reputation as a highly successful engine mechanic was beginning to stand in his way of becoming a pilot, and so he voluntarily started flying on sorties as an observer. McCudden soon impressed, particularly when acting as an aerial gunner, and so in early 1916 he was promoted to flight sergeant and sent back to England for pilot training.

With his training completed McCudden returned to France to join 20 Squadron at Clairmarais. The squadron was equipped with the Royal Aircraft Factory FE2b two-seat 'pusher' bomber and he had arrived during the height of the Battle of the Somme. However, he was not to remain with the squadron for long and soon found himself transferred to 29 Squadron at Abeele, a squadron equipped with the Airco DH2 single-seat fighter.

McCudden immediately took to the lighter DH2 and during a patrol along the Armentieres–Ypres sector on 6 September 1916, he scored his first success: a German Albatros. But he would have to wait until late in January 1917 for his next aerial success, although he had earlier sent a couple of enemy observation balloons to the ground to earn the Military Medal (MM). He had now been commissioned as a second lieutenant and by the following

Country of Origin: UK
Date: July 1918
Location: Imperial War Museum London
(© IWM)

month he was an ace, with five confirmed victories, for which he was awarded his first Military Cross (MC). He was then given a rest from the front line. The RFC was expanding at such a rate that experienced pilots were being taken from the operational squadrons in France to train the large numbers passing through the training system back home.

After returning to France, first with 66 Squadron and then as a flight commander with 56 Squadron, McCudden was a captain and flying the Royal Aircraft Factory SE5a fighter. It was the summer of 1917 and the Third Battle of Ypres, and the squadron was in constant battle with the best of the German fighters. McCudden scored his first success flying the SE5a on 18 August when he sent an Albatros spinning out of control. Things now started happening at pace. In October, he was awarded a Bar to his MC having been credited with eighteen victories – many falling to his guns when he used his preferred technique of diving beneath the height of his intended victim and then pulling up unseen from below.

Major James McCudden. (AHB)

Although described as being recklessly brave, McCudden was also professional in every respect. Being a former mechanic he had a thorough knowledge of his machine and was even known to carry out inspections of his flight's aircraft to ensure they were being maintained to the highest standard. Five more victories followed in November and then a remarkable fourteen in December, including several during the Battle of Cambrai, earning him the Distinguished Service Order (DSO) and Bar. By the end of January 1918, he had taken his total to forty-six, surpassing the score of the leading ace Albert Ball VC DSO & two Bars MC who had been credited with forty-four aerial victories before his death the year before.

McCudden added eleven more victories to his tally in February, taking his personal score to fifty-seven; all but five had been achieved flying the SE5a. He had long hardened to the horror of the air war over the Western Front but was now reportedly suffering from combat fatigue and so he was sent home for a well-earned rest. At the end of March came the official announcement of his award of the Victoria Cross (VC), the country's highest award for gallantry; the investiture taking place in April, the same week as the RAF was formed.

On 9 July 1918, McCudden was flying a new SE5a (C1126) and was on his way to take command of 60 Squadron at Boffles in northern France. After taking off from Auxi-le-Château in the late afternoon for the final leg of his journey, his aircraft was seen to roll on its side and plunge into trees on the edge of the aerodrome. Although McCudden was pulled from the wreckage and taken immediately to a casualty clearing station, he died that evening from his injuries. It was a tragic end to such a short but gallant life; he was just 23 years old.

James McCudden is buried at the Wavans British Cemetery in France. He was one of the highest-scoring and most highly decorated British airmen in history, and his VC was one of just nineteen awarded for gallantry in the air during the First World War. His death came just days before the loss of Major Micky Mannock VC DSO & two Bars MC & Bar, the highest-scoring British fighter pilot of the First World War with seventy-three victories.

The shattered glass windscreen, with its surrounding rubber seal, from McCudden's SE5a is on display at the Imperial War Museum in London, as is his tunic bearing the ribbons of his impressive array of military decorations.

8

Officer's Dress Jacket and Cap

THE ESTABLISHMENT OF the RAF as an independent service meant the design of a new uniform. It was initially decided that the officer uniform was to be pale blue with gold braid trimmings, although the khaki pattern of the RFC was still to be worn until the transition was complete. And so there was a period when either khaki or pale blue could be worn. In fact, the changeover period was particularly slow, not helped by many new RAF recruits being issued with the older khaki pattern and because the new pale blue was unpopular, even amongst the most senior of officers.

The khaki uniform continued to be worn until as late as 1924 when it was finally replaced by a new blue-grey colour uniform, the colour and style still worn today, which had replaced the rather unpopular and impractical idea of pale blue with gold braid.

Shown here is a khaki 1918-pattern RAF officer's service dress jacket and cap that belonged to Lieutenant Frederic Hopkins. Born in Sheffield in 1899, Hopkins joined the RFC in 1917 and after serving as a cadet at Corpus Christie College, Oxford, was commissioned as a second lieutenant. After transferring to the newly formed RAF, he served briefly at Waddington in Lincolnshire before being posted out to France where he served with 108 Squadron at Capelle.

The uniform is made of cloth, single-breasted and has an open collar and four pockets. It features brass buttons and the RAF pilot wings are sewn above the left breast pocket. At this stage the rank is still that of the army, as the RAF's new rank structure had yet to be implemented.

Country of Origin: UK
Date: 1918
Location: Newark Air Museum, Nottinghamshire (By kind permission of the Newark Air Museum)

The cap is khaki fabric with a black patent leather peak and fitted with a black mohair band.

Sadly, though, this uniform jacket and cap provides a poignant reminder of a lost generation. Hopkins was killed in action on 1 October 1918 when his DH9 two-seat bomber was shot down over Belgium; he was just 19 years old. Frederic Hopkins is buried in the Harlebeke New British Cemetery in Belgium. His service dress jacket and cap, along with other personal items, are currently on display at the Newark Air Museum, Nottinghamshire.

9

Cap and Badge of the Women's Royal Air Force

THE CAP AND badge shown here belonged to Maude Lowe of the Women's Royal Air Force (WRAF) who served as a station cook during 1918. She was one of more than 9,000 women who had volunteered to join the newly formed female branch of the RAF.

Formed on the same day as the RAF, the decision to establish the WRAF, with Lady Gertrude Crawford as its first commandant, had followed concerns about what would happen to the specialised female workforce working during the First World War as members of the Women's Army Auxiliary Corps (WAAC) and the Women's Royal Naval Service (WRNS). As things were to turn out, those already serving with the WAAC and WRNS were given the option to join the new service and the WRAF's numbers were swelled further by the enrolment of civilians to boost its ranks. The minimum age for female volunteers was 18, although selection from outside the military was complex and included stringent health checks. Those from educated and upper-class families were generally enrolled as officers, whilst the majority were recruited as members and fell into one of two categories; Mobiles, who lived on or near the workplace and could be transferred anywhere if required; or Immobiles who continued to live at home and were attached to their local station.

The original intention was that the WRAF would provide female mechanics so that men could be released for combat service, but such was the response to enrolment that women volunteered for many positions. Most were employed in basic trades, such as clerks or in stores; some worked in the Technical section covering a wide range of trades, many of which were highly skilled, such as fitters

Country of Origin: UK
Date: 1918
Location: RAF Scampton Heritage Centre, Lincolnshire (By kind permission of the Station Commander RAF Scampton)

The Women's Royal Air Force, the female branch of the RAF, formed as a wartime force and was disbanded in 1920, by which time some 32,000 women had served in the WRAF. (Ken Delve)

and welders; while others worked in the Household section where they often worked the longest hours doing back-breaking work for the lowest pay.

The early days of the WRAF were not without difficulty. When Lady Gertrude Crawford realised she was being seen as little more than a figurehead, and was unable to run the service in her own way, she resigned. Her successor, Violet Douglas-Pennant, did not last long either. She quickly formed the impression that the RAF was not fully committed to supporting its female branch and was removed after a report on the state of the WRAF, commissioned by the Secretary of State for Air, Lord Weir, was highly critical of Douglas-Pennant's performance as its commandant.

It had not taken long for the Air Ministry to become frustrated with the WRAF, although the decision to remove its second commandant was itself questioned. Nonetheless, the outcome was the appointment of Helen Gwynne-Vaughan, a former Chief Controller of the WAAC in France, as the WRAF's third commandant in its first six months.

Helen Gwynne-Vaughan stood firm throughout the political debates that followed. Again, the value of a women's service was questioned, but not only did she stem the tide, she quickly proved to be a formidable leader and an inspirational speaker. As well as working on RAF bases at home, it was not long before women were being sent across the Channel to bases in France and Germany to assist the army of occupation and to replace men being demobilised from the service. And as the WRAF continued to expand, more trades became available to women, such as catering, driving, tailoring and photography. Women were quickly proving to be equal in the workplace, thus releasing men for other duties. Furthermore, their presence helped keep morale high. In addition to their main duties they would often help organise sporting and social events.

The WRAF had finally won many of its critics over and had become an invaluable asset to the RAF. The high standards achieved soon led to it gaining the reputation of being the most professional and disciplined of all the women's services. However, it had been formed as a wartime force and with the RAF having to cut back in the post-war era, the WRAF was disbanded in April 1920, just two years after it had formed. During that time 32,000 women had joined the WRAF with the last surviving veteran from this era believed to have been Florence Green, who died in 2012.

Helen Gwynne-Vaughan's work as Commandant of the WRAF was recognised by her being made a Dame Commander of the Order of the British Empire (DBE). She had laid the foundations and set the standards, and her professionalism helped change male attitudes towards women in the air service. The WRAF paved the way for women in the future; so much so that it would have a second incarnation in 1949 that would last for forty-five years.

10

King's Message to the Royal Air Force

FOLLOWING THE CESSATION of hostilities on 11 November 1918, HM King George V sent a message of heartfelt congratulations to all ranks of the RAF. The message was sent via the Secretary of State for Air and President of the Air Council, Lord Weir, and in it the king states:

> The birth of the Royal Air Force, with its wonderful expansion and development, will ever remain one of the most remarkable achievements of the Great War.

By the end of the First World War the RAF's strength had grown to more than 313,000 personnel and some 22,000 aircraft. Ninety-nine squadrons were based in France, another thirty-four were based elsewhere overseas, fifty-five squadrons were providing home defence and there were a further 200 training squadrons. At its peak the RAF had around 100,000 personnel on the front line. But war had come at a heavy cost. Many casualty figures have been produced since the end of the First World War, but the Commonwealth War Graves Commission states that it commemorates 1.1 million casualties of the First World War. Of this figure, somewhere around 750,000 were either killed or missing military personnel from the British Isles. In relative terms, the number of those from the newly formed RAF will be low due to the late formation of the service, but the RAF Museum states that 9,349 personnel lost their lives while serving in the British air services during the First World War.

Establishments such as the Commonwealth War Graves Commission, The National Archives, and the

Country of Origin: UK
Date: 11 November 1918
Location: Private Collection

The King's Message to the Royal Air Force.

To the Right Hon. Lord Weir, Secretary of State and President of the Air Council.

IN this supreme hour of victory I send greetings and heartfelt congratulations to all ranks of the Royal Air Force. Our aircraft have been ever in the forefront of the battle; pilots and observers have consistently maintained the offensive throughout the ever-changing fortunes of the day, and in the war zones our gallant dead have lain always beyond the enemies' lines or far out to sea.

OUR far-flung squadrons have flown over home waters and foreign seas, the Western and Italian battle lines, Rhineland, the mountains of Macedonia, Gallipoli, Palestine, the plains of Mesopotamia, the forests and swamps of East Africa, the North-West frontier of India, and the deserts of Arabia, Sinai, and Darfur.

THE birth of the Royal Air Force, with its wonderful expansion and development, will ever remain one of the most remarkable achievements of the Great War.

EVERYWHERE, by God's help, officers, men and women of the Royal Air Force have splendidly maintained our just cause, and the value of their assistance to the Navy, the Army, and to Home Defence has been incalculable. For all their magnificent work, self-sacrifice, and devotion to duty, I ask you on behalf of the Empire to thank them.

November 11th, 1918

George R. I.

RAF Museum all hold extensive records relating to RAF personnel, with records covering all theatres of operations. The records are not always complete but much information can be gleaned from them. The last known founder member of the RAF to have died was Henry Allingham, a former aircraft mechanic, who died in 2009 at the age of 113.

Part 2
Building Foundations

11

DH9A

THE DH9A, OFTEN referred to as the 'Nine-Ack' or 'Ninak', was the RAF's standard aircraft type in the post-war era. A development of the disappointing two-seat Airco DH9 light bomber, which had an under-performing and often unreliable engine, the DH9A, with its new 400hp American V-12 Liberty engine, slightly larger wings and a strengthened structure, was to prove far more successful.

The DH9A entered service with the RAF in July 1918. The first squadron to receive the new type was 110 Squadron at Kenley and the following month the squadron moved across to France where the DH9A saw brief operational service with the RAF's Independent Force – its first mission being flown on 14 September 1918 against the German airfield at Boulay.

The RAF had placed an order for more than 2,000 DH9As and with it being its standard type, production was relatively easy and quick. By the end of 1918, nearly 900 had been built and this number was doubled the following year. After Airco became the de Havilland Aircraft Company in 1920, production resumed and by the time it ended some 2,300 DH9As had been built, including several dual-controlled trainers.

Country of Origin: UK

Date: 1918

Location: RAF Museum Hendon, London

(© RAF Museum)

The DH9A had a maximum speed of 114mph (183km/h) at 10,000ft (3,050m) and could reach a height of over 16,500ft (5,100m). As a combat aircraft it could carry 450lb (204kg) of bombs on underwing and fuselage racks, and was armed with a forward-firing 0.303in (7.7mm) Vickers machine gun and one rearward-firing 0.303in Lewis gun aft. But it was its endurance of more than five hours, its flexibility when on task and its ease of operation because of its standard design that made the DH9A an ideal aircraft for operating overseas in support of British foreign policy. Its first post-war operations were flown in southern Russia during 1919, supporting the White Army against the Bolsheviks in the Russian Civil War, and then, in 1922, a squadron was sent to Turkey in response to the Chanak Crisis. The Ninak also proved ideal for policing duties and so a further five squadrons of DH9As served in the Middle East to manage territories under British control following the collapse of the Ottoman Empire at the end of the First World War.

DH9As of 47 Squadron pictured during the 1920s over Mesopotamia. (Ken Delve)

The DH9A had performed well under difficult conditions, even when operating in high temperatures, and so a number were sent to India in a policing role on the North-West Frontier – reducing the need for large numbers of troops on the ground. Meanwhile at home, the DH9A was used for a variety of purposes and was part of the build-up of the Royal Auxiliary Air Force (RAuxAF).

By the time the DH9A was retired from service in 1931, twenty-four RAF squadrons had been equipped with the type, both at home and abroad, plus seven squadrons of the RAuxAF. So successful was the design that a large number of unlicensed copies were built in the Soviet Union as the Polikarpov R-1, which became the standard Soviet light bomber and reconnaissance aircraft during the 1920s. An American version had also been planned, although the end of the First World War brought an end to this idea.

The magnificent DH9A shown in the main image is F1010, which is on display at the RAF Museum Hendon. It was built in June 1918 as one of the first production batch of 150 aircraft and so was one of eighteen assigned to 110 Squadron, the RAF's first squadron to receive the new type. All these aircraft were financed by His Serene Highness, the Nizam of Hyderabad. It was the first time a squadron had been funded in this way and in appreciation each aircraft was marked with a suitable inscription on both sides of the nose: 'PRESENTED BY HIS HIGHNESS THE NIZAM OF HYDERABAD', underneath which was the aircraft's individual number. In F1010's case, it reads 'HYDERABAD No. 12A'. Although it was the thirteenth aircraft delivered to the squadron, the number thirteen was considered unlucky and so it became 12A instead and given the squadron code letter of 'C'. From then on the squadron became known as 110 (Hyderabad) Squadron with the Nizam's crest, depicting a demi-tiger, used as the basis of the squadron badge.

F1010 took part in the DH9A's first operation on 14 September 1918 against the German airfield of Boulay but did not bomb due to low cloud and poor visibility in the area. The following day, though, conditions were better and F1010 took part in another attack against a German airfield, this time at Buhl. Then, on 25 September, with Captain Andrew Inglis at the controls and Lieutenant William Badley as his observer, the target was the railway yard at Frankfurt and during this mission the crew claimed the destruction of a German Fokker DVII fighter. F1010's fourth and final mission of the war was flown on 5 October 1918 when it was one of twelve aircraft sent to attack Kaiserslautern and Pipmasens, but it was forced to land behind German lines – either as the result of flak damage or an engine problem. The aircraft was undamaged but Inglis and Badley were both taken as prisoners of war. F1010 then remained in German hands and in 1936 was put on display at the Berlin Air Museum. During the Second World War, it was moved to Poland with other exhibits to save them from the Allied bombing, and so after the war F1010 became part of the Polish Aviation Museum. Finally, in 1977, the much-travelled F1010 returned to the UK when it was part of a swap involving a Spitfire from the RAF Museum. Restoration on F1010 was then carried out and in 1983 the aircraft was put on display.

Army Book 425.

Pilot's Flying

Log Book.

Pilot Officer.

C. A. D. Brook.

Royal Air Force.

12

Army Book 425

ASK ANY NUMBER of aircrew to name their most precious personal belonging from their time in the RAF and their log book (or log books for the seasoned campaigners) will feature heavily amongst the answers. Log books have changed little over the years, but in the early days of the RAF those brave young men in their flying machines were still recording details of their flights in the Army Book 425.

The wonderful early example shown here belonged to Pilot Officer William Arthur Darville Brook who joined the RAF in February 1920, on his nineteenth birthday, as one of fifty-six ambitious young men making up No. 1 Entry at the RAF Cadet College, Cranwell. By the time his flying training was finished, Brook had recorded nine hours as an observer, seventeen hours as a pilot dual with an instructor and twenty hours solo, all in Avro 504s.

Brook was then posted to 5 Squadron in India and arrived at Quetta in May 1922. The squadron was equipped with the two-seat Bristol F2B and its role was to work with land forces in policing and securing the historically troubled North-West Frontier Province between 'British India' and Afghanistan. It was a vast area of difficult mountainous territory and home to hostile warrior tribes with little or no respect for British rule or law.

These were difficult times and operating aircraft thousands of miles from home was never without its problems. A shortage of spares meant that flying opportunities were limited, particularly for new young pilots like Brook. During his six months with the squadron he flew just ten hours as pilot plus a further twenty hours as observer, which included sorties such as aerial photography and communication exercises with the infantry.

Country of Origin: UK
Date: 1920
Location: Brook Family
(© Kenneth Boardman and reproduced with the kind permission of the Brook family)

Bill Brook's Army Form 425 showing his lucky escape on 12 March 1923. (Kenneth Boardman via the Brook family)

With such few flying hours to be had, it is of little surprise that flying incidents and serious accidents were all too common. Nonetheless, the value of the RAF controlling rebel tribes was beginning to show, particularly because an aircraft could be on task relatively quickly and with fewer casualties being suffered than might otherwise have been expected on the ground. Furthermore, and probably the most important benefit as far as the politicians back in London were concerned, the overall cost of policing the vast area of the frontier with a few aircraft in the air was far less than having to use large numbers of infantry on the ground.

Brook was next posted to 27 Squadron at Risalpur where he flew his first operational sortie as an observer on 17 December 1922. His new squadron was equipped with the DH9A and had moved to Fort Dardoni to conduct a series of bombing raids during a period of local unrest following the decision to construct a road through a potentially hostile tribal zone in central Waziristan. Having then completed his pilot conversion and operational work-up on the DH9A, Brook flew more bombing sorties, usually with his regular observer, LAC Murphy. These typically lasted over two and half hours, during which they bombed villages to the south of Dardoni and shot up any targets of opportunity.

On 12 March 1923, Brook and Murphy took off for a raid on the village of Sperkai. Armed with one 230lb (104kg) and two 112lb (50kg) bombs, they successfully attacked their target but then their engine cut out, forcing Brook to crash-land in a riverbed near to the village they had just bombed. Having climbed out of their crippled machine, he and Murphy fell straight into the hands of the Waziris. Their aircraft was set alight by the disgruntled natives but the two airmen were fortunate to be allowed to live after Brook, brandishing a chit written in the local language, had managed to persuade their captors that a ransom would be paid if they were to be returned alive. After a tough journey through the night they arrived at Wana Fort where the negotiations for the ransom ensued and the following day Brook and Murphy were picked up in a DH10 and flown back to Dardoni. Within days the crew were back on operations but it had been a lucky escape.

Brook remained in India until the end of his tour in early 1926 when he returned home. He would go on to enjoy a long and distinguished career in the RAF, reaching the rank of air vice-marshal, but Bill Brook's life came to a tragic end in 1953 while undertaking a jet conversion course shortly before his promotion and next appointment as Vice-Chief of the Air Staff. He was flying a Meteor near Stafford when his aircraft was seen to suddenly turn and dive into the ground.

The Army Book 425 has long been replaced by the RAF Pilot's Flying Log Book, or the RAF Form 414 to give its official name (the flying log book for other crew positions is the RAF Form 1767). It records many details, such as the date and type of aircraft flown, its serial number, the duty performed and the length of flight (day/night). It also records whether the individual flew as 1st pilot or 2nd pilot (co-pilot), whether the flight was made in a single-engine or multi-engine aircraft, and whether instrument flying was carried out. Times in hours and minutes are recorded in the appropriate columns.

But a log book is not only a personal treasure, it provides a very useful source for those researching the history of an individual, unit, station or aircraft, or when researching a specific operation or campaign. Indeed, every log book tells a story. Bill Brook's Army Book 425 is shown here with the kind permission of his son, Air Vice-Marshal David Brook, and the Brook family.

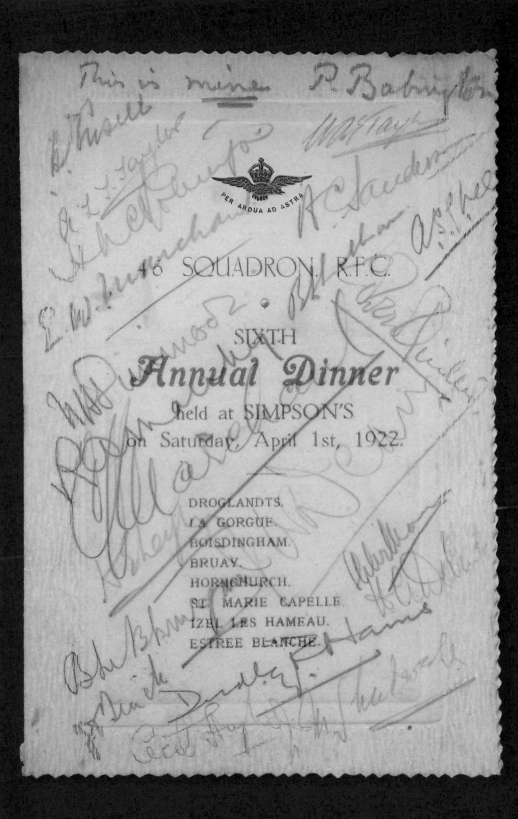

PER ARDUA AD ASTRA

46 SQUADRON, R.F.C.

SIXTH

Annual Dinner

held at SIMPSON'S
on Saturday, April 1st, 1922.

DROGLANDTS.
LA GORGUE.
BOISDINGHAM.
BRUAY.
HORNCHURCH.
ST. MARIE CAPELLE.
IZEL LES HAMEAU.
ESTREE BLANCHE.

13

Menu Card

THROUGHOUT ITS 100 years, members and former members of the RAF have come together at certain times of the year for a variety of reasons. Reunions and remembrance days remain an important part of the RAF way of life, and today we can all too easily take them for granted. But they had to start somewhere and were often started by founder members of squadrons or organisations who wanted to get together – be it to celebrate or commemorate.

The biggest national event today, of course, is Armistice Day, first hosted by HM King George V in the grounds of Buckingham Palace on the morning of 11 November 1919 to mark the signing of the armistice at the end of the First World War. But in addition to large national events, many lower-key occasions are held each year and amongst these are squadron reunions. These are marked in a variety of ways and provide an opportunity for members and former members of a squadron to get together to catch up on old times as well as to remember those no longer with them.

One early example of a squadron reunion is that held by 46 Squadron at Simpson's in the Strand on Saturday 1 April 1922. It marked the fourth anniversary of the formation of the RAF and was the squadron's sixth annual dinner having formed in 1916. It had then been equipped with the two-seat Nieuport 12 and had trained as a reconnaissance unit before moving to France. After flying over the Western Front as an artillery observation unit, 46 then became a fighter squadron, initially equipped with the Sopwith Pup and latterly with the Sopwith Camel. Then, when hostilities were over, the squadron returned to the UK before disbanding in 1919.

Country of Origin: UK

Date: 1 April 1922

Location: Private Collection

The menu card shown here belonged to Philip Babington (later Air Marshal Sir Philip Babington) who had commanded 46 Squadron from July 1916 until December 1917. It has been signed by former members of the squadron attending the dinner. Babington's signature can clearly be seen top right. He has written along the top of the card 'This is *mine*'. Inside the card, and for those interested, the menu reads:

Hors d'oeuvres – Native Oysters

Soup – Clear mock turtle or tomato

Fish – Boiled turbot with lobster sauce

Joints – Roast Saddle of Mutton with red currant jelly or Roast Sirloin of Beef and Yorkshire pudding

Vegetables – Cauliflower and roast potatoes

Sweets – Peach Melba

Savoury – Welsh Rarebit

Also for the record, the toasts were to the king, the squadron (both by Babington), absent friends (the Padre) and to the guests (Dimmock).

Like most RAF squadrons disbanded at the end of the First World War, 46 Squadron would later re-form in time of need only to be later disbanded once again. But although the squadron disbanded for the fourth and last time in 1975, the annual reunions have continued. Sir Philip Babington and his colleagues from the squadron's very early days during the First World War would be immensely proud that their reunions lived on.

14

Drill Shed

THE OLD DRILL shed shown here has stood for nearly 100 years. Today it is the Trenchard Museum and proudly represents the importance of the station where it stands – RAF Halton in Buckinghamshire.

One of the RAF's first stations, Halton's origins date back to before the First World War when the owner of the Halton Estate, Alfred de Rothschild, first invited the army to use his land for summer manoeuvres. After hostilities broke out the estate was again made available for military training and by 1917 the pressing need to expand technical training in the RFC had seen Halton become the main training unit for aircraft mechanics.

With this background in mind it can easily be seen why Halton was a major part of Trenchard's early vision for the RAF. He firmly believed that the only way to produce the high-quality mechanics needed for what would become an increasingly technical air force was to train them internally. At the heart of his thinking was the recruitment of well-educated boys between the ages of 15 and 16 who could absorb the necessary technical knowledge during an apprenticeship lasting just three years, rather than the five-year apprenticeships generally on offer in the civilian world at the time. These highly trained young men would then go on to form the backbone of the RAF's skilled technical force.

The RAF aircraft apprentice scheme was initially set up at Halton in 1920, but because the camp was not quite ready to accept its first apprentices the first four entries were trained at Cranwell. The first boy entrants, some 500 of them, and soon to become known as 'Trenchard's Brats', arrived at Halton in 1922, by which time additional facilities and accommodation had been constructed to

Country of Origin:
UK
Date: 1922
Location:
RAF Halton,
Buckinghamshire
(By kind
permission of
the Station
Commander RAF
Halton)

improve on the more basic conditions endured by trainees only a few years before.

The RAF's apprentice scheme soon earned international recognition with many boys from the Commonwealth and other overseas nations being trained at Halton prior to returning to their own air forces. Over the years the apprentices earned a reputation for being the best trained technicians in the RAF and were usually expected to reach senior non-commissioned officer ranks. Indeed, many

The same drill shed at RAF Halton as it appeared on 3 June 1927. (Trenchard Museum)

were subsequently commissioned as officers and nearly a hundred went on to achieve air rank.

By the time the last Halton apprentices marched off the parade square in 1993, some 40,000 boys had been trained under the scheme. But Halton has never been just about RAF apprentices. Over the years, it has welcomed young trainees in many other trades, not just technical, and today it is the gateway to the RAF where all young recruits, male and female, undergo basic training before embarking on their professional trade training.

The old drill shed shown here stands next to the parade square and has been there since 1922 when it was built at the same time as the accommodation blocks overlooking the square. It is believed the front of the shed was closed off during the early 1930s as the building was used in that era for dances and band practices. The dances were held once a month, although standing orders stated that no females were to be invited! Many ex-apprentices will remember the building being used as a gym. It was certainly used as a gym during the 1940s and was also used for the fortnightly pay parades. During the 1950s the gym doubled-up as a band hut and it later included a boxing ring for the apprentices as part of their physical training.

After the apprentice scheme ended in 1993 the building was left derelict and by 1998 it was on the verge of being demolished, but thanks to the efforts of several volunteers the building was retained to become a museum. The museum now preserves and displays items relating to the history of RAF Halton and is named in honour of Lord Trenchard who founded the aircraft apprentice scheme, with which the name Halton has become synonymous. Opened in 1999 by his grandson, the Viscount Trenchard, the museum is open to the public at specified times and is one of many original buildings that have survived. Others include the neighbouring accommodation blocks, adjacent to the original parade square, still being used by the RAF's young recruits. Indeed, the first impression for many of today's recruits when arriving at RAF Halton is like it is taking a giant step back in time. They have a point. At first glance very little has changed!

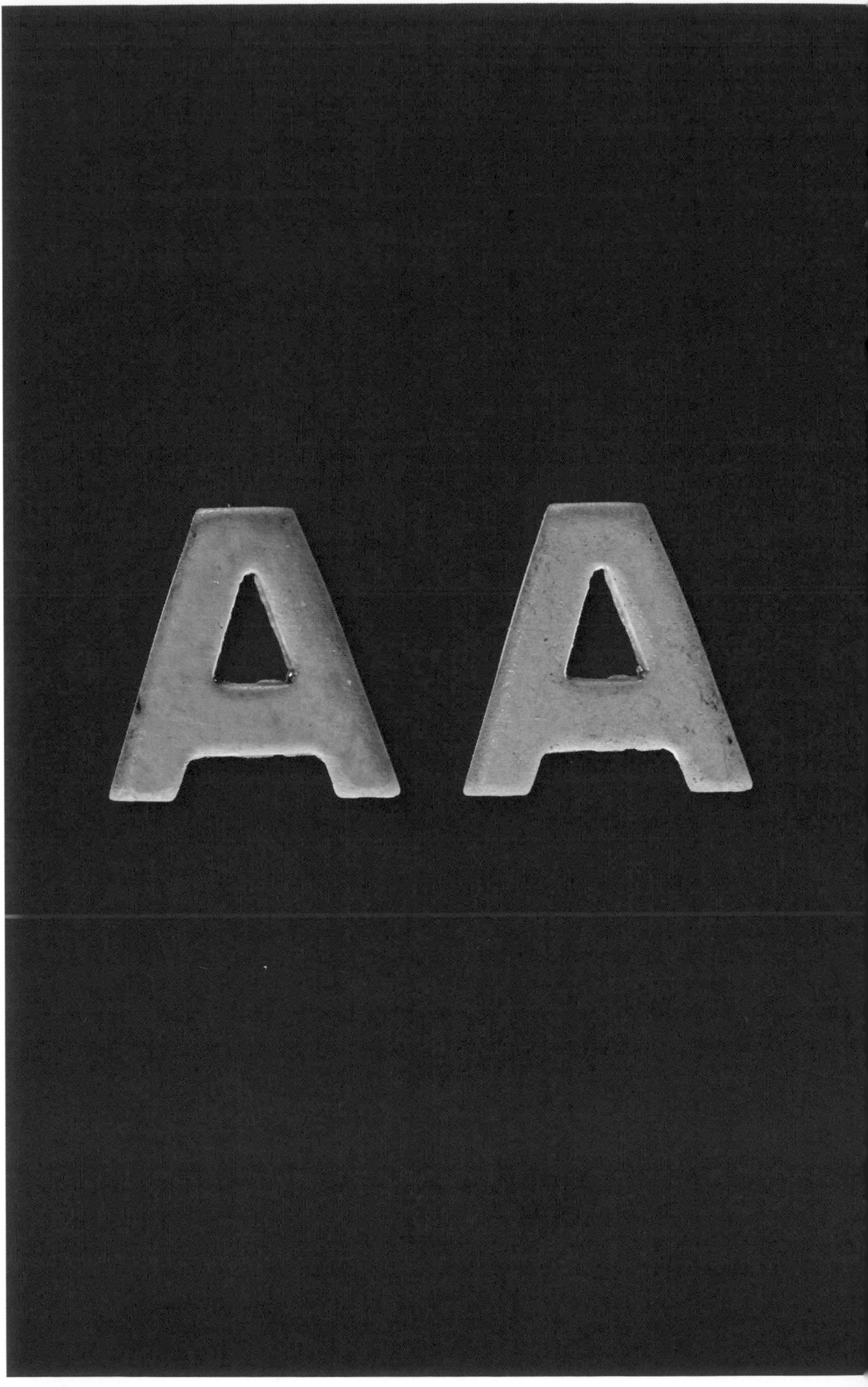
AA

15

The 'A's of the Royal Auxiliary Air Force

THE 'A'S PICTURED here are from the uniform of Squadron Leader Alfie Hall, the executive officer of 607 (County of Durham) Squadron, a reservist General Service Support squadron based at RAF Leeming in North Yorkshire. They represent all members, past and present, of the Royal Auxiliary Air Force (RAuxAF), now more commonly known as the RAF Reserves.

For most of the RAF's 100 years, its volunteer reserve element has provided trained personnel as a primary reinforcement capability in support of the regular service. It was another of Trenchard's early visions and came into being in 1924, with the first Auxiliary Air Force (AAF) squadrons forming the following year. The squadrons were then town-based and used facilities at an aerodrome nearby. Members were generally recruited locally, along similar lines to the Territorial Army, although the auxiliary squadrons tended to be formed from the wealthier classes. Pilots were required to obtain their licence at their own expense and serve for a minimum period of five years, flying a few hours every year and attending one annual training camp of fifteen days.

Country of Origin:
UK
Date: 1924
Location: RAF Leeming, North Yorkshire.
(Crown Copyright and reproduced with the kind permission of the RAuxAF)

In 1936 the RAF Volunteer Reserve (RAFVR) was formed to supplement the AAF as a way of providing a reserve of aircrew for use in the event of war. These were generally either civilians recruited from reserve flying schools and trained by the RAF before returning to their civilian employment until called up, or former members of the RAF who had left the service. By the time the Second World War broke out the RAFVR comprised more than 10,000 aircrew, two-thirds being qualified pilots and these were used as the principal means for reinforcing the RAF,

while more than twenty auxiliary flying squadrons were incorporated into the RAF's structure. The AAF was also responsible for anti-aircraft balloon defences of the UK, with more than forty units involved in this role. At its peak in 1944 there were more than a hundred auxiliary squadrons.

Officers of the RAFVR wore a 'VR' lapel badge while other ranks wore a cloth badge on the shoulder, but during the war the Air Ministry decided these should be removed as they were viewed as being divisive. However, there was no similar order for members of the AAF, who retained their 'A's on their uniform, and one notable figure often seen proudly wearing the 'A's on his RAF uniform was the British Prime Minister, Winston Churchill, in his capacity as Honorary Air Commodore of 615 (County of Surrey) Squadron.

In 1947, HM King George VI recognised the AAF's achievements during the Second World War by the approval of the prefix 'Royal'. The pre-war squadrons were reformed as fighter squadrons and so the RAuxAF played a major part in the UK's defence. During the Korean War, for example, the auxiliary squadrons provided much of the nation's air defence by replacing regular squadrons deployed overseas. However, these auxiliary fighter squadrons were disbanded in 1957 along with other associated squadrons, but the RAuxAF was not to be dormant for long. By the end of the decade its renaissance

Seen wearing 'A's on his RAF uniform during the Second World War is the British Prime Minister, Winston Churchill, in his capacity as Honorary Air Commodore of 615 (County of Surrey) Squadron. (RAuxAF)

had begun with the formation of three Maritime Headquarters Units and a Maritime Support Unit.

Things essentially remained this way for the next twenty years until the RAuxAF gradually began expanding again with field squadrons, a movements squadron and an aeromedical evacuation squadron – all of which have performed with great distinction during recent conflicts. The RAFVR, meanwhile, had remained the focus for former regulars who had a continuing obligation to reserve service but in 1997 it was finally absorbed into the RAuxAF, although the RAFVR (T), whose members usually operate part-time with air experience flights and volunteer gliding schools in conjunction with the Air Cadet Organisation, and RAFVR (UAS) continued unaffected. There has also been the introduction of RAFVR (DTUS), the Defence Technical Undergraduate Scheme.

RAF Reserves wear the same uniform as that of regular service personnel with the exception that RAuxAF officers wear the gilt 'A' badges on the lapels of their No. 1 dress uniform, while RAFVR (T) officers wear 'VRT' insignia on their lapels as well as on the rank braid on the epaulettes of their working dress uniforms.

In 2003 the RAuxAF was involved in the first large-scale mobilisation since the Korean War when nearly 1,000 personnel deployed to support RAF operations overseas. There are currently twenty-five RAuxAF squadrons in the UK, plus other specialist units, made up of paid male and female part-time volunteers, which provide trained manpower to the regular service in many different trades. The concept of auxiliaries may have moved away from its early days of flying squadrons manned by the wealthy, but Trenchard's vision more than ninety years ago has well and truly stood the test of time.

16

Tenor Drum

THE TENOR DRUM pictured here is believed to be one of the original set of drums belonging to the pipe band of No. 1 School of Technical Training (No. 1 SofTT) in 1926. It has a wooden shell and hand-painted royal crest, and was used by the band until the 1950s.

Established at RAF Halton in 1919, under the leadership of its first Commandant, Air Commodore Francis Scarlett, No. 1 SofTT was another key part of Trenchard's early vision for the training of aircraft mechanics and for the next seventy years trained thousands of aircraft apprentices. The school even received royal recognition in 1952 when HM Queen Elizabeth II presented it with her colour.

Made up of apprentices undergoing training, the pipe band was always an important part of the school's tradition and part of everyday life at Halton. For the apprentices accommodated in barrack blocks alongside Henderson Square, the day started by marching behind the band down to the station's workshops on the other side of the Tring–Wendover road. Then, at lunchtime, the parade would return up the hill only to go back down an hour or so later with stomachs full. Finally, when the day was done, all marched back up the hill to the accommodation blocks once more.

When the RAF's apprentice scheme finally ended in 1993, the school moved to Cosford where it now forms part of the Defence College of Aeronautical Engineering. However, the RAF Halton Pipes and Drums band survived and still performs on a voluntary basis, its members being recruited from across all ranks of serving personnel, civil servants and civilians from the surrounding area. From its earliest days as an apprentice band it has always been held in high regard across the piping community.

Country of Origin: UK
Date: 1926
Location: Trenchard Museum, RAF Halton, Buckinghamshire (By kind permission of the Station Commander RAF Halton)

On a wider scale, music has always been an important part of the RAF. The RAF School of Music was established soon after the service formed and led to the formation of the Central Band of the RAF at Uxbridge and the Band of the RAF College at Cranwell. In the lead-up to the Second World War there was a huge expansion of RAF Music Services, with many civilian professional musicians being drafted directly into the new ensembles. After the war, bands were organised on a geographical basis, including overseas, with RAF Music Services boasting ten established bands. Since then the branch has gradually reduced in size to what it is today: the Headquarters Music Services and three bands; the Central Band of the RAF, the Band of the RAF College and the Band of the RAF Regiment, with each band capable of providing many different ensembles. The RAF was the first service to recruit women into mixed bands and, in addition to their musical role, RAF musicians are also trained to provide support for operations around the world.

Cap, belt and saxophone belonging to a member of the RAF Central Band. Since its formation in 1920, the Central Band of the RAF has boasted a proud and distinguished heritage. (Crown Copyright 2015)

17

Lawrence Letter

PICTURED HERE, ALBEIT protected by a plastic cover, is a letter. The reason the letter is protected is because of its historical importance as it was written by Thomas Edward Lawrence, better known to most as Lawrence of Arabia, who was then serving in the RAF under the name of T.E. Shaw in order to protect his true identity. The fact that Lawrence served in the RAF seems to be little known. He did, in fact, serve in the RAF twice during the 1920s.

Born in Wales in 1888, Lawrence was a graduate of Jesus College, Oxford, with a first in history. He then practised as an archaeologist in the Middle East before joining the British Army, but it was while working as a liaison officer in the Middle East during the First World War that he became a household name for his part in the Arab Revolt against the Ottoman Empire. After the war, Lawrence returned to the UK as a colonel and then worked for the Foreign Office and as an advisor to Winston Churchill at the Colonial Office. But the mental scars of war had left him in a state of turmoil and so Lawrence decided to take a different path in life.

Country of Origin: India
Date: 16 October 1928
Location: RAF College Cranwell, Lincolnshire (By kind permission of the Commandant RAF College Cranwell)

Lawrence first enlisted into the RAF in August 1922 as an aircraftman under the name of John Hume Ross, but he was forced out six months later after his identity had been exposed. Lawrence then changed his name to Thomas Edward Shaw and joined the Royal Tank Corps but he repeatedly asked to return to the RAF and finally got his way. He re-joined the RAF in August 1925 under the name of Shaw and by the following year was serving at RAF Cranwell where he was employed as a runner and clerk for the mechanics maintaining the aircraft used to teach the cadets to fly. A keen motorcyclist, Lawrence bought a new Brough Superior motorcycle, which he called George V,

Mianshah

16·X·28

Dear Corporal

We are all happy here. It is a good detachment. The cooking is ~~very~~ Hayton ~~is sick off~~. He has two of everything, and would go three, if the flesh wasn't so weak.

Also he and Corpl. Stone have had three days each in dock with fever. I ran stores: the stores also ran, as Corpl. Leitch says.

No rifle parades: we do not march to work. We breakfast & then trickle down. Mr. Smetham is a treat. He has asked Wing to wash out guards: Wing replied that the Wing Commander was away.

Is it not true that very shortly a lorry comes up from you to us? I'm still worrying about my hot bath. The weather here is getting chilly. What is needed is a ..... Have you any, not on charge? At Depot I had a b.... Dope-drum: that was very good: but it's the sort of thing one found at Depots. A petrol drum (4 gallon) would do: or two four-gallon oil-cans, which I could have stuck together by the coppersmith for whom I rely on Serjt.-Major Buchan. I am sure he will want a coppersmith for the Test Bench.

May I remind you also of my overalls? They could come up by lorry, too, I expect.

Hayton sends his love. Corpl. Stone is in Bannu, to check a broken case of photographic goods.

Au revoir

TES.

5 Sqdn. were much in credit on last month's messing. So we forgot about your C.R.A's? Teeh?

Lawrence pictured on his motorcycle in 1927 while serving with the RAF. (RAF College Cranwell)

and he was often seen riding it around the local country lanes. He was also a prolific writer and it was while at Cranwell that he finished writing his autobiographical *Seven Pillars of Wisdom*.

At last Lawrence seemed to have found happiness. He had made friends among his RAF airmen colleagues and his life had entered a new phase, but a fresh outburst of publicity following the publication of his book *Revolt in the Desert*, an abridged edition of *Seven Pillars*, resulted in him being posted to a remote base in India. And it was while serving in India that Lawrence wrote the letter shown here.

When he wrote this letter to a colleague, dated 16 October 1928, Lawrence was detached to a wireless station at Miranshah Fort, a fort constructed by the British in 1905 to control North Waziristan on the North-West Frontier, where he was employed as a clerk. The letter shows Lawrence to be in a cheery mood, starting with, 'We are all happy here. It is a good detachment.' The rest of the letter is routine chat, although at the end he refers to working with 5 Squadron, which at that time was based at Risalpur from where its Bristol F2bs were working as an army co-operation unit over the North-West Frontier. Lawrence signs the letter 'TES'.

This letter is one of a number known to have been written by Lawrence during his time in India. In an earlier letter, he describes Miranshah Fort as a 'dust-hole ringed by mountains close to Afghanistan, with the peaks sharp like bottle-glass and the fort in a pit'.

Lawrence returned to the UK at the end of the year and for a while served at RAF Bridlington in Yorkshire, where he specialised in high-speed boats. For a man scarred by the events of war, his time in the RAF seems to have been a happy one. He left the service in March 1935 at the end of his enlistment but, tragically, just two months later he was fatally injured in a motorcycling accident near his home in Dorset. Lawrence died on 19 May 1935 at the age of 46.

Amongst Lawrence's works was *The Mint*, which he wrote in 1922 about his first period in the RAF. It was written under his service name of Aircraftman Ross and has since been reprinted many times. The letter shown here is kept at the RAF College Cranwell where the library contains a large quantity of Lawrence-related material.

18

College Hall

THE RAF'S ICONIC Grade 2* listed College Hall at Cranwell, with its impressive Rotunda and Founders Gallery, and its many wonderful rooms that preserve the history of this marvellous building, stands as an impressive landmark on the Lincolnshire landscape.

The establishment of the Cadet College at Cranwell was another key part of Trenchard's early plans for the RAF. His vision was to establish an air academy for officers, along the same lines as the Royal Navy's Dartmouth and Sandhurst for the British Army, that would provide basic flying training for the cadets, while also providing them with an intellectual education and to engender an *esprit de corps* within the RAF's future leaders. This would, he felt, provide tangible evidence that the RAF was to be a permanent feature of Britain's military landscape.

Cranwell had previously been used by the Royal Navy as the training establishment HMS *Daedalus* but Trenchard felt that its remoteness, with no distractions for the cadets, made it an ideal location for the new college. On 1 November 1919 the RAF Cadet College formed under its first commandant, Air Commodore Charles Longcroft, to become what is now the oldest military air academy in the world. During the early days training took place in old corrugated-iron huts. The decision to replace these with the permanent college structure seen today was made as early as 1922, but the foundation stone was not laid until seven years later when the dignitaries attending the formal ceremony included Lord Trenchard, Air Vice-Marshal Charles Longcroft and the architect of College Hall, Sir James Grey West.

The College Hall architecture conforms to English tradition, being built of rustic and moulded brick work with the more important features in Portland Stone.

Country of Origin:
UK
Date: 1929
Location: RAF College Cranwell, Lincolnshire

With its frontage of 800ft (244m) and the main tower 150ft (46m) tall, it was built with the accommodation around quadrangles to mirror Britain's prestigious old universities. In front of the College were gravel paths leading around a circular area of grass, known as the Orange, towards the parade ground immediately in front of the building.

The new college was first used by cadets in 1933, although it was not formally opened until 11 October 1934 by Air Marshal HRH Edward, Prince of Wales. Following the outbreak of the Second World War, the training of officer cadets was suspended but Cranwell remained open to train pilots as the RAF College Flying Training School. Then, after the war, the college returned to its former function and even broadened its training to include the equipment and secretarial branch cadets to train alongside the traditional flight cadets. In those days, graduates received a permanent commission in the RAF after a residential course of two to three years. All pilot training was being conducted at Cranwell but when the academic syllabus was further improved it meant that only basic flying training could be completed within the three-year course and so advanced flying training moved elsewhere.

Improvements to the college to support the academic syllabus included the building of Whittle Hall, opened

A Grob Tutor training aircraft over College Hall. (Crown Copyright 2002)

in 1962 by Sir Frank Whittle who had formulated many of his ideas for the jet engine while serving at Cranwell during the 1920s. Cranwell's link with engineering was formalised during the mid-1960s when the RAF's Technical College at Henlow, a similar cadet college for the training of engineering officers, merged with Cranwell. Then, in 1970, the graduate entry scheme was introduced to replace the flight cadet system. Under this new scheme university graduates completed a shortened initial officer training course before going on to their specialist training, while non-graduate entrants were trained at the RAF Officer Cadet Training Unit, Henlow. However, since 1980, all initial officer training has been carried out at Cranwell.

Cranwell had become the entry point for all officers entering the RAF. The College's responsibilities were also extended to include administrative control of the university air squadrons and, in 1992, the Directorate of Recruiting and Selection was formed at Cranwell, which included the Officers and Aircrew Selection Centre following its move from Biggin Hill. Amongst its many responsibilities today, the RAF College Cranwell continues to select and provide initial officer training for all RAF cadets and to develop them to become the RAF's leaders of the future.

19

Schneider Trophy

THROUGHOUT THE HISTORY of aviation, speed has always been an important factor, whether it is to reduce the time it takes to fly between two points or, in the case of military aviation, to give a fighter the edge over its opponent. There can be few greater eras in the quest for speed than the interwar years when aircraft designers and the early pioneers of high-speed flight pushed the aeroplane to its physical limits. With this in mind, there cannot be any greater object to define the RAF's early conquest of speed than the Schneider Trophy.

To encourage early technical advances in civil aviation, Jacques Schneider, a French financier and aircraft enthusiast, came up with the idea of a trophy and financial prize to be awarded annually to the winner of a race for seaplanes and flying boats. The trophy, which Schneider called the Coupe d'Aviation Maritime, was competed for the first time at Monaco in 1913 and won by the French. The following year, again in Monaco, Britain won the race with a Sopwith Tabloid flown by Howard Pixton. The competition was then interrupted by the First World War but resumed in 1919 at Bournemouth, this time with the Italians winning, although they were later disqualified and the event declared void.

Country of Origin:
France
Date: 1931
Location: Science
Museum, London
(© Science
Museum)

The competition was all about speed, with laps raced over a course and staged as time trials with competing aircraft setting off at specified times several minutes apart. Each nation could enter up to three competitors with an equal number of alternatives. The race was supervised by the Fédération Aéronautique Internationale and the aero club of the hosting country.

These contests had become extremely popular events, attended by crowds said to be in their hundreds of

thousands. Each year the race was hosted by the previous winning country, and it was always the intention that if a nation won the event for three consecutive years then it would retain the trophy.

Pictured at Calshot on 11 August 1931 is the S.6B that just a few weeks later won the Schneider Trophy outright for Britain. (© Science Museum)

In 1926, won by the Italians, both the Americans and Italians used military pilots. So competitive had the event become that the Air Ministry agreed to support the British team. Pilots were drawn from the RAF and the High Speed Flight was formed at the Marine Aircraft Experimental Establishment at Felixstowe. The following year, in Venice, a strong British presence included six aircraft from three manufacturers – two Supermarine S.5s, three Gloster IVs and a Short Crusader – all flown by RAF pilots of the High Speed Flight. The two S.5s, designed by the English aeronautical engineer Reginald Mitchell, took first and second place with the winning aircraft (N220), flown by Flight Lieutenant Sidney Webster, having been timed at an average speed of 281.6mph (453.3km/h).

The 1927 event was the last year the competition was held annually. From then on it was held biennially to allow designers more time to develop their aircraft. In 1929 the Schneider Trophy was held at Calshot, with Britain again winning; this time with the improved and refined Supermarine S.6, an all-metal construction powered by a new engine, the Rolls-Royce R. The winning aircraft (N247) was flown by Flight Lieutenant Dick Waghorn at an average speed of 328.6mph (528.9km/h).

By the time of the next meet in 1931, again held at Calshot, the British government had withdrawn funding, but a private and very generous donation from Lady Houston allowed Supermarine to compete once again and win the competition with the S.6B. The winning aircraft (S1595) was flown by Flight Lieutenant John Boothman (later Air Chief Marshal Sir John Boothman) and set a new average record speed of 340.1mph (547.3km/h). Boothman's success had meant a third straight win for Britain and so the Schneider Trophy was retained. Having won the trophy outright, the High Speed Flight was disbanded.

The Schneider Trophy had enabled aircraft designers to explore the boundaries of high-speed flight, with significant advances made in aerodynamics and engine design. It had also provided a testing ground for the ideas behind some of the best fighters of the Second World War; an example being the Spitfire, which was developed from the Supermarine S.6.

The Schneider Trophy is now on display at the Science Museum in South Kensington, London. It is a truly magnificent sculpture of silver and bronze set on a marble base, depicting a zephyr skimming the waves, and a nude winged figure is seen kissing a zephyr recumbent on a breaking wave. The heads of two other zephyrs and of Neptune, the god of the Sea, are surrounded by octopus and crabs. It symbolises speed conquering the elements of sea and air.

20

Air Force Cross

INSTITUTED BY A Royal Warrant dated 3 June 1918, the Air Force Cross (AFC) is awarded for an act, or acts, of valour, courage or devotion to duty whilst flying, though not in active operations against the enemy. The cross was designed by the Liverpudlian sculptor E. Carter Preston, and until 1921 the crosses were made by Messrs John Pinches Ltd of London, and thereafter by the Royal Mint.

The design of the cross represents aircraft propellers with wings between the arms. The obverse depicts Hermes riding on the wings of a Hawk holding a laurel wreath. At the top of the upper arm is the royal crown, while the other three arms bear the royal cypher of the reigning monarch at the time of issue. There have been four types of AFC: George V (with the four letters 'G V R I'); George VI first type (with the letters changed to 'G R I VI'); George VI second type ('G R VI'); and Elizabeth II ('E R II'). Awards are mentioned in the *London Gazette* and recipients are entitled to use the post-nominals 'AFC'. In the event of a recipient being awarded the AFC for a further act, a Bar is awarded and worn on the ribbon. The ribbon is of red and white alternate stripes, originally horizontal but in July 1919 the design was changed to the stripes running at an angle of 45 degrees from left to right.

The AFC was originally awarded to RAF officers and warrant officers (other ranks were entitled to the Air Force Medal) but could also be formally awarded to officers of Commonwealth countries. It has also been awarded to individuals from non-Commonwealth nations who rendered distinguished service to aviation in actual flying – an example being the award to the well-known American airman, Charles Lindbergh, for his transatlantic flight from New York to Paris in 1927. After the Second World War,

Country of Origin: UK
Date: 1918
Location: Private Collection (© Cecilia Cooper-Colby by kind permission of Richard Black at the London Medal Company)

eligibility for the award was expanded to include the other services. Then, in 1993, all ranks became eligible for the AFC following the discontinuation of the Air Force Medal.

One recipient of the AFC during the interwar years, and heavily linked with the previous object, was Flight Lieutenant George Stainforth, a member of the High Speed Flight, who helped Britain win the Schneider Trophy outright. The son of a solicitor, George Hedley Stainforth was born in 1899. He was educated at Dulwich College and Weymouth College, and then first joined the army before transferring to the RAF in 1923. After pilot training, Stainforth served with 19 Squadron but he was then posted to the Marine Aircraft Experimental Establishment for duties with the High Speed Flight.

Stainforth was due to compete in the 1929 Schneider Trophy competition held in Venice but his Gloster VI aircraft developed technical problems and so it had to be withdrawn. The event was won by a colleague but on the following day, 10 September 1929, Stainforth attempted to break the record over a measured mile in the Gloster VI. He managed to achieve a top speed of 351.3mph (565km/h) and a ratified world absolute speed record, averaged over four runs, of 336.3mph (541km/h). But he was to hold the record only briefly as a later run by a Supermarine S.6 achieved an average of more than 350mph (563km/h).

At the next event, in 1931, Stainforth was again part of the team. It was the historic third straight win, giving

Britain the right to keep the Schneider Trophy. Just days later, on 29 September 1931, Stainforth set a new world record for high-speed flight. Flying a S.6B (S1595) he became the first person to exceed 400mph (644km/h), flying the course at an average speed of 407.5mph (655.8km/h). For this achievement and his work with the High Speed Flight, George Stainforth was awarded the AFC.

Stainforth was later promoted to the rank of squadron leader, and by the time the Second World War broke out he was serving with the Central Flying School at Upavon. He then served at Farnborough carrying out various trials before being promoted to wing commander to command 89 Squadron, and it was while commanding the squadron in the Middle East that he was killed in action on 27 September 1942 at the age of 43. George Stainforth AFC was buried with full military honours at the British Cemetery at Ismailia in Egypt.

Flight Lieutenant George Stainforth. (Richard Black)

Stainforth's AFC is shown here with his other medals (from left to right): British War Medal 1914–20, Victory Medal, 1939–45 Star, Africa Star, and War Medal 1939–45.

21

Tiger Moth

NO BOOK ABOUT the history of the RAF would be complete without including some of its iconic aircraft, one of which is the Tiger Moth, a 1930s biplane operated by the RAF as a trainer for twenty years.

Designed by Geoffrey de Havilland in response to an Air Ministry specification for an *ab initio* training aircraft, and designated by the company as the DH82, the Tiger Moth I entered service with the RAF Central Flying School in 1932 as a two-seat primary trainer. In terms of its size, the aircraft was 24ft (7.3m) in length and had a wingspan of just over 29ft (8.8m). The first Tiger Moths were powered by a Gipsy III piston engine (120hp), although the subsequent Tiger Moth II (DH82A) was powered by the Gipsy Major I (130hp), giving the aircraft a top speed of just over 100mph (160km/h) – although its cruising speed was around 65mph (105km/h) – and an operating height up to 13,000ft (3,962m).

From the outset the Tiger Moth proved to be a robust aircraft and an excellent trainer. Although it required a positive and confident input from the student to fly, many instructors felt this helped them early identify an inept student pilot. The aircraft also proved simple and cheap to maintain. By the start of the Second World War more than 500 were in service and eventually 7,000 Tiger Moths were built in Britain, of which 4,000 were built during the Second World War specifically for the RAF. Thousands of RAF pilots got their first taste of flight in this wonderful aircraft until it was phased out of service in 1952 to be replaced by the de Havilland Chipmunk.

The Tiger Moth continues to be a huge success worldwide and remains in widespread use as a recreational aircraft in many countries. This wonderful example shown

Country of Origin: UK

Date: 1932

Location: Temple Bruer, Lincolnshire (Courtesy of David Porter)

R4959 landing at its home landing strip at Temple Bruer in Lincolnshire. (Graham Robson)

here is a DH82A Tiger Moth built by de Havilland at Hatfield in 1939. With the RAF registration of R4959 it was initially allocated to No. 5 Maintenance Unit at RAF Kemble in February 1940 for issue to service and later that year was delivered to No. 16 Operational Training Unit at RAF Upper Heyford where it served as a communications aircraft. The following year R4959 was transferred to No. 1 Elementary Flying Training School (EFTS) at Hatfield and then, in February 1942, to No. 26 EFTS at Theale near Reading, where it remained until the end of 1944 when it suffered damage in a major accident. After the war, R4959 was refurbished and had various homes as a training aircraft until it was struck off RAF charge in 1953. It was then bought by Rollasons and overhauled for use by the Tiger Moth Club at Redhill. In 1960 it was civilian registered as G-ARAZ and has since been further refurbished and painted in its RAF wartime training colours. The aircraft has changed hands many times since leaving the RAF. It is now owned by David Porter and is operated from his home in Lincolnshire.

22

Browning 0.303in Machine Gun

WHETHER FITTED IN aircraft for offensive or defensive purposes, machine guns needed to be light in weight, reliable and have sufficient firepower to be effective. Achieving all three proved to be a difficult challenge but machine guns had come a long way since they had first been adapted from army models used during the First World War. In 1934 the RAF selected the Browning machine gun to fire its standard 0.303in (7.7mm) ammunition as a replacement for the earlier Vickers machine gun, and it was to be the Browning that was to become the standard machine gun fitted to RAF fighters and in the gun turrets of most British bombers during the Second World War.

Named after the successful American firearms designer John Browning, the gun was manufactured under licence in the UK by Vickers-Armstrongs and the Birmingham Small Arms Company (BSA). It was designed as a wing-mounted machine gun for fighters and was essentially a 1930-pattern belt-fed Colt-Browning machine gun

Country of Origin:
USA
Date: 1934
Location:
Trenchard
Museum,
RAF Halton,
Buckinghamshire
(By kind
permission of
the Station
Commander RAF
Halton)

with just a couple of modifications required for use with cordite-based British ammunition. The gun measured 3ft 8in (1.1m) in length and weighed nearly 22lb (10kg). It had an impressive 1,150 rounds per minute rate of fire, a muzzle velocity of 2,660ft per second (810m/sec) and a maximum range of around 1,000 yards (914m).

By the start of the Second World War, the RAF's two principal fighters – the Hawker Hurricane and Supermarine Spitfire – were armed with eight Brownings. During those early days, ammunition belts were made up

manually by armourers using belt-making machines but these were later replaced by ones that were electrically powered. The Browning was also adapted for use in the gun turrets of RAF bombers and reconnaissance aircraft, and it was the MkII (almost identical to the MkI but with a modified muzzle attachment) that became the standard machine gun used in most gun turrets during the Second World War; for example, in all three of the four-engine heavy bombers – the Short Stirling, the Handley Page Halifax and the Avro Lancaster – and the Short Sunderland of Coastal Command.

The Browning 0.303in machine gun proved to be reliable and accurate, and only towards the end of the war did the RAF start to use heavier-calibre 0.5in machine guns in its bombers. More than 500,000 Browning machine guns were manufactured in the UK during the Second World War, mostly by BSA, after which production came to an end.

23

Rolls-Royce Merlin Engine

THE ROLLS-ROYCE MERLIN was one of the most important aircraft engines ever built, although it was initially developed as a private venture when Rolls-Royce realised there was a need for a larger engine than their 21-litre (1,296cu. in) Kestrel in service at the time.

The new design, known as the PV-12 (standing for private venture 12-cylinder), first flew in a Hawker Hart biplane in 1935. From the PV-12 came the Merlin B (of which just two were built) to follow the company's convention of naming its engines after birds of prey. Then came the Merlin C, a development of the B with the crankcase and cylinder blocks having become separate castings to alleviate earlier problems. After further modifications, the early production engines, designated the Merlin I, were completed in 1936 for the Fairey Battle. From this engine came the main production version, the Merlin II, which produced 1,030hp at 3,000rpm at 5,500ft (1,676m), to power the RAF's new fighters, the Hurricane and the Spitfire.

The Merlin continued to be built in large numbers and a series of rapid developments, brought about because of wartime needs, meant that around fifty marks were eventually built – making the Merlin one of the most successful engines of the Second World War. Amongst

Country of Origin: UK

Date: 1936

Location: Science Museum, London (© Science Museum)

A stunning image of a Merlin-powered Spitfire of the Battle of Britain Memorial Flight performing a 'hot start'. (Crown Copyright 2013)

the many RAF types to be powered by the Merlin were the Boulton Paul Defiant, Bristol Beaufighter, de Havilland Mosquito, Vickers Wellington, Armstrong Whitworth Whitley, Handley Page Halifax and the Avro Lancaster, an aircraft for which the Merlin was built in vast numbers – more than for any other aircraft type.

Because of the demand, Merlin production was spread far and wide. They were built in Derby, Crewe and Glasgow by Rolls-Royce, as well as in Manchester by Ford of Britain and also under licence in the United States by Packard. By the time production came to an end in 1950, more than 160,000 Merlin engines had been built. Several have survived with some even still in operation, for example with the RAF's Battle of Britain Memorial Flight or in private ownership worldwide. The main image is of a Merlin on display at the Science Museum in London.

24

Mitchell Statue

THIS WONDERFUL IMAGE is of the most impressive Mitchell Statue, a slate sculpture of Reginald Mitchell by Stephen Kettle, displayed at the Science Museum as part of an exhibition titled 'Inside the Spitfire: Personal stories of Britain's most famous plane'. It shows Mitchell standing at his lectern, next to a model of his most famous design.

Born in 1895, Mitchell was one of the country's most famous aeronautical engineers. He gained an apprenticeship at the age of 16 but it was working at a locomotive engineering works that he first learned his trade. He ended up working in the company's drawing office but his spare time was spent studying engineering and mathematics and, in 1917, he joined the Supermarine Aviation Works at Southampton. Within two years he was the chief designer and by the time he marked his tenth year with the company he had become its technical director.

Supermarine was primarily a seaplane manufacturer. Several of Mitchell's designs were flying boats, but also amongst his designs were racing seaplanes built by the company to compete in the Schneider Trophy. These included the S.6, which won the competition in 1929, and then the S.6B, which won the trophy outright for Britain two years later.

Mitchell was made a Commander of the Order of the British Empire (CBE) in 1932 for his contribution to high-speed flight. His technical expertise in the design of these highly successful racing seaplanes soon led to him proceeding with a new aircraft, an all-metal monoplane fighter that would eventually become the iconic Spitfire.

Sadly, though, Mitchell would not live to see just how successful the Spitfire would go on to be. He died of cancer in 1937.

Country of Origin: UK
Date: 1895–1937
Location: Science Museum, London
(© Science Museum)

SIR SYDNEY CAMM
CBE, Hon. FRAeS
1893 - 1966

25

Bronze Bust of Sydney Camm

THIS BRONZE BUST of the British aeronautical engineer Sir Sydney Camm, designer of the legendary Hawker Hurricane, stands proudly in the entrance corridor at the RAF Club in Piccadilly, a stunning building in the West End of London and officially the RAF's club since 1922. The bronze bust is by Ambrose Barber and stands alongside another of Reginald Mitchell. Between them, their aircraft designs helped save Britain during the Second World War.

Sydney Camm was born in 1893. The eldest of twelve children, he followed his father into carpentry and soon found a passion for aeronautics. By the start of the First World War he was working as a carpenter at the Martinsyde aircraft company at Brooklands in Surrey. He was later promoted into the drawing office and in 1923 joined the Hawker Aircraft Company at Kingston-upon-Thames as a senior draughtsman. His first success was the design of the Cygnet and by 1925 he was Hawker's chief designer.

Camm soon started developing a form of metal construction and among his early designs were the Hawker Hart, a two-seat biplane light bomber, which entered service with the RAF in 1930, and its counterpart, the Hawker Fury, a fast and agile single-seat biplane fighter capable of more than 200mph (322km/h), which entered service the following year.

By now Camm had become convinced that the future of aviation lay in a monoplane design. Using the knowledge gained from his two latest biplanes, combined with the improved engine technology becoming available at the time, he was confident he could design a contemporary monoplane fighter that would be faster and more deadly than ever before to replace the RAF's ageing biplanes.

Country of Origin: UK
Date: 1893–1966
Location: RAF Club, London
(© Dan Soliman by kind permission of the RAF Club)

However, his proposal to build a low-wing monoplane fighter was initially received with uncertainty at the Air Ministry, as were many ideas at that time, as some considered there to be no point in risking large sums of money on new and uncertain designs.

Fortunately, though, the foresight of the private aircraft industry led to the project being funded by the company. Work began in 1933 on a design that was essentially a scaled-up Fury, and so the project was initially known as the Fury Monoplane. The project gained momentum the following year when increasing instability in Europe led to the Air Ministry issuing Specification F.36/34 calling for a high-speed monoplane single-seat fighter.

The specification had been based on Hawker's design, now being referred to as the Hawker Monoplane Fighter, and powered by a new Rolls-Royce Merlin C engine, the prototype (K5083) first flew at Brooklands on 6 November 1935. With Hawker's chief test pilot, Flight Lieutenant George Bulman, at the controls, the overall silver appearance of the new aircraft presented a spectacular sight.

There then followed a series of successful company test flights, during which the aircraft reached a top speed of 325mph (520km/h) at 16,500ft (4,950m), before K5083 was delivered to the Aeroplane and Armament Experimental Establishment at Martlesham Heath to undergo service trials before acceptance into the RAF. By now, the new

The highly successful Hawker Hurricane, the design of Sir Sydney Camm. Shown here is LF363 of the Battle of Britain Memorial Flight, which is believed to have been the last Hurricane delivered to the RAF. (Crown Copyright 2015)

fighter had been given the name Hurricane. With an order for 600 aircraft, production began immediately. The first production airframe, L1547 (powered by a Merlin II engine), made its first flight in October 1937 and just weeks later the first four Hurricane MkIs were delivered to 111 Squadron at Northolt. By September 1939 there were seventeen Hurricane squadrons serving with Fighter Command.

The Hurricane was one of the finest aircraft of its generation and one of the most important of the Second World War. Not only was it a great fighter, its rugged construction and excellent manoeuvrability meant that it went on to become a highly effective ground-attack aircraft in all of the RAF's operational theatres, carrying larger weapons than ever anticipated. But its finest hour was undoubtedly the Battle of Britain.

Camm went on to design the Hawker Typhoon and Hawker Tempest, two aircraft that helped pave the way for the Allied victory in 1945. After the war, he was instrumental in many jet-powered designs, most notably the Hawker Hunter and the Hawker P.1127, the forerunner to the Harrier, and was knighted for his contribution to British Aviation before he finally retired as Hawker's chief designer in 1965.

Sydney Camm died the following year at the age of 72. Of all his designs, it is probably the Hawker Hurricane that he will be best remembered. It will forever be one of the RAF's most iconic aircraft and is one to which the British public owe so much.

26

Swingate Chain Home Station

THE IMPORTANCE OF radar is well understood today, but in the 1930s it was a new concept. And so two surviving transmitter towers at Swingate, high up on the cliffs overlooking the town of Dover, provide a historic reminder of just how important the new technology was to Britain's survival during the early months of the Second World War.

From the earliest days of radio technology, signals had been used to aid navigation using the radio direction-finding technique, but it had been the observation that moving objects caused a noticeable pattern to develop in a received signal that caused much excitement. Although the principles were widely recognised at the time, it was British scientists and technicians that were to make it work.

The idea of detecting an aircraft at range was clearly of interest to the RAF. One man to be impressed by the concept was Air Marshal Hugh Dowding, then the Air Member for Supply and Research, who agreed to fund further development provided that a practical demonstration could be carried out. What followed in February 1935 became known as the Daventry Experiment. Using the BBC transmitter at Borough Hill near Daventry, a Handley Page Heyford bomber passing through the area produced notable effects on the receiver.

The concept had been demonstrated and led to the idea of building a network of stations, with separate transmitters and receivers, along the east coast of England, each separated from the next by about 20 miles. In early

Country of Origin: UK

Date: 1938

Location: Swingate near Dover, Kent

1936 a team moved in to Bawdsey Manor in Suffolk to establish the Air Ministry Experimental Station and later that year work began on a second station at Swingate near Dover in Kent.

There were soon five operational stations covering the approaches to London and by the outbreak of the Second World War there was an entire network of twenty-one. With a range of up to 150 miles (240km), each station was designed to detect an air raid and then report the information to its group's operations room which, in turn, would direct RAF fighters to intercept the raid. Given the code name Chain Home, it was the world's first integrated air defence system capable of detecting and tracking aircraft, and within months the network stretched from the north of Scotland to the south coast of England. Improvements would soon see the installation of an Identification Friend or Foe system that enabled controllers to differentiate between friendly and enemy aircraft, and the addition of Chain Home Low radars to fill the gaps in low-level coverage left by the original technology. The British had radar and without it the outcome of the Battle of Britain, and indeed the Second World War, might well have been quite different.

The Chain Home station at Swingate shown here was completed in 1938. During the summer of 1940 it came under the control of Fighter Command's No. 11 Group and given its proximity to France was firmly in the front line of Britain's defence. It was one of a number of radar stations targeted by the Luftwaffe in August 1940, resulting in some damage to one of the towers as well as some huts. However, Swingate remained operational throughout the battle; albeit with some reliance on emergency equipment.

Swingate was retained after the war but its days as a front-line radar station ended in 1955 when a new early warning and control radar at nearby RAF Ash came online, although Swingate continued to be used until the late 1980s when technological advances finally made it redundant. Three of the original transmitting towers survived until 2010 when one was removed. However, because of their historical importance, these two towers have survived, along with the original transmitter building, on what is now a Grade 2 listed site.

Part 3
The RAF at War

Telephone Nos.: BUSHEY HEATH 1661 (6 lines).
　　　　　　　　 BUSHEY HEATH 1646 (4 lines).
Telegraphic Address :
"AIRGENARCH, STANMORE."

Reference :— FC/S.19048.

HEADQUARTERS, FIGHTER COMMAND,
ROYAL AIR FORCE,
BENTLEY PRIORY,
STANMORE,
MIDDLESEX.

SECRET.

16th May, 1940.

Sir,

      I have the honour to refer to the very serious
calls which have recently been made upon the Home Defence
Fighter Units in an attempt to stem the German invasion
on the Continent.

2.   I hope and believe that our Armies may yet be
victorious in France and Belgium, but we have to face the
possibility that they may be defeated.

3.   In this case I presume that there is no-one who
will deny that England should fight on, even though the
remainder of the Continent of Europe is dominated by the
Germans.

4.   For this purpose it is necessary to retain some
minimum fighter strength in this country and I must request
that the Air Council will inform me what they consider this
minimum strength to be, in order that I may make my
dispositions accordingly.

5.   I would remind the Air Council that the last
estimate which they made as to the force necessary to defend
this country was 52 Squadrons, and my strength has now been
reduced to the equivalent of 36 Squadrons.

6.   Once a decision has been reached as to the limit
on which the Air Council and the Cabinet are prepared to
stake the existence of the country, it should be made clear to
the Allied Commanders on the Continent that not a single
aeroplane from Fighter Command beyond the limit will be sent
across the Channel, no matter how desperate the situation
may become.

7.   It will, of course, be remembered that the estimate
of 52 Squadrons was based on the assumption that the attack
would come from the eastwards except in so far as the defences
might be outflanked in flight. We have now to face the
possibility that attacks may come from Spain or even from the
North coast of France. The result is that our line is very
much extended at the same time as our resources are reduced.

8.   I must point out that within the last few days
the equivalent of 10 Squadrons have been sent to France, that
the Hurricane Squadrons remaining in this country are
seriously depleted, and that the more squadrons which are sent
to France the higher will be the wastage and the more
insistent the demands for reinforcements.

/I....

The Under Secretary of State,
  Air Ministry,
    LONDON. W.C.2.

27

Dowding Letter

ANOTHER HISTORIC LETTER held by the RAF College Cranwell, again protected by its plastic covering, is the original letter written by Air Chief Marshal Sir Hugh Dowding, the Air Officer Commanding-in-Chief of Fighter Command, on 16 May 1940 to the Under Secretary of State at the Air Ministry, in which he puts forward his views on the sending of more RAF fighters across the English Channel to France.

Dowding wrote this historic letter from his headquarters at RAF Bentley Priory, near Stanmore in Middlesex, following the Nazi invasion of France and the Low Countries, which had begun on 10 May. In response to the rapid German advance, the French Prime Minister, Paul Reynaud, had asked Britain for more squadrons of RAF fighters to be sent across the Channel, to which the British Prime Minister, Winston Churchill, had agreed to provide support to France in every possible way.

Dowding's letter contains ten short, but to the point, paragraphs. The final two crucial paragraphs over the page are worth repeating here. They read as follows:

Country of Origin: UK
Date: 16 May 1940
Location: RAF College Cranwell, Lincolnshire (By kind permission of the Commandant RAF College Cranwell)

9.   I must therefore request as a matter of paramount urgency the Air Ministry will consider and decide what level of strength is to be left to the Fighter Command for the defences of this country, and will assure me that when this level has been reached, not one fighter will be sent across the Channel however urgent and insistent the appeals for help may be.

10.   I believe that, if an adequate fighter force is kept in this country, if the fleet remains in being, and if Home Forces are suitably organised to resist invasion, we should be able to carry on the war single handed for

Air Chief Marshal
Sir Hugh Dowding
was the Air Officer
Commanding-in-Chief
of Fighter Command
during 1940.

some time, if not indefinitely. But, if the Home Defence Force is drained away in desperate attempts to remedy the situation in France, defeat in France will involve the final, complete and irremediable defeat of this country.

I have the honour to be,

Sir,

Your obedient Servant

Dowding's letter has since been described as the letter that changed the course of history. There is nothing else to say!

28

Aircraft Location Instrument

BRITAIN'S AIR DEFENCE system during the summer of 1940 was not just about the technology of radar and the heroics of 'The Few'. The RAF's fighter pilots needed as much accurate information as they could get and this was delivered to them from a ground controller, with information being provided from a variety of sources. Amongst these sources were the visual observations of hostile aircraft (including number, course and height) provided by members of the Observer Corps, a civil defence organisation on the ground. In fact, once enemy aircraft had crossed the English coastline it was such observations that provided the best means of tracking the enemy raid.

The origins of the Observer Corps date back to the First World War when an early form of an integrated defensive system was set up in response to the Zeppelin airship raids on London. The system in place then included observers, searchlights, guns, aircraft and the police to warn the public, and its success led to the formation of the Observer Corps in 1925. During the Battle of Britain, its members worked around the clock – twenty-four hours a day, seven days a week – plotting enemy aircraft and passing essential information to an Observer Centre. The information was then passed on to RAF Fighter Command, which, in turn, passed it on to the pilots.

Observer posts were formed into groups, identified by a letter and number: for example, A3. Each post was typically established with up to sixteen observers (although only two observers were required to be on duty at any one time) and equipped with an Aircraft Location Instrument, like the one shown here, a grid-squared chart attached to a circular table, a telephone connected to the Observer Centre and

Country of Origin:
UK
Date: 1940
Location:
Trenchard
Museum,
RAF Halton,
Buckinghamshire
(By kind
permission of
the Station
Commander RAF
Halton)

binoculars. The No. 1 Observer was responsible for sighting the instrument on an enemy aircraft and estimating the grid square of its position, from which its height could be approximated. This information was passed to the Observer Centre by the No. 2 Observer who acted as the telephonist. He also listened out for the bearing passed by a neighbouring post, and with the two posts working together the aircraft's bearing could be cross-plotted on each other's chart to determine the actual position of the aircraft. Once the actual position was known the corrected height could be read off the instrument.

By taking information from three posts at any one time, it was possible to obtain even more accuracy through triangulation, and from reports received from various posts the centre could then work out the track of the enemy aircraft. The only limitation of the instrument was when trying to assess low-flying aircraft – in which case the observers had to estimate height and position as best they could.

Following its success during the Battle of Britain, the Observer Corps was awarded the title 'Royal' by HM King George VI in 1941, after which the ROC became a uniformed civil defence organisation administered by Fighter Command. Women were soon allowed to serve in

Observer post of the Royal Observer Corps, showing the Aircraft Location Instrument in use and its two-man team. (AHB)

the ROC and when the first V-1 flying bombs appeared over southern England during 1944 it was like going back to the summer four years before; only this time the observation posts would also fire illuminating flares to visually alert the RAF's patrolling fighters of the position of the V-1s.

With the Second World War over, the ROC was stood down but it was soon revived as a civil defence organisation during the Cold War – albeit with a different role. With the risk of a nuclear attack shaping British defence policy, the United Kingdom Warning and Monitoring Organisation was established under Home Office control and the ROC given the task of providing primary data on the position and magnitude of atomic weapons during any attack. Composed mainly of civilian part-time volunteers, ROC personnel wore a uniform of the style of the RAF and latterly came under the administrative control of RAF Strike Command (with the Commandant ROC being a serving RAF air commodore) and the operational control of the Home Office. In its latter years the ROC had more than 10,000 personnel but following the 1990 Defence Review *Options for Change*, its main field force element was stood down before the Headquarters ROC at Bentley Priory finally disbanded in 1996.

29

Fordson Sussex Balloon Winch Vehicle

AT THE HEIGHT of the Battle of Britain there were around 2,000 barrage balloons defending key targets around London and south-east England, and so lorries such as this Fordson Sussex balloon winch vehicle were once a common sight. They are, of course, a much rarer sight these days and this example, PHX 376, has been lovingly restored in all its detail and is now on display at the RAF Museum Hendon.

Vehicles such as this were an essential part of the RAF's Balloon Command. The command had been formed in November 1938 under the command of Air Vice-Marshal Owen Boyd. With responsibility for controlling all UK-based barrage balloons, its headquarters was set up at RAF Stanmore Park, close to HQ Fighter Command at Bentley Priory, and by the outbreak of the Second World War there were around 800 balloons available and 600 balloon winch vehicles in service with the RAF.

The balloon barrage was an important part of Britain's overall defence system. The large balloons, fixed on steel cables and measuring over 60ft (18.3m) in length, were raised to form a barrage around important locations, such as vital factories or ports, to protect them against attack by low-flying aircraft.

The balloon was carried on the vehicle in a large green package behind the winch, which was designed to wind in and out at a controlled speed. The balloon was simply a means of supporting the steel cable. Any aircraft flying into the cable would be brought down or, at least, suffer significant damage, and so the sight of the balloons would at least make an enemy crew think twice before carrying out a low-level attack. They would instead be forced to

Country of Origin: UK
Date: 1939
Location: RAF Museum Hendon, London
(© RAF Museum)

make their attack from a higher altitude where it was much harder to ensure bombing accuracy. However, the balloons not only provided a deterrent against enemy aircraft, they occasionally proved a hazard for the defending fighters as well.

The establishment of Balloon Command varied during its six years in existence. In the summer of 1940, for example, the command controlled five groups, with each group covering a geographic area and with its organisation based on squadrons. The brunt of the action was seen by No. 30 (Balloon Barrage) Group, which covered London. Led by the former First World War pilot, Group Captain William Guilfoyle, the group had four Balloon Centres and more than 500 balloons. No. 1 Balloon Centre, with three auxiliary squadrons – 901, 902 and 903 (County of London) (Balloon) Squadrons – and more than 150 balloons (including forty waterborne), was located at Kidbrooke in south-east London. No. 2 Balloon Centre (with two squadrons) was at Hook in Surrey while No. 3 (also with two squadrons) was at Stanmore in Middlesex. No. 4 Balloon Centre, with three squadrons, was the largest of the centres. It had nearly 160 balloons (including thirteen waterborne) and was located at Chigwell in the Epping Forest district of Essex. The other groups (Nos 31–34 (Balloon Barrage) Groups) covered the Midlands, northern England and Scotland.

By the end of 1941 the number of balloons had risen to around 2,500 of various types and they again provided a valuable line of defence during the V-1 flying-bomb attacks of 1944. Whereas four years before the balloons had mainly been used as static defences, the mobility of the winch lorry meant that balloons were now moved into positions depending on the direction of attack. And unlike a bomber crew who could see the balloons and, therefore, try to avoid them, the V-1s could not and it has

Winch vehicles such as the Fordson Sussex were an essential part of the RAF's Balloon Command during the Second World War. (RAF Museum)

been estimated that more than 250 were brought down by the cables of barrage balloons. Balloon Command was also responsible for providing squadrons for service overseas. However, once the war was over, there was no further need for barrage balloons and so the command was disbanded in June 1945.

PHX 376, shown here, is a Fordson Sussex Type E917T. Fordson was the brand name given to the mass-produced trucks (and tractors) manufactured by Henry Ford & Son in America and the UK, with the 'E' standing for English, the '9' the year of manufacture, i.e. 1939, and the 'T' for truck. It is a fine example of one of the more common balloon winch vehicles used during the Second World War. Powered by a 30hp 3621cc V8 engine, and fitted with a Wild MkIV winch (made by M.B. Wild & Co. of Birmingham) for raising and lowering the balloon, it weighs 4.9 tons (4,400kg) and has a maximum speed of 20mph (32km/h). It has a steel wire mesh safety cage to protect the winch operator from injury in case the balloon cable should break and for protection during the lowering of the balloon in windy conditions when handling lines were flying around. Behind the cage is the cable drum housing and the cable pulley is at the rear of the vehicle. PHX 376 was restored in its pre-war air force blue paint scheme by Ken Kelly and Eddie Smith, and presented to the RAF Museum during the mid-1990s. It stands on display as a marvellous tribute to the activities of RAF Balloon Command during the Second World War.

30

Plotting Table

THE PLOTTING TABLE shown here is in the former underground operations room at RAF Uxbridge in Middlesex, home to Headquarters No. 11 Group during the Second World War. Now known as the Battle of Britain Bunker, this historic room has been restored to how it looked on 15 September 1940 – remembered today as Battle of Britain Day.

During the summer of 1940, RAF Fighter Command was divided into groups, each covering a geographical sector of the UK. Bearing the brunt of the Luftwaffe onslaught was No. 11 Group, under the command of Air Vice-Marshal Keith Park, with responsibility for planning and co-ordinating the air defence of London and south-east England. And so, it was from this operations room that most of Fighter Command's participation in the battle was co-ordinated and where key decisions were made that ultimately decided the fate of the nation.

Park's group was divided into seven sectors around London – Tangmere (Sector A), Kenley (Sector B), Biggin Hill (C), Hornchurch (D), North Weald (E), Debden (F) and Northolt (Z) – with his headquarters at Hillingdon House within the grounds of RAF Uxbridge. One of the key parts of the underground operations room was the plotting table. Information coming in from a variety of sources, such as from the radar stations and Observer Corps posts, was first filtered for its relevance before being fed to the operations room for display on the table and surrounding boards, with crucial information then passed on to the fighter pilots by the controllers.

The plotting table consisted of an outline map centred on the group's area of responsibility. As enemy raids built in size the details were fed to the plotters through

Country of Origin: UK
Date: 1940
Location: Battle of Britain Bunker, Uxbridge, Middlesex (Image shown with the kind permission of the Battle of Britain Bunker)

their headphones and then displayed on the table using magnetic rakes and a coloured system of counters – red, yellow and blue – to represent aircraft formations. The colours used changed every five minutes according to the colour-coded clock on the wall. This meant that information being displayed to the controllers, and therefore passed on to the fighter pilots, was as accurate as possible and never more than fifteen minutes old. The senior controller, with overall tactical control of the air battle, was positioned in a soundproofed central box, portioned off from the main working areas by glass screens, overlooking the plotting table and the tote board providing squadron readiness states and other relevant information. On 15 September 1940, the British Prime Minister, Winston Churchill, visited the operations room and by chance witnessed a significant moment of the battle. It was then that he famously asked what reserve squadrons were available, to which the answer was 'none'.

As well as playing a key part in the Battle of Britain, the operations room had also been responsible for controlling fighter operations during the evacuation at Dunkirk and was also used extensively during the D-Day Normandy landings in 1944.

In 1958, No. 11 Group was relocated to Martlesham Heath and the operations room closed. It was restored during the 1970s and has since become a force development asset and public attraction. Although RAF Uxbridge closed in 2010, the Ministry of Defence and Hillingdon Council have worked together to secure the future of the Battle of Britain Bunker and preserve the site's heritage for generations to come. It is open to the public for guided tours with prior arrangement.

The Air Training Corps
Gazette

| Vol. I No. 1 | MARCH 1941 | Price 6d |

In this Number

To the Air Training Corps
From the Commandant, AIR COMMODORE J. A. CHAMIER C.B., C.M.G., D.S.O., O.B.E.

A New Chapter
By Mr. J. F. WOLFENDEN, Director of Pre-entry Training

The Royal Road to the Royal Air Force

News from the Squadrons

Other features include

Captain W. E. Johns
To Bale or Not to Bale
Biggles Flies Alone

Aeroplane Recognition Drawings
By JAMES H. STEVENS

Wireless
By JOHN CLARRICOATS

Goering's Semi-Secret Weapons

The Journal of
THE AIR TRAINING CORPS

31

First Edition of the *Air Training Corps Gazette*

SHOWN HERE IS a rare first edition of the *Air Training Corps Gazette*, issued in March 1941 as the new monthly journal of the newly formed youth organisation. For the record, it was on sale for 6*d* (six old pence).

The gazette was the work of William Earl Johns, a former RAF pilot and prolific author of adventure stories (usually written under the pen name of Captain W.E. Johns), who is probably best remembered as the creator of Biggles. Included in this first edition (Vol. 1, No. 1) is a message to the new Air Training Corps (ATC) from its commandant, Air Commodore John Chamier, now remembered as its founding father, and the opening episode of 'Biggles Flies Alone' – the one Biggles story to be serialised in these wartime periodicals and later to become a book titled *Biggles Defies the Swastika*.

The idea of military cadets was not new. They date back to the mid-nineteenth century when several schools around the country first formed armed, uniformed units, made up of older boys and adults, with the purpose of protecting Britain in the event of an attack from overseas. By the turn of the century there were units in over a hundred schools and in 1908 these became the Officers' Training Corps (OTC). During the 1920s and '30s, individual sections within these cadet units started to form, with those in the Air Sections wearing an RAF armband with the army uniform. Then, in 1938, the Air Defence Cadet Corps (ADCC) was founded.

The ADCC had been the vision of John Chamier, a retired RAF officer and the secretary of the Air League of the British Empire. His passion for aviation and determination to raise awareness of the RAF, and its vital

Country of Origin:
UK
Date: 1941
Location:
RAF Scampton
Heritage Centre,
Lincolnshire
(By kind
permission of Mark
Wood and the
station commander
RAF Scampton)

role in any future war, led to him coming up with the idea to attract and train young men with an interest in aviation. From his own experience as a pilot during the First World War he knew that training time would be very limited in any future conflict, and so the sooner people could be trained the better prepared and more experienced they would be in combat. His plan, therefore, was to set up squadrons of young cadets across the country, in as many cities and towns as possible.

Chamier knew that he would have to rely on local people to organise and run the squadrons, and he would also have to rely on cadets paying a subscription to fund the new organisation. But Chamier need not have worried. His idea quickly captured the imagination and mood of the country. The Second World War was looming and in their eagerness to help the nation prepare for war, young men joined in the thousands.

When the Second World War broke out, many squadron buildings were taken over by the military and adult instructors joined the armed forces, and so the cadets were moved on to RAF stations where they were used for a variety of tasks. These included filling sandbags, moving aircraft and equipment, carrying messages, and loading belts of ammunition.

The Chief of the Air Staff, Air Chief Marshal Sir Stephen Hillier, himself a former cadet, inspecting RAF Air Cadets on a parade held at Cranwell on 13 August 2016 to mark the 75th anniversary of the organisation. (Crown Copyright 2016; credited to Cranwell Serco Photographic)

The government soon realised the value of the cadets and so in 1940 took control of the ADCC with the idea of reorganising and renaming it. The outcome was the ATC, which was officially established on 5 February 1941 with HM King George VI as its Air Commodore-in-Chief. The OTC Air Sections were soon absorbed into the new ATC and by the end of the war, just seven years after the ADCC had first formed, it is estimated that almost 100,000 cadets had gone on to join the RAF.

After the war the school-based OTC units became part of the Combined Cadet Force (CCF), made up of cadets of all three services, with many of the original Air Sections of the OTC becoming CCF (RAF) units. Today, the RAF Air Cadet Organisation is sponsored by the RAF and offers young people, boys and girls aged between twelve and twenty, the chance to get involved in a hands-on experience of activities and courses that are designed to challenge and develop individual skills. It currently has more than 40,000 members, made up of those in the ATC (which currently consists of more than 900 squadrons within communities around the UK) and the RAF section of the CCF (in around 200 independent and state schools across the country). The three aims of the RAF Air Cadets are: to promote and encourage a practical interest in aviation and the RAF among young people; to provide training which will be useful in the armed forces and civilian life; and to encourage the spirit of adventure and develop qualities of leadership and good citizenship. There is also the fact, of course, that being an RAF air cadet is fun!

32

Flying Helmet

PICTURED HERE IS a Second World War flying helmet, a Type C, which replaced the earlier Type B (synonymous with fighter pilots during the Battle of Britain) in 1941. The Type C is of brown leather chamois-lined, with rubber earpieces with circular-shaped ear telephones. The early models had no integral wiring, although this was remedied later in the war, and had leather chinstraps; these were eventually replaced with elasticated fabric ones. The metal pop fasteners are on the left side of the face and a metal guide place is fixed to the right.

This is an early version of the Type C (wired) flying helmet with a bell-shaped jack plug connecting the helmet to the aircraft communication system. It is displayed with a rare G-Type oxygen mask and more common MkVIII angled flying goggles, as typically worn by crews of Bomber Command during the latter years of the war.

Flying helmets, masks and goggles were continuously improved during the Second World War. For example, earlier goggles, with curved celluloid lenses fitted into narrow blackened metal frames as worn by fighter pilots, were superseded by split-lens glass after it was found that the earlier version melted during a cockpit fire and so gave the pilot little or no eye protection.

The set of flying helmet, goggles and mask shown here is on display at the RAF Scampton Heritage Centre where it is on long-term loan from the Thorpe Camp Visitors Centre, situated on what was once the communal site of RAF Woodhall Spa.

Country of Origin:
UK
Date: 1941
Location:
RAF Scampton
Heritage Centre,
Lincolnshire
(By kind
permission of
the Station
Commander RAF
Scampton)

The RAF's legendary fighter pilot Douglas Bader. (AHB)

33

Douglas Bader's Wings

THESE WINGS BELONGED to the legendary Douglas Bader, probably the RAF's most famous fighter pilot of all time. His story is a quite extraordinary one and his name became widely known after Bader's life was immortalised on screen in the 1956 biographical film *Reach for the Sky*.

Born in London in 1910, Bader joined the RAF as an officer cadet at the RAF College Cranwell. After graduating in 1930 he was posted to 23 Squadron at Kenley and the following year represented the squadron in an aerobatics competition at the Hendon air display. Later that year, though, he crashed his Bristol Bulldog while attempting to roll the aircraft at low level. Miraculously, Bader survived but he lost both of his legs, one above the knee and one below, and so began his personal story of extreme courage.

Bader initially remained in the RAF but was clearly unable to fly and so he left the service and ended up working for a petroleum company. However, when the Second World War broke out he asked to return to flying and with the RAF suffering a shortage of pilots, he finally managed to persuade the service to give him a chance.

After successfully completing a flying assessment at the Central Flying School, Bader re-joined the RAF and after a short refresher course joined 19 Squadron at Duxford. It was now February 1940 and the squadron was equipped with Spitfires but his stay with 19 was to be short-lived. The following month he was promoted to flight lieutenant and posted across the airfield to 222 Squadron, another Spitfire squadron, as a flight commander.

On 1 June 1940, Bader scored his first aerial success; a Messerschmitt Bf 109 near Dunkirk. He was then promoted to squadron leader and given command of 242 Squadron at Coltishall. This time he was to fly the

Country of Origin:
UK
Date: 1941
Location:
Imperial War
Museum Duxford,
Cambridgeshire
(© IWM)

Hurricane but recent losses and poor serviceability had reduced morale and so Bader's first task was to get his squadron back into shape. By the end of the Battle of Britain he had claimed nine more enemy aircraft destroyed, for which he was awarded the DSO – his citation stating that he had 'displayed gallantry and leadership of the highest order'.

Bader was then posted to Tangmere on promotion as Wing Commander Flying. The wing was equipped with Spitfire IIs and was on the offensive. Bader soon took his personal score to nineteen, plus several more shared, earning him the Distinguished Flying Cross (DFC) and Bar, and a Bar to his DSO. However, on 9 August 1941 he was leading the Wing during a bomber escort mission over France when he was engaged by several Bf 109s. After claiming one, his twentieth victim, he collided with another, taking the tail off his aircraft. Bader baled out to spend the rest of the war in captivity.

Bader returned home to become a group captain and was given the honour of leading the victory flypast over London. However, life in the post-war era was going to be very different to that in wartime where he had excelled and so Bader left the RAF in 1946 to join Shell. He was later knighted for services to the disabled but after attending a dinner in honour of Sir Arthur Harris in 1982, the courageous Douglas Bader died on his way home at the age of 72.

Bader's wings shown here were donated to the Imperial War Museum by Mr L. Judd who served at Duxford from 1939 to 1942. Judd was the batman to various officers in the east wing of the Officers' Mess and the wings were taken from one of Bader's old tunics when new wings were attached.

The wings are the symbol of qualification and worn by trained pilots. When the RAF was formed in 1918 the design was changed slightly from the earlier RFC design, with the wing shape taking the form of an eagle and the monogram becoming RAF. The wings were the first of their kind and have formed the basis of many designs worldwide. They are still worn today but now bear the Queen's crown to reflect the reign of HM Queen Elizabeth II.

34

Hillman Minx

THIS ORIGINAL 1938 Hillman Minx has been restored in the colours and markings of RAF Bomb Disposal Squad No. 15 during the Second World War. It is now part of the Shuttleworth Collection, an aeronautical and automotive museum located at the Old Warden aerodrome in Bedfordshire; one of the most prestigious collections of old and well-preserved aircraft and vehicles in the world.

The Hillman Minx is now best described as a classic old-fashioned mid-sized family car. With a 30bhp 1185 cc engine, it was built from 1931 and became the first mass-produced car with an all-synchromesh gearbox. Many versions of the type were built before production ended in 1970, and this wonderful example is the final pre-war model. It was civil-registered as HSL 958 and purchased in Leeds but was commandeered by the Air Ministry following the outbreak of the Second World War and given the registration RAF 184832.

Bomb disposal had previously been left to the army but once the first German bomb fell on mainland Britain the War Office accepted responsibility for the future disposal of unexploded bombs. Each service was given its own responsibilities, the RAF's defined as being responsible for all unexploded bombs and ordnance (from whatever nationality) found on or near to crashed aircraft. It was initially felt the task of dealing with an unexploded bomb should fall to the armourers but the RAF soon had its own highly trained specialists. By 1940 there were eighty RAF Demolition Sections, supplemented by mobile squads and soon to be renamed RAF Bomb Disposal Flights. These flights were located at airfields across the country, each being established with around thirty personnel and allocated a wide range of motor vehicles, such as

Country of Origin:
UK
Date: 1938
Location:
Shuttleworth
Collection,
Old Warden
Aerodrome,
Bedfordshire
(© Malcolm
English and shown
by kind permission
of the Shuttleworth
Collection)

Another splendid image of HSL 958. (Malcolm English; shown with the kind permission of the Shuttleworth Collection)

the Hillman Minx shown here.

In the first two years of the war, the RAF's bomb disposal specialists dealt with more than 1,500 enemy bombs. At that stage the Air Ministry remained the controlling body but in 1943 the RAF Bomb Disposal Organisation was restructured into a wing headquarters and six squadrons. The squadrons were given a four-figure number beginning with '5', for example 5131 (BD) Squadron (which happened to be based at airfields in the north of England), and their flights a four-figure number starting with '6'; in 5131's case, its five flights were numbered 6205-9.

After the war a huge disarmament programme began, involving some 8,000 RAF personnel, of which around 800 were qualified BD specialists. For the next two years they disposed of more than 16,000 tons of high explosives, as well as other pyrotechnic devices and millions of rounds of ammunition. Clearly, bomb disposal was (and remains) a highly dangerous job and its dangers are reflected in the high number of gallantry awards made to bomb disposal specialists; at least six George Crosses and nine George Medals are known to have been awarded to RAF personnel for their courage during or in the immediate aftermath of the Second World War.

5131 (BD) Squadron is still undertaking bomb disposal duties. Now based at RAF Wittering in Cambridgeshire, its primary role is to provide an explosive ordnance disposal (EOD) capability, both for the RAF and across Defence. As for HSL 958, after its time with the RAF it was later owned and restored by Graham Church of Kempston in Bedfordshire before being purchased by the Shuttleworth Collection in 2006. Over the years, it has appeared at many military events and similar displays.

35

Metal Standing Cross

THE WAR IN the Far East is often referred to as the Forgotten War. Those captured in the Far East after the fall of Singapore in February 1942, arguably Britain's greatest military disaster of the Second World War, would certainly have felt like they had been forgotten. But from adversity came extraordinary tales of courage and this metal standing cross, together with a wooden wafer box, still containing the remains of a wafer, provides an example of one such story of courage.

The cross belonged to The Venerable (Air Vice-Marshal) Alan Giles, the RAF's Chaplain-in-Chief from 1953 to 1959, who had been a prisoner of war of the Japanese during the Second World War. Born in Dublin in 1902, Giles joined the Chaplains' Branch in 1934 and, as a squadron leader, was Senior Chaplain in Singapore and the Far East when Japan entered the war in December 1941.

With the arrival of Japanese forces imminent, his family were evacuated from Singapore but Giles volunteered to stay behind with the defending troops. He finally managed to make his escape on one of the many small craft heading for safety just before the British surrender. Despite his boat being hit twice by bombs he eventually made it to Batavia, only to be captured later by the invading Japanese forces.

Giles would spend the rest of the war in captivity and during his time as a prisoner of the Japanese was interred in ten different camps, the principal camp being at Surabaya on the Indonesian island of Java. Although worship was usually not permitted, the prison camps provided a setting for chaplains to fulfil their role of maintaining morale and attending the educational, physical and the spiritual needs of the prisoners.

Country of Origin: Java

Date: 1942

Location: HQ Air Command, RAF High Wycombe, Buckinghamshire (Image courtesy of The Venerable (Air Vice-Marshal) Jonathan Chaffey by kind permission of the Giles family)

Supported by the other chaplains in captivity, Giles provided spiritual welfare to the prisoners for the rest of the war. The cross shown here was secretly made by prisoners inside the camp, using small scraps of metal they had collected, for the purpose of secret worship. For use in administering the Holy Communion one prisoner carved the simple wooden box to hold communion wafers.

Simply but lovingly crafted these two objects became in time symbols of faith, courage and hope in a situation of extreme deprivation, hardship and cruelty. They were central to the work of the chaplains in the camp and were successfully concealed from the Japanese guards for the duration of the war. At one camp, Holy Communion was held in a drain while lookouts were posted to warn those prisoners participating of the approach of any camp guards. Many prisoners who would not normally have classed themselves as religious found great strength and comfort in such a horrific situation from the hope that faith gave.

Giles was able to bring the two objects home at the end of the war. In recognition of his conduct as a prisoner of war he was awarded the Order of the British Empire and was mentioned in despatches. After heading the Chaplains' Branch, he retired from the RAF and was the Dean of Jersey until 1970. Alan Giles died in 1975 at the age of 72.

The Chaplains' Branch remains an established part of service life. Its mission today is to serve the RAF Community through prayer presence and proclamation. The work of the chaplain remains as varied as ever – as pastor, worship leader and educator – depending on the unit served, which can vary enormously from a main operating base to serving in a hospital or at a training establishment. Padre's hours, for example, have been a feature for every young trainee. In more recent times, RAF chaplains have deployed on all major operations and are now considered as essential to any operational deployment.

The metal standing cross and wafer box shown here, together with other items of memorabilia, are on display in the RAF Chaplain-in-Chief's office at Headquarters Air Command, RAF High Wycombe.

36

Bomber Harris' Desk

THE DESK SHOWN here was used by Air Chief Marshal Sir Arthur Harris, otherwise known as Bomber Harris, while he was Commander-in-Chief Bomber Command during the Second World War. His headquarters was located at RAF High Wycombe in Buckinghamshire and his elevation to lead the command in February 1942 was one of the RAF's key appointments of the Second World War.

After frequent changes of commander – Harris was Bomber Command's sixth C-in-C since its formation less than six years before – his appointment was seemingly welcomed amongst the bomber crews as it came at a time when the command's fortunes and spirits were at a low ebb. Harris appreciated the great strain under which his crews were operating. As a group commander during the early months of the war he had tried to introduce a policy where every crew received two nights of rest between operations. But while this had proved hard to sustain, his thinking was to stand him in good stead as the command's new head.

Harris had also become increasingly concerned about the way the strategic bombing offensive was being conducted during the early years of the war, but he could now ensure it would be run his own way and no longer allow his command's valuable resources to be misused or bled away. While his strong views often resulted in heated discussions, arguments even, at the highest of levels, Harris would inspire and lead Bomber Command until the end of the war. He later said:

Country of Origin: UK
Date: 1942
Location: RAF College Cranwell, Lincolnshire (By kind permission of the Commandant RAF College Cranwell)

> The bomber force of which I assumed command on 23 February 1942, although at that time very small, was a potentially decisive weapon. It was, indeed, the

only means at the disposal of the Allies for striking at Germany itself and, as such, stood out as the central part in Allied offensive strategy.

After the war, Harris was promoted to marshal of the Royal Air Force but with some disquiet in post-war Britain about the level of destruction caused by the area bombing of German cities, he moved to South Africa – only to return to the UK just a few years later to see out the rest of his life at his home in Goring-on-Thames. He died in 1984 at the age of 91.

While his bombing strategy might have made Harris one of the controversial figures of the Second World War, there is no doubt that he commanded extraordinary respect and admiration from the men under his command. The enormous strength of loyalty is still evident amongst the Command's last surviving wartime members.

37

Avro Lancaster

ONE OF THE MOST famous aircraft of all time, the Avro Lancaster was the RAF's main strategic heavy bomber of the Second World War. Today, just over a dozen examples remain as complete airframes worldwide.

Designed by Roy Chadwick from the ill-fated twin-engine Avro Manchester, the Lancaster was over 69ft (21m) long and had a wingspan of 102ft (31m). With a crew of seven (pilot, navigator, flight engineer, bomb aimer, wireless operator and two air gunners) and powered by four Rolls-Royce Merlin XX engines, the MkI could reach a speed of 280mph (450km/h) and an operational ceiling of around 21,500ft (6,500m), depending on its fuel and bomb load. Perhaps most importantly though, the Lancaster's operational range of some 2,500 miles (4,000km) meant that targets deep into Germany and Nazi-occupied Europe could be reached from bases in England.

Country of Origin:
UK
Date: 1942
Location:
Lincolnshire
Aviation
Heritage Centre,
East Kirkby,
Lincolnshire
(By kind
permission of
the Lincolnshire
Aviation Heritage
Centre)

The Lancaster entered the operational arena on the night of 3/4 March 1942 when four aircraft of 44 Squadron based at RAF Waddington carried out minelaying in the Heligoland Approaches off the north-west coast of Germany. Although it was a low-key start to its operational life, the Lancaster would soon be at the forefront of all of Bomber Command's strategic bombing campaigns. Within weeks of its introduction more than seventy Lancasters took part in the first Thousand Bomber raid (against Cologne on the night of 30/31 May 1942) and within a year the number regularly involved on operations had risen to 200. The build-up of the Lancaster force continued at pace and just two years after its introduction more than 600 took part in a raid for the first time. The number then peaked on the night of 13/14 February 1945 when 796 Lancasters bombed

Dresden. By then there were forty-five bomber squadrons equipped with the type.

By the end of the war the Lancaster had flown over 150,000 individual sorties and dropped more than 600,000 tons of bombs. It had taken part in all of Bomber Command's major efforts during the latter half of the war as well as many specialist raids, with the daring low-level attack on the Ruhr Dams in May 1943 being its most famous. Then, with hostilities over, the Lancaster was used to drop food into Holland (Operation Manna) and to repatriate British prisoners of war from Europe (Operation Exodus).

A total of 7,377 Lancasters were built in several different variants. One of the aircraft's main strengths was its long and unobstructed bomb bay, giving the Lancaster the ability to carry a variety of bomb loads; the largest being the 12,000lb (5,400kg) Tallboy, as used in 1944 to destroy the German V-weapon sites in northern France and to sink the mighty German battleship *Tirpitz* in a Norwegian fjord, and then the 22,000lb (10,000kg) Grand Slam earthquake bomb, used in 1945 to destroy strategic targets such as bridges, viaducts and submarine pens.

The story of the Lancaster is a remarkable one. Not only was it such a versatile bomber during the war but its design lived on through the Avro York, the Lancastrian, the Lincoln, and finally the Shackleton – long after the

The Lancaster of the Battle of Britain Memorial Flight. (Crown Copyright 2005)

Second World War was over. Such is the legacy of this famous bomber, there are still two flying Lancasters in existence today – one with the Battle of Britain Memorial Flight at RAF Coningsby and the other in Canada – while others unable to take to the air are lovingly preserved by enthusiasts at museums and heritage centres across the world.

The wonderful example shown on the previous page is NX611 *Just Jane* belonging to the Lincolnshire Aviation Heritage Centre, a family-run museum at the former wartime bomber airfield of East Kirkby. Built by Austin Motors at Longbridge and completed in 1945, NX611 was too late for operations in Europe and so it was one of the first 150 MkVIIs completed to the Far East standard and destined for Tiger Force. However, the Japanese surrender brought an end to the war in the Pacific and so NX611 was put into storage at No. 38 Maintenance Unit at Llandow. Then, in 1952, it was one of several aircraft bought by the French government for service in its naval air arm.

After retiring from service in 1964, NX611 returned to the UK via Australia. It was then flown by the Historical Air Preservation Society before being delivered to Squires Gate where it became the main attraction at the Blackpool Aeronautical Museum. In 1972, NX611 was offered for auction but its future became uncertain when it failed to realise its reserve price. However, it was bought by Lord Lilford of Nateby so that it could remain in Britain and it was at that point that a Lincolnshire farmer, Fred Panton, became interested in the aircraft. With the help of the RAF, Panton managed to secure NX611 on loan. It was then dismantled and transferred to RAF Scampton where its restoration was completed before it was placed at the main entrance to the station as gate guardian. It remained there for the next ten years but with the loan period at an end, NX611's future again became uncertain. This time, though, Fred Panton and his brother Harold were able to buy the aircraft. For the next five years it remained as gate guardian at Scampton. Then, in 1988, it was dismantled once again and moved to East Kirkby where the brothers were establishing the Lincolnshire Aviation Heritage Centre as a memorial to Bomber Command and a tribute to their eldest brother, Christopher Panton, a flight engineer serving with 433 Squadron RCAF, who was shot down and killed during a bombing raid over Nuremberg on the night of 30/31 March 1944.

38

Pathfinder Force Badge

THE COVETED PATHFINDER Force badge was worn by the specialist Pathfinder crews of Bomber Command during the Second World War, and the example shown here belonged to a young air gunner who was fortunate to have a rather lucky escape on just his third Pathfinder sortie.

The creation of the Pathfinder Force (PFF) in August 1942 was a source of some of the bitterest arguments within Bomber Command of the war. Some feared the Pathfinders would be seen too elitist and, therefore, its existence would have an adverse effect on morale across the whole command. But as things were to turn out, this was not to be the case, although there was always healthy rivalry between the crews of the different bomber groups, and for many the award of the PFF badge was a genuinely sought after achievement.

The PFF was given group status in January 1943 as No. 8 (Pathfinder Force) Group. Led by its redoubtable young Australian commander, Air Vice-Marshal Donald Bennett, its crews led the way in improving navigation and target-marking techniques to light up the path for Bomber Command to achieve the accuracy and concentration of bombing effort that had previously eluded it. Its crews were volunteers from across Bomber Command's main force squadrons and were required to complete forty-five ops rather than the usual thirty. The PFF went on to fly more than 50,000 individual sorties during the Second World War, against nearly 3,500 targets, but with more than 3,700 men killed on operations, losses were incredibly high.

The PFF badge was awarded under Air Ministry Order No. A 1244/42, and was accompanied by a certificate or letter confirming its award. Recipients were entitled to

Country of Origin: UK
Date: 1942
Location: Private Collection

19-1-45 / P.F.F. Badge issued

HEADQUARTERS,

PATH FINDER FORCE,

ROYAL AIR FORCE.

10th January 1945.

To : 1618195 Flight Sergeant Orchard A.

AWARD OF PATH FINDER FORCE BADGE

You have to-day qualified for the award of the
Path Finder Force Badge and are entitled to wear the
Badge as long as you remain in the Path Finder Force.

2. You will not be entitled to wear the Badge
after you leave the Path Finder Force without a further
written certificate from me authorising you to do so.

Air Vice-Marshal, Commanding
Path Finder Force.

ROYAL AIR FORCE PATHFINDER FORCE BADGE
(Air Ministry Order No. A 1244/42)

To be worn on left hand pocket flap underneath Pilot's
Wing or Aircrew Brevet & Medal Ribbons.
This coveted wing is permitted to be worn only by those
personnel holding the Pathfinder Certificate.

AMO No. A 1244/42

Flight Sergeant Arthur Orchard pictured wearing his Pathfinder Force badge.

wear the badge on the left-hand pocket flap underneath their aircrew brevet and medal ribbons, but only during their time serving with the PFF.

The badge shown here was awarded to Flight Sergeant Arthur Orchard, a Lancaster rear gunner serving with 156 Squadron at RAF Upwood. A former employee of the Vauxhall Motor Company in his hometown of Luton, Orchard volunteered for aircrew service as soon as he was aged 18. He was accepted as an air gunner and having completed his training in August 1943 he was posted to 101 Squadron based at RAF Ludford Magna in Lincolnshire. But having flown just five ops with the squadron, the second of which was against the Nazi V-weapon research establishment at Peenemünde on the Baltic coast and the last two being even longer trips to Berlin, Orchard's crew volunteered for the PFF.

After a brief period of further training, the crew joined 156 Squadron at RAF Warboys in Cambridgeshire. However, disaster struck on just their third Pathfinder sortie; against Bochum on the night of 29/30 September 1943. While overhead the target their Lancaster was hit. The aircraft's flying instruments and radio were put out of action, making it impossible to communicate with anyone or determine their height. After nursing the stricken bomber back towards base, and estimating the aircraft was somewhere over south-east England, they started their descent in search of an airfield.

In the briefing before the raid the crew had been told the cloud base would be no lower than 3,000ft, and so they would hopefully be able to break through the cloud and then make an emergency landing at any airfield they could find. With no way of communicating with anyone, or being certain of where they were, all the crew could do was to hope and pray. Down and down they went, edging closer to the ground. Suddenly they broke through the cloud but were alarmed to see just how low they were. They caught a quick glimpse of an airfield on their port side but it was at that point the Lancaster hit the ground. The next thing Orchard remembered was opening his eyes and seeing the dark sky above. The rear turret had broken away from the rest of the fuselage on impact with the ground, and he had been thrown clear.

The Lancaster had come down in Norfolk. Orchard was later found and rushed to hospital in Ely and was remarkably lucky to get away with just a broken leg and a bruised spine. But, sadly, the rest of his crew were killed. It was a year before Orchard returned to the squadron, now based at RAF Upwood, to continue his Pathfinder tour. He flew with his new crew for the first time in October 1944 and was awarded his Pathfinder Force Badge on 10 January 1945. By the end of the war, Arthur Orchard had completed thirty-four ops as a Pathfinder; he was still just 20 years old.

39

Guy Gibson's Office

WING COMMANDER GUY Gibson became a household name after leading the legendary Dams Raid by 617 Squadron in May 1943. The raid, later immortalised on screen in the 1955 film *The Dam Busters*, was carried out from RAF Scampton in Lincolnshire, where Gibson's original office has today been restored by volunteers at the station's Heritage Centre.

A former night fighter pilot and now with two Bomber Command tours behind him, 24-year-old Gibson arrived at Scampton in March 1943 to set up 617 Squadron for a specialist raid. The squadron's task, as Gibson would later find out, was to attack the dams in the heart of Germany's industrial Ruhr. Any breach of the dams would impact on hydro-electricity generation, as well as causing mass destruction in the area through severe flooding.

Called Operation Chastise, the plan was for nineteen Lancasters, each carrying a new specialist weapon, code-named Upkeep, to attack the dams in three sections. The first section of nine aircraft, led by Gibson, was to attack the Möhne dam and, if successful, would then fly on to attack the Eder. The second section of five would attack the Sorpe dam while the third section, also of five aircraft, would act as a mobile reserve and briefed to attack any of the primary targets should they not already have been breached.

Country of Origin:
UK
Date: 1943
Location:
RAF Scampton
Heritage Centre,
Lincolnshire
(By kind
permission of
the Station
Commander RAF
Scampton)

Just after 9.30 p.m. on the night of 16/17 May 1943, Gibson led the first section off in three waves of three. Everything seemed to be going well until crossing the Rhine when one aircraft in the second wave was shot down by anti-aircraft flak. Gibson's lead wave, meanwhile, arrived unscathed over the Möhne soon after midnight. The Lancasters had now been spotted and when Gibson ran in to make the first attack he was greeted with intense

anti-aircraft fire. Still he pressed on and moments later his Upkeep hit the target, causing a huge rise of water above the dam. But the excitement soon turned to disappointment after the water settled and the crew could see the dam was still intact.

The second aircraft was repeatedly hit by ground fire and was last seen staggering away from the dam before blowing up. Gibson now decided to escort the others during their individual attacks and one by one the Lancasters ran the gauntlet of fire to deliver their attack. Then, just as the fifth Lancaster was running in to release its Upkeep, the dam was suddenly seen to collapse.

Circling above the reservoir the crews watched the spectacular sight as thousands of tons of water burst into the valley below. But there was still more to be done and so Gibson led the remaining Lancasters on to the Eder. It took a while to locate the dam but the crews were relieved to find it undefended. However, its position meant that it would take great skill to complete an attack. While Gibson watched over, the first Lancaster ran in and then the second but its Upkeep was released too late and hit the dam without bouncing, exploding on impact, and catching the Lancaster full in the blast. The third attack, though, was delivered with devastating accuracy. Again, the crews watched the breach gradually widen before a great tidal wave swept down the valley.

Wing Commander Guy
Gibson. (AHB)

With the Möhne and Eder dams breached, the surviving Lancasters of the first section were on their way home. The second section, meanwhile, had suffered badly. Two aircraft had been forced to return home early but what had happened to two others is unclear. This left just one crew to attack the Sorpe dam alone. Although they hit the target there was no breach. The third section had also suffered badly with only two aircraft managing to reach the dams. One attacked the Sorpe while the other attacked the Ennepe dam; both without success.

With two of the primary dams breached, resulting in widespread flooding and devastation, Operation Chastise was considered a success. But it had been a costly night for the squadron. Eight of the nineteen Lancasters had failed to return and fifty-three aircrew were missing. Thirty-four gallantry awards were made to the survivors, the most notable being the award of the Victoria Cross to Guy Gibson for leading the raid. His citation concluded:

> Throughout his operational career, prolonged exceptionally at his own request, he has shown leadership, determination and valour of the highest order.

Sadly, though, Gibson would not survive the war. After leading the dams raid he first went to the United States with the British Prime Minister, Winston Churchill, after which he was posted to the Air Ministry. But Gibson was determined to return to a front-line station and eventually found himself at RAF Coningsby for another ground tour. He even managed to persuade his superiors to let him fly the occasional op, but, in the end, his keenness and enthusiasm for operational flying was to cost him his life. On the evening of 19 September 1944, Gibson took off from nearby RAF Woodhall Spa in a Mosquito belonging to 627 Squadron to act as Master Bomber for a raid against Rheydt and Mönchengladbach. Flying with him was Coningsby's station navigation officer, Squadron Leader James Warwick, but their Mosquito failed to return. Gibson was last heard over the target area late that evening, after which his aircraft was seen to come down in flames at Steenbergen in Holland where it exploded on impact.

At first it was not known that Gibson's aircraft was overdue. With Woodhall Spa and Coningsby being so close together, each airfield assumed the Mosquito had landed at the other. And when that turned out not to be the case, it was hoped the aircraft had landed elsewhere. However, it then became apparent the Mosquito was lost. At the time of his death, Guy Gibson was aged 26. Of all the RAF's gallant VC winners, few, if any, will be better known than Wing Commander Guy Gibson VC DSO & Bar DFC & Bar.

40

The 'Bouncing Bomb'

THE 'BOUNCING BOMB', or Upkeep to give its official name, known for breaching the Ruhr dams on the night of 16/17 May 1943, was the result of months, if not years, of hard work by its designer, Barnes Wallis.

Long before the raid took place, Wallis, then the assistant chief designer at the Vickers-Armstrongs Aviation section at Weybridge in Surrey, had been working on ideas to breach the dams in the German industrial heartland of the Ruhr. Initially he had worked on the principle of designing a massive bomb to be dropped from high altitude that would create a shockwave underground and cause large-scale destruction in the area, but at that stage of the war there was neither the weapon nor the aircraft to deliver such an attack. And so, Wallis turned to other ideas and after countless experiments concluded that the explosion of a weapon against the surface of a dam would cause a shock wave capable of weakening the structure, and that successive detonations would eventually result in the destruction of the dam.

Trials began in 1942 with Wallis working on a method to deliver such a weapon accurately onto its target, while further tests determined the amount of explosive required. Wallis concluded that just 6,000lb (2,720kg) of explosive would be required to breach a dam. The construction of prototype weapons, initially spherical in shape and designed to be dropped from very low altitude and then bounce across the water to the target, then began.

The bouncing bomb, as it became known, was effectively a conventional depth charge. It weighed 9,250lb (4,195kg), of which 6,600lb (2,994kg) was the main explosive charge, and was designed to be carried beneath the Lancaster by two v-shaped arms. By rotating the

Country of Origin:
UK
Date: 1943
Location:
RAF Scampton
Heritage Centre,
Lincolnshire
(By kind
permission of
the Station
Commander RAF
Scampton)

weapon backwards, it meant that on impact with the water it would start decelerating as it bounced towards the target. Having calculated the rate of deceleration, Wallis was then able to determine its release point. However, there would be little or no margin for error. The weapon would have to be dropped 400–450 yards (around 400m) from the target and from a height of just 60ft (18m), while the aircraft maintained a steady speed of 220mph (350km/h).

Five practice drops were made using a modified Wellington bomber before the decision was made to install the new weapon, now given the code name Upkeep, into a Lancaster. Modifications to the aircraft included the removal of the bomb doors to mount the gear for rotating the weapon, the removal of the dorsal gun turret to reduce the weight and a hydraulic motor to drive the rotating gear installed in the cabin.

The Upkeep shown here can be seen at the RAF Scampton Heritage Centre. It was reconstructed from casing recovered at the Fording Bridge bombing range by No. 14 Group Royal Observer Corps and presented to 617 Squadron. It was unveiled in October 1975 by members of the squadron who had flown on the raid that had breached the dams. It now stands outside the Heritage Centre in front of Gibson's office.

41

Pigeon Container

FOR HUNDREDS, IF not thousands, of years homing pigeons have been selectively bred for their ability to find their way home over extremely long distances, and during the Second World War many RAF airmen owed their lives to these heroic stout-bodied birds. It has been estimated that nearly a quarter of a million birds were used during the war, not only by the RAF but also by the army and the Civil Defence Service; in fact, homing pigeons were used in operational theatres all over the world.

When the Second World War broke out, many pigeon fanciers gave up their birds to aid the war effort. The birds served with the National Pigeon Service and came from all over the country, including the Royal Lofts at Sandringham. In fact, the first pigeon to make a successful home-run with a message from a downed RAF aircraft in occupied Europe was a bird owned by HM King George VI called Royal Blue – or to give his official identification NURP.40. GVIS.453 – when, on 10 October 1940, he flew 120 miles (190km) from Holland in four hours, ten minutes to deliver his message; it later earned the young Royal Blue the Dickin Medal, otherwise known as the 'Animal VC', for conspicuous gallantry and devotion to duty.

Country of Origin: UK

Date: 1943

Location: RAF Linton-on-Ouse Memorial Room, North Yorkshire (By kind permission of the Station Commander RAF Linton-on-Ouse)

The pigeons were considered so crucial that all RAF bombers and long-range reconnaissance aircraft carried at least one, often two. The idea was simple. If the aircraft came down, the crew would release the pigeon and it would fly back to its home base with a message giving the approximate position of where they had come down. In the case of an aircraft coming down in the sea, the Air–Sea Rescue Service would then initiate a rescue of the crew.

The award of the Dickin Medal to Royal Blue was the first of thirty-two awards to pigeons during the Second

World War. Another example of the extraordinary courage of these birds was White Vision from Scotland, awarded the Dickin Medal in 1943 for delivering a message under exceptionally difficult conditions and so contributing to the rescue of the crew of a Catalina flying boat of Coastal Command that had come down in the Hebrides. A thick morning mist had made it impossible for a normal search to be carried out and it was not until late afternoon, more than eight hours after the Catalina had come down, that White Vision arrived at her loft, having crossed the heavy sea in poor visibility and against a strong headwind, to deliver the life-saving message.

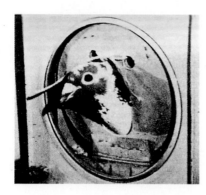

Pigeons were considered so crucial that all RAF bombers and long-range reconnaissance aircraft carried at least one, often two, and many airmen owed their lives to these heroic stout-bodied birds.

The stories of Royal Blue and White Vision are just two of many heroic tales involving pigeons and the RAF. Others include Dutch Coast, who delivered an SOS message from a ditched crew close to the enemy coast, covering 288 miles (460km) in seven and a half hours in unfavourable conditions, and Billy, who returned from a downed bomber in exceptionally bad weather, although in a state of complete collapse. And then there was Cologne who returned all the way home from a crashed aircraft near Cologne despite being seriously wounded, Gustav who delivered the first message from the Normandy beaches on D-Day, and Flying Dutchman who three times successfully delivered messages from agents in Holland before going missing in 1944 while on his fourth operation with the RAF. The stories go on and on.

The pigeons were trained at regional training centres and lofts were built at the RAF bases, with trained staff to look after the birds; usually one corporal and two airmen. The pigeons carried their message in special containers on their legs or in small pouches looped over their backs.

Aircrew carried their pigeons in special containers, like the one shown here, and part of their pre-flight routine was to pick up their pigeon. The container was usually made of Bakelite or metal, with push-on lids to make them watertight in the event of ditching. The container included a partially completed message form giving details of the station where the crew were based, the aircraft number and date. In the event of an emergency the crew would then complete the rest of the form with their location and time, with any other message, before releasing the bird.

The pigeon container shown here is from 1943. It was used at the bomber airfield of RAF Linton-on-Ouse in Yorkshire, and clearly shows the scars of war. Its occupant, Sam, had a lucky escape when the Halifax bomber in which he was being carried was hit by anti-aircraft flak over Berlin. Fortunately for Sam, the piece of shrapnel had only clipped his container. Although injured in his beak, Sam made a full recovery and suddenly found himself the centre of attention back at Linton once his story had become known!

42

Victoria Cross Awarded to Flight Lieutenant Bill Reid VC

THE NATION'S HIGHEST award for gallantry is the Victoria Cross. Since its introduction by HM Queen Victoria in 1856 to honour acts of valour during the Crimean War, it has been awarded fifty-one times for exceptional courage in the air. Thirty-two of these were awarded during the Second World War and one recipient was a young Scot, 21-year-old Flight Lieutenant Bill Reid, a Lancaster pilot serving with 61 Squadron at RAF Syerston in Nottinghamshire, who was awarded the VC for his supreme courage and leadership during a raid against the German city of Düsseldorf on the night of 3/4 November 1943.

Reid was flying his tenth op that night. His aircraft was first attacked by an enemy night fighter, a Messerschmitt Bf 110, soon after crossing the Dutch coast at 21,000ft (6,400m). The windscreen was shattered and Reid was wounded in his head, shoulder and arms, and the damage meant the Lancaster was becoming increasingly difficult to control. Furthermore, the compasses and communications were no longer of any use and the rear turret had been badly damaged. But having first ascertained that his crew were unscathed, and saying nothing of his own injuries, Reid pressed on. However, another enemy night fighter soon appeared, this time a Focke-Wulf FW190, and the Lancaster was attacked once again. Cannon shells raked the fuselage from stem to stern, hitting the flight engineer, killing the navigator, and fatally wounding the wireless operator. It was a devastating blow. The Lancaster's

Country of Origin: UK

Date: 1943

Location: Private Collection (© Spink & Son, London)

mid-upper turret was also out of action and its oxygen and hydraulics systems had been ruptured.

Without the use of the main aircraft compass, two turrets out of action and with two of his crew either dead or seriously wounded, Reid would have been fully justified in turning the aircraft back towards home but he pressed on. Using the stars to aid navigation, Düsseldorf was reached an hour later and using all his strength to hold the bomber steady, and with his arms wrapped around the aircraft controls, Reid continued until the bombs had gone.

Flight Lieutenant Bill Reid. (via Bill Reid)

The crew's bombing photos would later show the Lancaster to have been right over the centre of the target when the bombs were released. Reid turned for home but it was now intensely cold inside the aircraft and he was steadily getting weaker through the loss of blood. Nonetheless, with the support of his surviving crew members, and again using the stars to aid navigation, he nursed the crippled bomber back towards home.

Reid was now lapsing into semi-consciousness but, somehow, he managed to get the bomber back over the English coast where an airfield was sighted. Ground mist partially obscured the runway lights but Reid was not going to give up. Not now. With the aircraft's hydraulic system being out of action, the undercarriage had to be lowered using the emergency hand pump. Using all his strength, and with blood flowing from his gaping head wound and into his eyes, Reid touched the aircraft down. He managed to hold it steady for some time but then the leg of the damaged undercarriage collapsed and after sliding across the concrete runway the aircraft finally came to rest.

The Lancaster had landed at the American base at Shipdham in Norfolk. It was just after 10 p.m. – five hours after they had taken off. Reid was rushed to hospital and it was there that he later learned of his award of the Victoria Cross. His citation concluded:

Wounded in two attacks, without oxygen, suffering severely from cold, his navigator dead, his wireless operator fatally wounded, his aircraft crippled and defenceless, Flight Lieutenant Reid showed superb courage and leadership in penetrating a further 200 miles into enemy territory to attack one of the most strongly defended targets in Germany, every additional mile increasing the hazards of the long and perilous journey home. His tenacity and devotion to duty were beyond praise.

Reid eventually made a full recovery and went on to serve with 617 Squadron at RAF Woodhall Spa. On 31 July 1944, he was taking part in a raid against a German V-weapon storage site located in a railway tunnel at Rilly-la-Montagne in France, when a bomb dropped from an aircraft above passed straight through the mid-section of his Lancaster, severing the control cables. Unable to maintain control, Reid gave the order to his crew to bale out but as the crew tried to make their escape the aircraft went into a dive, pinning Reid to his seat. Struggling against the forces, he finally managed to release the escape hatch and get out, just seconds before the Lancaster broke in two; he was one of just two crew members to escape.

Reid was captured to become a prisoner of war and after repatriation he left the RAF and returned to Scotland, working in the agricultural industry until his retirement in 1981. Bill Reid died in 2001 at the age of 79. Reid's VC was later sold in 2009 to a private collector for £348,000 – then a world-record auction price for a VC to a British recipient. The main image is of the rarely seen reverse of the VC, showing Reid's name, rank and unit on the suspender. Rather interestingly, though, and for no obvious reason, the date engraved in the circle is 7 December 1943, which is not the date of the act, as would usually be the case, nor is it the date the award was promulgated in the *London Gazette*.

43

Leather Gauntlet

HEAVILY LINKED TO Bill Reid's VC is the object shown here: a standard 1941-pattern angle-zip brown leather flying gauntlet, made in soft russet goatskin, as issued to Bomber Command aircrew during the Second World War. At first glance it is unlikely to arouse much interest but this is the leather gauntlet that belonged to 22-year-old Flight Sergeant Jim Mann of 61 Squadron, the wireless operator who was fatally wounded on the night that Reid's courage led to the award of his Victoria Cross.

Known as 'Bim' to his family but Jim to his crew, John James Mann was born in Liverpool in 1920. After joining up as a wireless operator, he was posted to No. 29 Operational Training Unit at RAF North Luffenham for training on Wellingtons and it was there that he became part of Bill Reid's crew. Having completed their OTU course together, the crew next went to No. 1654 Heavy Conversion Unit at RAF Wigsley to convert to the Lancaster, after which they were posted to 61 Squadron at RAF Syerston.

It was while on the way to Düsseldorf on the night of 3/4 December 1943, during the second night fighter attack in the space of just a few minutes, that Mann was fatally wounded. The devastating burst of fire had caught all four crew members in the cockpit area, instantly killing the navigator and sending him to the floor while Mann had collapsed on top of him seriously wounded.

Country of Origin:
UK
Date: 1943
Location:
Birchwood Leisure
Centre, Lincoln,
Lincolnshire

Mann was still alive when the Lancaster finally crash-landed at Shipdham in Norfolk and was immediately evacuated from the aircraft and rushed to the station's medical centre for treatment, but he sadly succumbed to his wounds two days later.

Jim Mann is buried in Bootle Cemetery, Liverpool, and his death was clearly a sad and personal loss to Bill Reid.

His crew had always been made to feel so welcome during their visits to Mann's family home when enjoying a short period of leave. While recovering from his own wounds in hospital at Ely, Reid wrote to Mann's parents:

> Jim's loss must be still such a great shock to you and so hard to understand. It is hard for me to express myself in sympathy to you. But, having known and flown with Jim well over a year now, it just seemed we were part of a family, and I know you will understand the deep regret I have for this sad bereavement. At the time I never thought Jim was so badly wounded since he said not a word about it ... I was glad to hear that the others did manage to attend Jim's funeral and am sorry I was unable to pay my respects to such a fine member of our crew as Jim was. When I get my sick leave however, I'll most certainly visit you and let you know anything you want to hear about. If I can possibly help you in any other way please don't be afraid to ask me. Should you have any trouble about Jim's personal kit I'll see what I can do.

Flight Sergeant Jim Mann. (via Deborah Mitchelson)

After Mann's death, this leather gauntlet was lovingly kept with other personal belongings by his younger sister Kathleen, who, it has been said, never truly recovered from the death of her older brother. After Kathleen died in 2014, Mann's personal belongings, including the leather gauntlet, were donated to the 50 & 61 Squadrons' Association by her daughter. While Bill Reid's story is one of great courage, the story of his wireless operator that night, Jim Mann, is one of great sadness.

44

Flying Scarf

THE FLYING SCARF shown here was worn by Les Bartlett, a Lancaster bomb aimer, throughout his tour with Bomber Command during the Second World War. He always considered it to be his lucky scarf and after completing each op he added the name of the target to the list. He was, however, always worried should he be shot down and captured, as the scarf would show the raids he had previously participated in. And so, he had decided that should he ever have to bale out over enemy-occupied territory then he would dispose of the scarf rather than be captured with it. Fortunately, though, this was not necessary. Bartlett successfully completed his tour of operations and the only time he had to take to his parachute was during a training sortie over Lincolnshire.

Les Bartlett joined 50 Squadron at Skellingthorpe, near Lincoln, in October 1943. On the evening of 19 November, he was involved in a dinghy search to look for a downed crew, unfortunately without success; but because the search had taken place along the enemy coast it was later counted as an op, hence its feint entry at the top of the scarf above the first 'Berlin', his first bombing op flown on the night of 22/23 November.

Bartlett's first visit to the Nazi capital was during the opening phase of what was to later become known as the Battle of Berlin. The sortie had lasted more than seven hours and it was his first of five visits to Berlin in his first eight ops. Then, after raids on Stettin and Brunswick, he returned for his sixth visit on the night of 20/21 January 1944, and just twenty-four hours later he was back over Berlin again.

It was relentless and there was to be little or no rest for the crews as Bomber Command ordered two further raids

Country of Origin: UK
Date: 1943
Location: Bartlett Family (Courtesy of Les Bartlett)

against Berlin before the end of the month. For Bartlett, the first of these, flown on the night of 27/28 January, was just five minutes short of nine hours long while on the second, just twenty-four hours later, his actions led to the possible destruction of an enemy night fighter. He had just released the bomb load over the target when a Junkers Ju 88 was spotted ahead and about to attack another Lancaster. Bartlett promptly manned the front turret and started firing. The Ju 88 was seen to do a slow turn to the left and then spiral down to earth.

In between the operational sorties there were the occasional training flights and during one of these, a fighter affiliation exercise, Bartlett had a close escape when the port outer engine caught fire. All attempts to extinguish the fire failed, leaving the crew with no option other than to bale out; sadly, though, two of his colleagues were killed.

Bartlett now learned that he had been awarded the Distinguished Flying Medal (DFM) for proving himself 'a most competent and efficient bombardier' during his eighteen ops completed so far and for damaging the enemy night fighter during the raid on Berlin at the end of January. By the end of March, he had been commissioned as a pilot officer and the hard-fought campaign against the Nazi capital was over. During the sixteen raids against Berlin, spanning four months, more than 9,000 sorties had been flown (80 per cent by Lancasters) and nearly 30,000 tons of bombs dropped. At no other stage of the war was such a sustained bombing campaign against a single target carried out.

Bartlett had been to the Nazi capital ten times that winter but the end of the Battle of Berlin did not bring an end to the heavy losses. Ninety-five aircraft failed to return from a raid against Nuremberg on the night of 30/31 March 1944. It was Bomber Command's costliest raid of the war.

Nuremberg had been Bartlett's twenty-first op. Bomber Command now turned its attention away from targets in Germany to support preparations for the Allied landings in northern France, now just a matter of weeks away. And so all but two of Bartlett's final eight ops were flown against targets in France. The first of these was a successful attack on an aircraft factory at Toulouse on the night of 5/6 April, an all-No. 5 Group effort involving 144 Lancasters and lasting seven hours. It was also a memorable night for

Pilot Officer Les Bartlett. (via Les Bartlett)

Bartlett as his daughter had been born earlier that day. The next two raids were against railway marshalling yards around Paris, at Juvisy and La-Chapelle, and then at the end of April there were two more ops shown on Bartlett's scarf as Bordeaux. The target for both of these ops was an explosives factory at St-Médard-en-Jalles but on the first night, 28/29 April, haze and smoke prevented most of the attacking force from bombing, and so the bombers returned the following night to finish off the attack. Bartlett's last op was flown on the night of 1/2 May 1944. It was another attack against a target in France – this time an aircraft assembly factory at Toulouse.

The fact there are only twenty-nine raids shown on his treasured scarf is because Bartlett missed his crew's trip to Aachen on the night of 11/12 April 1944; he was on compassionate leave at the time following the birth of his daughter. After the war, Bartlett returned to his pre-war occupation of pharmacy. He always treasured his memories and belongings from his days as a Lancaster bomb aimer, and became one of Bomber Command's great characters in the later years of his life. Les Bartlett died in 2013 at the age of 96.

Royal Air Force Station Wickenby.

A/C	Sqdn	Captain	Out	In	3/4th May 1944 Mailly le Camp
	12	F/Sgt S.J. Carroll	21·50	03·27	
	12	P/O S.B. Black	21·58	03·44	
	12	F/Sgt S.W. Payne	22·04		Failed to return
	12	P/O J.O. Carter	21·48		Failed to return
	12	P/O E.K. Farfan	21·59	03·40	
	12	F/L H.I. Gray	21·50	03·53	
	12	P/O N. Rollin	21·38	03·33	
	12	F/Sgt J.K. Richardson	22·02	00·30	Returned early
	12	P/O P.F. Thompson	21·42	03·53	
	12	F/O P.G. Maxwell	21·39		Failed to return
	12	P/O O.H. Pollard	21·40	03·29	
	12	Lt L.K. Dawley	21·37	03·24	
	12	P/O A.W. Moore	21·44	03·09	
	12	F/O J.H. Ormrod	21·43		Failed to return
	626	F/L A.J. Wright	21·52	03·37	
	626	F/Sgt P.J.W. Barkway	21·57		Failed to return
	626	F/Sgt A. Bladon	21·47	03·26	
	626	P/O R.S.J. Bennett	22·14	00·25	Returned early
	626	P/O J.F.V. Butcher	21·51	03·22	
	626	F/Sgt E. Grisdale	21·54	03·41	
	626	P/O R.F. Ayres	22·09	03·47	
	626	P/O C.R. Marriott	22·10	03·52	
	626	P/O N.J. Fisher	22·08		Failed to return
	626	F/L A.W. Ravenhill	22·13	03·31	
	626	F/L W. Breckenbridge	22·07	03·34	
	626	F/Sgt G. Smith	22·15	03·35	
	626	P/O D.S. Jackson	22·11		Failed to return

45

Ops Board

THE ORIGINAL OPERATIONS board shown here can be seen in the old watch office at Wickenby airfield in Lincolnshire, where it has been restored to its state on the night of 3/4 May 1944. The target that night was a German military camp near the French village of Mailly, but it was to be a costly one for the crews taking part.

For three months leading up to D-Day on 6 June 1944, Bomber Command had switched its focus from Germany to targets in northern France in preparation for the Allied landings. Many of these attacks were to soften up the enemy's defences in the region and one such example was Mailly-le-Camp, involving 346 Lancasters, including twenty-seven from RAF Wickenby, and fourteen Mosquitos.

Wickenby's Lancasters – fourteen from 12 Squadron and thirteen from 626 Squadron – got airborne around 10 p.m. for a trip that would last around five hours. Although the initial low-level marking of the target seems to have been accurate, a breakdown in communications led to the main attack being delayed. It was a delay that proved costly for the Main Force. German night fighters swooped on the area and bomber losses were high. Forty-two of the Lancasters were lost, including seven from Wickenby (four from 12 Squadron and three from 626), more than one-quarter of those that had taken off from Wickenby that night. They had been part of the second wave, where most of the losses had occurred.

Although costly, the raid did have some success. Accurate bombing resulted in more than a hundred barrack buildings and nearly fifty transport sheds being destroyed, and without any reported French casualties from the bombing. Nonetheless, it was a night never to forget for those survivors that had taken part.

Country of Origin: UK
Date: 1944
Location: Wickenby Airfield, Lincolnshire (By kind permission of the Wickenby Memorial Collection)

46

Spitfire

NO BOOK ABOUT the RAF's 100 years would be complete without including the Spitfire. Often perceived by the British public to be *the* fighter of the Second World War, the Spitfire could in fact be included anywhere in the RAF's story between 1938, when it was first introduced into service, and 1957 when it was finally retired; even then it went on to serve with nations elsewhere. By the time production had finished, in excess of 20,000 Spitfires had been built – more than any other British combat aircraft before or since the Second World War – in twenty-two variants and for many different roles.

The vision of Supermarine's chief designer, Reginald Mitchell, the Spitfire was designed as a high-performance fighter. The prototype made its first flight in 1936 and two years later the MkI entered service with the RAF. The early Spitfires were powered by the new Rolls-Royce Merlin and its distinctive elliptical wing, with the thinnest possible cross-section, enabled it to out-perform other contemporary fighters at that time. The airframe was also strong enough to accommodate the more powerful Merlins that soon followed, as well as the Rolls-Royce Griffon engine that powered the later variants of Spitfire.

Whatever the engine, the Spitfire had outstanding performance. The MkVb, for example, powered by a Merlin 45 supercharged V12 engine, was capable of 370mph (595km/h), a rate of climb of 2,600ft/min (13m/s) and an operational ceiling of 36,000ft (11,000m). Furthermore, variations in the Spitfire's wing design as the war progressed meant that its initial armament of eight 0.303in Browning machine guns was replaced by up to four 20mm Hispano cannons, or a mix of both. Much

Country of Origin: UK
Date: 1936
Location: Battle of Britain Memorial Flight, RAF Coningsby, Lincolnshire (Crown Copyright by kind permission of the Station Commander RAF Coningsby)

loved by the pilots who flew it, the Spitfire served in all the RAF's operational theatres during the Second World War.

The stunning image shown here is of MK356, a Spitfire MkIX of the Battle of Britain Memorial Flight based at RAF Coningsby in Lincolnshire, and is titled 'Warming up for D-Day'. It was shortlisted for the RAF's 'People's Choice: Image of the Year' competition in 2014.

Built at Castle Bromwich, MK356 was initially allocated to 443 Squadron RCAF in early 1944. The squadron had formed at RAF Digby in Lincolnshire but soon moved south to RAF Holmsley South in the New Forest to work-up with two other Canadian Spitfire IX squadrons as 144 Wing, part of the RAF's newly formed 2nd Tactical Air Force.

With its work-up complete, the wing moved to RAF Westhampnett in West Sussex to commence operations and it was from there that MK356 flew its first op on 14 April 1944; a fighter sweep over northern France. In the

following two months, it flew sixty operational missions, sharing in the destruction of a Messerschmitt Bf 109G on the ground. The wing had now moved to nearby RAF Ford and it was from Ford that MK356 flew in support of the Normandy landings. But its operational life was cut short when it was damaged for the third time on 14 June 1944, resulting in the aircraft having to make a wheels-up landing.

The Spitfire will probably remain the RAF's most famous aircraft of all time. (Crown Copyright 2010)

MK356 needed to be repaired and so it missed out when the wing crossed the Channel to operate from an airstrip in northern France. It was instead on its way to a maintenance unit and would take no further part in operations during the war. It was then moved to Halton for use as an instructional airframe and from 1951 was a gate guardian at a handful of RAF bases. It was also used as a static airframe in the epic film *Battle of Britain* before becoming part of the RAF Museum collection.

Fortunately, though, MK356's flying days were not over. It was restored to an airworthy condition and in 1997 took to the air again for the first time in more than fifty years. It subsequently joined the Battle of Britain Memorial Flight and is seen here in markings representing a MkIX flown by Squadron Leader Johnny Plagis DSO DFC & Bar, who commanded 126 Squadron in July 1944. Plagis named his personal aircraft after his sister Kay and her name is seen on the port side of the fuselage next to the cockpit, beneath which are two scrolls displaying sixteen swastikas to represent his personal score. The black and white stripes, worn by Allied aircraft supporting the D-Day landings to aid identification, are clearly seen on the underside of the wings and rear fuselage.

The Spitfire played a major part in the Allied victory of the Second World War and truly deserves its place in history. It will probably remain the RAF's most famous aircraft of all time.

NOOR
INAYAT KHAN
1914-1944
G.C., M.B.E.
Croix de Guerre

47

Bronze Bust of Noor Inayat Khan

THE WOMEN'S AUXILIARY Air Force (WAAF) was established in 1939 for wartime duty and while WAAFs may not always have been seen by the British public to be in the front line in the same way as the men, some were no less heroic. Women, in fact, performed all kinds of roles during the Second World War. Some even paid the ultimate sacrifice, and one such example is Noor Inayat Khan.

Born of Indian origin in 1914 in pre-revolutionary Russia, and raised in England and then France, Noor escaped to Britain following the Nazi occupation. Her father had died many years earlier and as the eldest of four children she had taken on responsibility for the caring of her mother and younger siblings from an early age.

While Noor was undoubtedly devoted to her family, she also wanted to do her bit against Nazi tyranny and so she applied to join the WAAF. Her initial application was refused on the grounds she had been born in Russia, but after appealing to the Air Ministry she was finally accepted for training. Using the first name of Nora because it was more familiar to the British, Noor joined the WAAF in November 1940 as an Aircraftwoman 2nd Class. On completion of basic training at RAF Harrogate, she was posted to Balloon Command for specialist training as a wireless telegraphist, after which she was posted to Headquarters No. 6 Group at RAF Abingdon.

Noor was now an Aircraftwoman 1st Class. However, she had seemingly become bored and so looking for something more challenging she applied for a commission. For someone often described as gentle and shy, Noor is also said to have had strong views, which is probably why she

Country of Origin: UK

Date: 2012

Location: Gordon Square Gardens, London

returned to Abingdon unsuccessful. She was, however, soon promoted to Leading Aircraftwoman (LACW) but, unbeknown to her, her progress was being tracked elsewhere. The combination of her being bilingual in English and French, and her wireless telegraphist skills had brought her to the attention of the Special Operations Executive (SOE).

Noor was interviewed in November 1942 by the novelist Selwyn Jepson, a captain and recruiting officer for the SOE's F Section (F for France) and on 8 March 1943 she joined the SOE. Such was the secretive nature of everything to do with the SOE, and the bureaucracy associated with it, Noor was still officially in the WAAF but seconded to the First Aid Nursing Yeomanry. This allowed her to be trained in the use of firearms and provided female agents with a cover story while attached to the SOE. And because SOE operatives held a commissioned rank, Noor was officially discharged from the WAAF in the rank of LACW on 15 June 1943 and instantly given an honorary commission as an assistant section officer in the WAAF the following day – this date being when she went into France.

Noor Inayat Khan of the Women's Auxiliary Air Force.

Operating under the name Jeanne-Marie Renier, and with the code name 'Madeleine', Noor was F Section's first female radio operator to be sent into the field. She was inserted into France by Lysander on the night of 16/17 June 1943 and quickly made her way to Paris, but she soon found herself to be in one of the SOE's principal and most dangerous posts in France.

Noor had arrived in the French capital just days after a key circuit had been compromised and many notable agents arrested. She went straight into hiding but just three days after arriving in France she managed to inform London of the disaster unfolding in Paris; it was the quickest response from a radio operator after arriving in the field. London wanted to recall her immediately but Noor was determined to carry on. She knew that she was now the SOE's only radio operator in Paris. Constantly on the move, and keeping her transmissions short to avoid being intercepted by the many radio detection vans operating in the area, Noor kept London informed of developments at that most crucial time. She not only worked within her own circuit but she soon became the focal point for communicating with other circuits as well.

Noor was now in the most perilous of positions. Her superiors in London knew that it was only a matter of time before she was caught, but on the other hand she was the last link they had with Paris; the most crucial link of them all. Noor was virtually alone and although she had been instructed to lie low, she continued to transmit for SOE circuits and French Resistance groups in the area. She even helped in the escape of thirty Allied airmen who had been shot down over France, as well as organising supply drops of arms and other vital supplies to the Resistance groups. It was extremely dangerous work.

The Germans were now hot on the trail of the lady they only knew as Madeleine but who had become top of their most wanted list. Finally, in October 1943, Noor was betrayed. She was caught in a trap and arrested, and then taken for interrogation. But Noor gave nothing away. She even tried to escape before being transferred to Germany where she was imprisoned at Pforzheim and placed in solitary confinement. Chained hand and foot she was kept alive on the lowest rations. Then, in September 1944, she was taken to Karlsruhe and imprisoned with other SOE women before she was finally taken to the concentration camp at Dachau where the exceedingly brave Noor suffered further at the hands of her captors. Then, probably on 13 September 1944, she was taken to the camp's crematorium, made to kneel in front of a mound of earth, and shot through the back of her head.

At the time of her death Noor was aged 30. It was not until after the war that the full story of her time in France became known and her exceptional courage recognised by the award of the George Cross; the country's highest award for gallantry in such circumstances.

This bronze bust of Noor Inayat Khan by sculptor Karen Newman can be seen in Gordon Square Gardens, London, close to where Noor had lived and where she is known to have spent time relaxing when home on leave. It was unveiled by HRH the Princess Royal in November 2012.

48

Short Sunderland

ONE OF THE most widely used flying boats of the Second World War was the Short Sunderland. Essentially designed from the S.23 Empire flying boat, a passenger- and mail-carrying aircraft of the mid-1930s, the S.25 Sunderland was extensively modified for the military and entered service with the RAF in 1938.

It is probably fair to say that the Air Ministry's focus on Fighter Command and Bomber Command during the final months leading up to war meant that Coastal Command, the maritime arm of the RAF, did not always get the resources it required and so by the start of the

Second World War there were just three squadrons of Sunderlands in service; a total of forty aircraft.

With a typical crew of ten (two pilots, a navigator, two flight engineers/air gunners, three radio and radar operators/air gunners and two mechanics for in-flight maintenance), the Sunderland was a huge aircraft. More than 85ft long (26m), its wingspan was nearly 113ft (34m) and its height nearly 33ft (10m). Powered by four Bristol Pegasus engines, it cruised at around 180mph (285km/h) at a height of 5,000ft (1,500m) and had a maximum range of around 1,800 miles (2,850km). Its offensive weapons included a mix of bombs (250lb or 500lb), mines and depth charges, carried both internally and winched beneath the wings, and its defensive armament of sixteen 0.303in and two 0.5in Browning machine guns earned it the respectful nickname of the Flying Porcupine amongst the Germans.

Although the Sunderland was reportedly difficult to handle when taking off and landing in rough conditions, it was otherwise relatively easy to operate, particularly when in the hands of a skilled pilot. The Sunderland crews spent the early years of the war providing Royal Navy ships and the many naval convoys with protection from air attack and countering the threat posed by the German U-boats operating in the Atlantic. From the end of 1941 the Sunderland was fitted with air-to-surface vessel radar and in addition to operating over the waters around Britain and the Atlantic, the RAF also conducted long-range operations from bases overseas in Africa and the Far East.

Nearly 750 Sunderlands were built. Its design was so good that it remained in front-line service until 1959 and was the last flying boat to be operated by the RAF – the last aircraft being scrapped in Singapore.

The Sunderland shown here is ML824. It was built in 1944 as a MkIII and launched at the Shorts factory at Queen's Island, Belfast, after which it was converted to MkV standard and delivered to the RAF. It first served with No. 57 Maintenance Unit at RAF Wig Bay (a specialist flying boat base on the shores of Loch Ryan in Scotland) and then, in February 1945, it became the first Sunderland V to be transferred to 201 Squadron based at RAF Castle Archdale on the eastern shore of Lower Loch Erne in Northern Ireland. By the end of the war,

Country of Origin: UK
Date: 1944
Location: RAF Museum Hendon, London
(© RAF Museum)

ML824 had completed eleven operational sorties (ten anti-U-boat patrols and one convoy patrol), totalling nearly 130 flying hours, and had been transferred to 330 (Norwegian) Squadron based at RAF Sullom Voe in the Shetland Islands.

With hostilities over ML824 was initially struck off charge but it was then transferred back to No. 57 MU at Wig Bay. In 1951 it was one of fourteen Sunderlands to be transferred to the French navy under the Western Union Defence Programme. Ten years later its days with the French were over and having amassed some 2,900 flying hours, ML824 made its last flight to RAF Pembroke Dock where a display site had been leased in the dockyard. It was then hauled from the water for the last time, its French markings removed and the aircraft restored to its wartime condition with 201 Squadron.

ML824 became such a popular attraction that it was soon getting a reported 20,000 visitors a year, and so, in 1968, it was handed over to the RAF Museum, although it would be three more years before it was partially dismantled and moved by road to Hendon where ML824 remains on display.

49

Commonwealth War Graves Commission Headstone

THE COMMONWEALTH WAR Graves Commission commemorates the 1.7 million men and women of the Commonwealth forces who died in the two world wars. Its cemeteries, burial plots and memorials are a lasting tribute to those who died in some 154 countries across the world. One of those remembered is 30-year-old Flight Lieutenant David Lord VC DFC, the only member of Transport Command to have been awarded the country's highest award for gallantry, who is buried in the Arnhem Oosterbeek War Cemetery in Holland.

An experienced twin-engine Douglas Dakota pilot serving with 271 Squadron, Lord was killed on 19 September 1944 during the RAF's resupply of the British 1st Airborne Division at Arnhem. While approaching the drop zone at 1,500ft (457m), his aircraft was hit in the starboard wing by anti-aircraft fire from the ground, causing the engine to burst into flames. Lord would have been fully justified in abandoning his run-in but he knew how desperate the troops on the ground had become. They needed the supplies and having first established that his crew were OK, he decided to press on to complete the drop.

Lord took the Dakota down to its drop height. His burning aircraft had now been singled out for further attack from the ground, but Lord held the aircraft steady for long enough while the supplies were dropped. He might then well have turned for home but two containers were still on board. The wing was now burning ferociously and was in danger of falling off but Lord decided to take

Country of Origin:
Holland
Date: 1945
Location:
Oosterbeek War Cemetery, Arnhem, Holland

FLIGHT LIEUTENANT
D. S. A. LORD, VC., DFC
PILOT
ROYAL AIR FORCE
19TH SEPTEMBER 1944 AGE 30

GREATER LOVE
THAN THIS NO MAN HATH,
THAT A MAN LAY DOWN
HIS LIFE FOR HIS FRIENDS
R. I. P.

The twin-engine Dakota was the workhorse of Transport Command in support of the Allied advance towards Germany in 1944. (Crown Copyright 2015)

the aircraft around again for a second run to drop the remaining supplies. The Dakota was still under intense anti-aircraft fire and it took several minutes to complete the second drop, but only when his task was complete did Lord finally give the order for his crew to bale out. However, the aircraft was now dangerously low and just at the point the crew were preparing to jump, the starboard wing fell off and the Dakota fell to earth in flames.

The Dakota had come down at Reijerskamp to the north of Wolfheze. Those killed on board, including Lord, were initially buried alongside the aircraft wreckage until the bodies were reinterred to Oosterbeek in 1945. Miraculously, though, one of the crew had survived. He had been thrown clear of the aircraft to become a prisoner of war. It was only after he returned home at the end of the war that he could tell the story of Lord's heroic act and extraordinary sacrifice, leading to the posthumous award of the Victoria Cross to David Lord. His citation concluded:

> By continuing his mission in a damaged and burning aircraft, twice descending to 900 feet to ensure accuracy, and finally by remaining at the controls to give his crew a chance of escape, Flight Lieutenant Lord displayed supreme valour and self-sacrifice.

The Arnhem Oosterbeek War Cemetery contains the graves of, or commemorates, 1,691 Commonwealth servicemen of the Second World War, many of whom were killed during the airborne operation of September 1944. David Lord is buried in plot 4.B.5.

Part 4
Into the Jet Age

50

Whittle W.1 Jet Engine

WITH THE SECOND World War over, the RAF entered a new and exciting era – the jet age – and perhaps the best place to start this section is with the Whittle W.1 engine, which powered Britain's first jet aircraft. Designed by Frank Whittle, the engine is best described as a double-sided centrifugal compressor with ten reverse-flow interconnected combustion chambers and a single-stage turbine. It weighed 560lb (254kg) and produced 850lb (3,800kN) static thrust, and was the result of years of hard work, dating back to when Whittle had first shown an interest in engineering at a very early age.

Born in 1907, Frank Whittle joined the RAF as an apprentice. In those early days, it was not possible to train all apprentices at Halton and so he went to Cranwell instead. Often described as something of a mathematical genius, the young Whittle soon caught the eye of his superiors and, in 1926, he was recommended for officer training. He soon went solo in an aircraft and excelled when it came to his studies. Part of Whittle's course required a thesis and his was titled 'Future Developments in Aircraft Design', in which he wrote about flight at high altitude and speeds exceeding 500mph (800km/h). He showed that incremental improvements in existing engine designs – i.e. using propellers – were unlikely to achieve extreme altitudes or speeds. Instead, Whittle suggested that a conventional piston engine could provide compressed air to a combustion chamber and the resulting exhaust could be used directly for thrust. Furthermore, at high altitude the reduced outside air pressure would increase the efficiency of the design.

Whittle's thesis earned him a prize for aeronautical sciences. He continued to develop his idea but instead

Country of Origin:
UK
Date: 1941
Location: Science
Museum, London
(© Science
Museum)

of using a piston engine to provide the compressed air for the combustion chamber, he worked out that a turbine could be used to extract some power from the exhaust to drive a compressor and that the remaining exhaust thrust could be used to power the aircraft.

In 1928, Whittle joined III Squadron at Hornchurch, a squadron equipped with the Armstrong Whitworth Siskin, after which he was posted to the Central Flying School as an instructor. He remained convinced about his engine concept and after it caught the attention of his commanding officer his idea was sent to the Air Ministry for consideration, only to be returned as impracticable.

Air Commodore Sir Frank Whittle. (AHB)

Since the RAF was not interested in Whittle's concept, it was not declared secret and so he took the idea to the engineering company British Thomson-Houston (BTH), but although his idea was well received, the company did not want to put up the money required to develop the engine. For now, the idea went no further and so Whittle focused on his RAF career, first attending an engineering course at Henlow and then a two-year engineering course at Cambridge University.

Meanwhile, the discussions and debates about the potential of Whittle's concept had continued and, eventually, in 1936, the company Power Jets Limited was formed from a four-party agreement, which included Whittle and the Air Ministry. In 1938, the development and testing of the WU (Whittle Unit) began at BTH's Ladywood facility near Lutterworth. However, the problems of funding had never gone away and so the Air Ministry finally stepped in to help. But the secrecy now attached to the project, as well as the continual delays in securing additional funding, meant the development of the engine had slowed at a time when Germany's work on a jet-powered aircraft was far more advanced.

Because the WU was too large to develop into a flyable engine, Whittle started work on the contracted engine, the Whittle Supercharger Type W.1. To reduce the length of the engine and, therefore, its weight, it featured a reverse-flow design. Air from the double-sided centrifugal compressor was fed rearwards into the combustion chambers, then back towards the front of the engine and then finally reversing again into the cooled axial-flow turbine.

By now the Air Ministry had placed a contract with the Gloster Aircraft Company to build a simple aircraft specifically to air test the W.1. The result was a small low-wing aircraft of conventional configuration, with the jet intake in the nose, called the Gloster E.28/39 (standing for the twenty-eighth experimental specification issued by the Air Ministry in 1939).

Otherwise known as the Gloster Whittle, the aircraft was delivered to Brockworth in April 1941 for ground testing, after which it was moved to RAF Cranwell where, on 15 May 1941, Gloster's Chief Test Pilot, Flight Lieutenant Gerry Sayer, flew the jet-powered E.28/39 (W4041) for the first time. The flight lasted seventeen minutes and was followed by a series of flight tests, during which a maximum speed of 350mph (563km/h) was attained in level flight at 25,000ft (7,620m).

The experience gained from the E.28/39 paved the way for Britain's first operational jet fighter, the Gloster Meteor, which first flew in 1943 and entered operational service the following year; it was the Allies' only operational jet aircraft of the Second World War. In 1948, Frank Whittle, by then an air commodore, left the RAF, having received a knighthood for his work. He then moved to the United States where he died in 1996 at the age of 89.

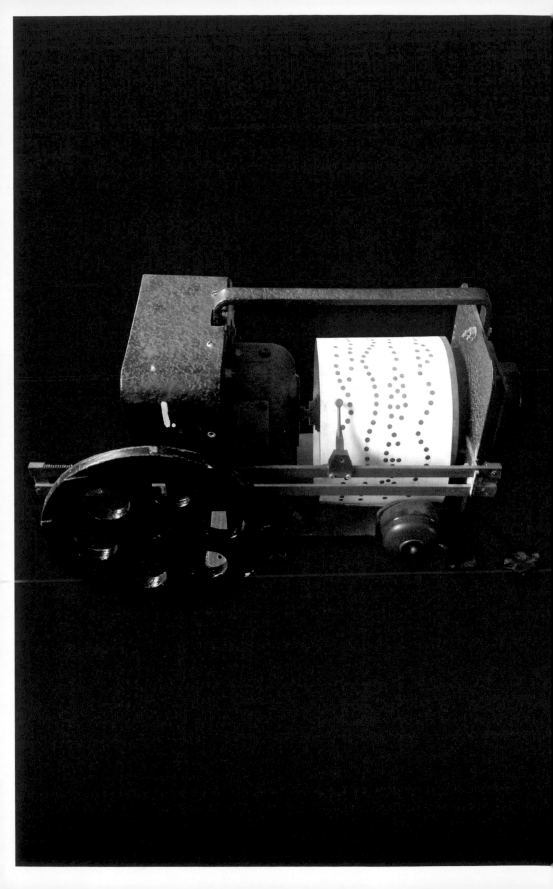

51

Control of Velocity Test

UNTIL THE SECOND World War the RAF had selected its aircrew based on an unstandardised interview. But, by 1941, the high number of failures in pilot training had become a concern. Furthermore, as much of the flying training was being carried out overseas, it was imperative that only those trainees that had shown high potential should occupy the training spaces available.

One of the first developments to help identify an individual's potential for pilot training was a new system called 'grading', which entailed a short period of flying, typically twelve hours, during which the student's performance was recorded, assessed and analysed. This produced an immediate effect, almost overnight, and cut the wastage in pilot training by half – from 1 in 2 to 1 in 4. But although grading had proved to be of some success, it was time consuming and relatively expensive. Besides, it made little or no contribution to the problem of selecting the wide range of aircrew categories now making up an aircraft's crew.

After much research in Britain and the United States, aptitude testing was introduced for all aircrew and by the middle years of the war a series of tests were being given to candidates at the newly formed Air Crew Receiving Centres. The tests were carried out over a couple of days and covered a multitude of disciplines – general intelligence, science, mathematics, table reading, mechanical comprehension, instrument interpretation and map reading to name just a few – all designed to identify skills relevant to each aircrew position. These tests were completed in a controlled environment and at that early stage were mostly done with paper and a pencil, but others were being introduced that

Country of Origin: UK
Date: 1943
Location: Adastral Hall RAF Cranwell, Lincolnshire (By kind permission of the Commandant RAF College Cranwell)

were carried out on apparatus that scored the candidate's performance mechanically.

One such test was the control of velocity test (CVT), as shown here, which had been developed at Cambridge University to measure one-direction pursuit tracking. It was first introduced into ACRCs during 1943 and enabled an assessment to be made of a candidate's hand-eye co-ordination and, therefore, his suitability for pilot training. The white drum rotated slowly and the candidate was required to follow the dots by keeping the pointer at the end of the mechanical arm over the dots by turning the large wheel at the bottom left. It sounds simple enough but when 'lag' was fed into the device, the candidate had to anticipate the movement of the pointer over the dots. Every time the pointer passed over the centre of the dot, a score was credited.

Aptitude testing has been an essential part of aircrew selection ever since. After the war a single Aircrew Candidate Selection Board was set up, first at RAF Hornchurch and then at RAF North Weald where, in 1947, it was joined by the Medical Board, and the Aptitude Test Centre (which moved from RAF Bridgnorth) to form the RAF Combined Selection Centre (CSC). The CSC moved back to Hornchurch in 1952 to become the Aircrew Selection Centre and then in 1962, when Hornchurch closed, the ASC merged with the Ground Officer Selection Centre at RAF Biggin Hill to become the newly formed Officers and Aircrew Selection Centre (OASC). In 1992 the OASC moved to RAF Cranwell where it remains today.

As the RAF entered the jet age, the importance of aptitude testing became increasingly more evident as the cost of flying training became ever more expensive. The CVT was an important part of the pilot selection process for more than forty years until it was replaced in 1985 by a computerised version. Many young would-be pilots will remember the CVT well!

52

Commer Commando Airfield Bus

AMONGST THE MANY vehicles found on large RAF bases in the post-war period was the Commer Commando airfield bus, used to transport large crews or passengers; for example, between an aircraft and a terminal. But very few have lasted to this day and this superb and rare example, XAT 368, is believed to be one of just half a dozen to have survived.

A post-war specification issued by the Ministry of Supply called for a bus capable of carrying twenty passengers and their luggage, with each passenger carrying their maximum allocation of 60lb (27kg). This led to the one-and-a-half-deck observation coach design and the result was the Commer Commando airfield bus.

Designed in 1946 and built by the Park Royal Coachworks in North London (a company that had made aircraft parts during the Second World War), a total of 315 of these vehicles were ordered by the RAF and the two British airlines, British Overseas Aircraft Corporation and British European Airways. Based on the well-established Commer Q4 Commando chassis, the bus was powered by a Humber Snipe 6-cylinder 4,086cc side-valve petrol engine, giving it a top speed of around 50mph (80km/h), and, with 180cu. ft of storage space, it could carry twenty-one passengers and all their luggage.

XAT 368 was delivered to the RAF in 1947 and remained in service for ten years. It was then used for a variety of purposes – by the Hull Cricket Club, as a factory staff bus and as a commercial bus – until 1972 when it was last used by the British Auto Racing Club as a control vehicle at the Silverstone racing circuit. XAT 368 then fell into disrepair but, in 1993, was donated by its owner to the RAF

Country of Origin:
UK
Date: 1947
Location:
Yorkshire
Air Museum,
Elvington, North
Yorkshire
(© Neill Watson
via the Yorkshire
Air Museum)

XAT 368 at Elvington where it is on display as part of the Yorkshire Air Museum. (Yorkshire Air Museum)

Benevolent Fund in recognition of the work the fund had done for his mother when her husband had been killed in a flying accident before the Second World War. It was then lovingly restored by the General Engineering Flight at RAF Cottesmore on behalf of the fund and is now on display at the Yorkshire Air Museum.

53

Martin-Baker Mki Ejection Seat

SINCE BEING INTRODUCED into military service, ejection seats have saved thousands of lives across the world. Today, they are common in all military combat aircraft but the origins of escaping from an aircraft date back to before the First World War, when a bungee-assisted escape first took place.

Ejection seats as we have come to know them today were first developed during the Second World War. Until then, of course, the only method of abandoning an aircraft was to bale out, but the difficulty of this, particularly in the event of incapacity or high g-forces, led to the idea of propelling a pilot or crew member from an aircraft. The first recorded ejection from an aircraft occurred in 1942 in Germany, where early ideas used compressed air, but within two years this concept had been developed further to use an explosive charge to fire gases up pipes and force the seat clear of the aircraft.

Country of Origin:
UK
Date: 1947
Location:
RAF Scampton
Heritage Centre,
Lincolnshire
(By kind
permission of
the Station
Commander RAF
Scampton)

In Britain, meanwhile, two men, James Martin and Valentine Baker, founded the company Martin-Baker as an aircraft manufacturer. They had also been investigating the idea of ejection seats and after Baker was killed during a test flight in 1942, Martin's primary focus became pilot safety. The company was then reorganised to concentrate on the design and manufacture of ejection seats. Martin also worked on the principle of using an explosive charge to force the seat up with the occupant still in it, and once clear of the aircraft the pilot would open the parachute manually. Finally, in July 1946, the company carried out its first ejection from a Gloster Meteor flying at 320mph (510km/h) at 8,000ft (2,400m).

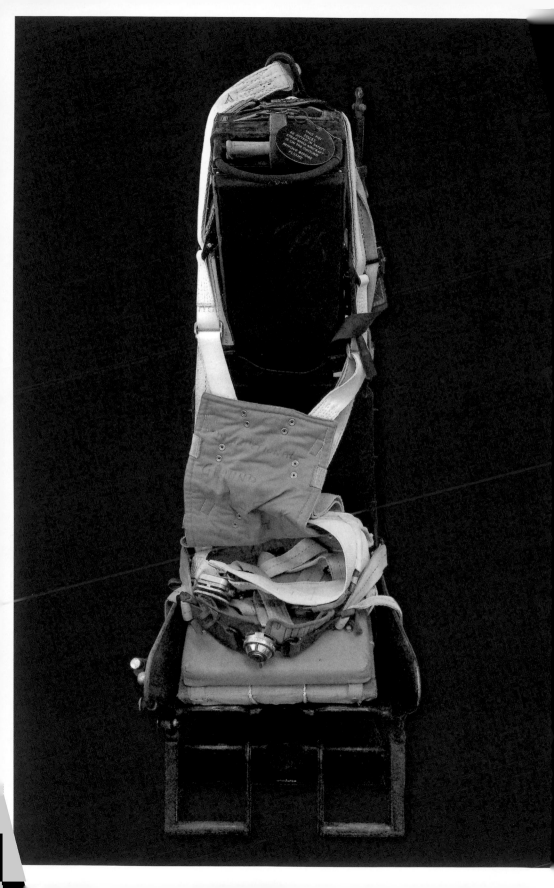

After a successful series of trials, it was decided to standardise the Martin-Baker ejection seat for installation in all new British military jet aircraft, and so the seat was re-designed to allow production on a large scale. The MkI seat, like the one shown here, had an adjustable seat pan that could be raised and lowered to suit the various statures of occupants, without increasing the height of the seat, adjustable foot rests and integral thigh guards to prevent the legs being forced apart by the air blast. During an ejection the seat was guided by rollers running in a guide rail assembly bolted to the aircraft structure. Sixty-nine lives were saved using the MkI seat.

The Martin-Baker company soon started exploring the operational envelope of the ejection seat. With the advent of new aircraft, it soon became necessary to reduce the weight of the seat, without impairing its operation and efficiency in any way, as well as automating more phases of the ejection sequence. Although initially fitted with a face screen firing control as shown here (red handle), an alternative firing handle was fitted in the leading face of the seat pan to allow the occupant to eject under extreme conditions of high-g. Indeed, it would be the seat pan handle that would eventually become the preferred method of use and was adopted for all later seats.

In the early years of its design the aircraft had to have some forward velocity for an ejection to be successful, but more research and trials meant that it was soon possible to eject from an aircraft in almost any situation, such as at low altitude and at low speed. This eventually led to the 'zero-zero' seat, meaning that aircrew could successfully eject on the ground with the aircraft stationary.

Martin-Baker has become the world leader in the design and manufacture of ejection seats for more than sixty-five years, having delivered over 70,000 seats to nearly a hundred air forces worldwide. More than 7,450 aircrew owe their lives to the Martin-Baker ejection seat.

This early MkI ejection seat was the pilot's seat of a Canberra jet bomber and is now on display at the RAF Scampton Heritage Centre.

54

1948 Olympics Running Vest

Country of Origin:
UK
Date: 1948
Location:
Trenchard
Museum,
RAF Halton,
Buckinghamshire
(By kind
permission of
the Station
Commander
RAF Halton)

AWAY FROM ITS professional branches and trades, fitness and sport have always been important ingredients of the military lifestyle. Indeed, the armed forces encourages excellence in sport and one airman to compete at the very top was Don Finlay, the British team captain for the 1948 Summer Olympics held in London.

Born in Hampshire in 1909 and educated in Taunton, Finlay joined the RAF as a 16-year-old aircraft apprentice at RAF Halton. He had been a promising athlete during his school days and soon found that he could pursue his athletics while in the service. He started hurdling, equalling the RAF's record in his first race, and in 1928 won the first of eleven consecutive Service Championships. The following year he earned his first international vest as a long jumper when he represented England against France.

For the next two years Finlay challenged the great Lord Burleigh for hurdling honours and in 1932 won the first of seven consecutive AAA (Amateur Athletics Association) championships. He also represented Britain at the 1932 Olympics in Los Angeles, earning a bronze medal in the 110m hurdles, and in 1934, at the Empire Games, he won gold in the 120-yard hurdles.

Finlay was then commissioned as a pilot but he still managed to find time to keep up his athletics and represented Britain at the Berlin Olympics of 1936. Then aged 27, he went one better than his previous Olympic performance by taking silver in the 110m hurdles with a time of 14.4 seconds. The following year he recorded his personal best of 14.1 seconds. Finlay not only excelled in the hurdles events. He had also run in Britain's 4 x 100m relay in both the 1932 and 1936 Olympics, he

was the inter-services champion in the long jump and the RAF champion in the high jump, as well as being an accomplished shot putter.

Don Finlay, fighter pilot and Olympic athlete.

The Second World War brought a temporary halt to his athletics prowess. As a Spitfire pilot during the Battle of Britain, Finlay first commanded 54 Squadron and then 41 Squadron at Hornchurch, during which he was credited with shooting down three Messerschmitt Bf 109s and shared in the destruction of two other enemy aircraft. He later served in the Mediterranean and Far East, ending the war as a group captain with a DFC and an AFC, having been credited with four confirmed victories and many more either shared or damaged.

Finlay remained in the post-war RAF, reverting to the rank of wing commander, and with hostilities over resumed his athletics career. In 1948, at the age of 39, he was the British team captain for the London Olympics and was chosen to take the Olympic Oath in Wembley Stadium on behalf of all the nations taking part. But age was now against him and in the first round of the 110m hurdles he hit the final hurdle with his leading foot and fell at the finish, and so was eliminated from the event at that stage.

Although Finlay's Olympic career had ended with disappointment, he won his eighth AAA title the following year at the age of 40. In 1950 he became a group captain for the second time and transferred to the engineering branch, and that same year competed in the British Empire Games; finishing fifth in the 120-yard hurdles. It was only then that he finally retired from international athletics.

The war years may well have denied Finlay from reaching the pinnacle Olympic gold that he desired but it had been a marvellous athletics story running alongside his extremely successful RAF career. He went on to serve as the Senior Technical Officer at No. 1 School of Technical Training at RAF Halton, where he regularly competed in the station sports days. Even at the age of 43 he won all the events he entered – the 100-yard hurdles, 100-yard sprint, 220-yard sprint, high jump and the long jump.

It was most fitting that Finlay had returned to the station where his RAF career had begun. In 1952, he proudly commanded the parade at which HM Queen Elizabeth II presented her colour to No. 1 School of Technical Training. Finlay retired from the RAF in 1959 but was later paralysed following a motoring accident. He died in 1970 at the age of 60. In 2012, 41 Squadron, based at RAF Coningsby in Lincolnshire, unveiled a Tornado GR4 with special tail markings to celebrate Don Finlay's command of the squadron and his immense achievements as an athlete, particularly in the Olympic Games.

55

Handley Page Hastings

THE END OF the Second World War brought much celebration and optimism for the future, but it had not been over long before Europe faced its first post-war major international crisis. It started in June 1948 during the multinational occupation of Berlin when the Soviet Union blocked access to the city – roads, railways and canals – under Western control. In response, the Western Allies organised what became known as the Berlin Airlift so that essential supplies could be flown in to the city and one of the many aircraft types taking part was the RAF's new Handley Page HP.67 Hastings, including TG517 shown here.

Powered by four Bristol Hercules 101 radial engines, and with a crew of five, the Hastings was the largest transport aircraft to have been designed for the RAF and would go on to become the mainstay of Transport Command for many years. The first C1s were rushed into service to join the airlift. They were delivered to 47 Squadron at RAF Dishforth, Yorkshire in September 1948 and just two months later the squadron detached to RAF Schleswigland in Germany (the RAF's northern-most post in the Berlin air bridge campaign) as part of Operation Plainfare.

Country of Origin:
UK
Date: 1948
Location: Newark Air Museum, Nottinghamshire (By kind permission of the Newark Air Museum)

Flying along a recognised air corridor just over 20 miles (32km) wide, aircraft from several nations flew in to the West Berliners nearly 9,000 tons of essential supplies each day. It was a staggering effort. Thankfully, the flights were unopposed, for fear of escalating what was already a politically delicate situation, and by the spring of 1949 it was clear the airlift was succeeding. Finally, on 12 May 1949, the Soviets lifted the blockade of West Berlin, although the airlift continued for a further four months.

By the end of the operation there were three RAF squadrons equipped with the Hastings, with thirty-two

aircraft operating from Schleswigland. Between them they had delivered 55,000 tons of supplies, mostly coal to keep Berlin's industries going. The total Allied effort is estimated to have delivered around 2.3 million tons of supplies; 500,000 tons of which were carried by the RAF on more than 280,000 sorties. At its peak, one transport aircraft was landing in West Berlin every thirty seconds.

Hastings of 70 Squadron pictured in 1956 with Suez stripes. (Crown Copyright)

It had been a busy start to the aircraft's operational life and for the next twenty years the Hastings continued to provide transport support to British operations around the world; including the dropping of paratroopers on El Gamil airfield during the Suez Crisis in 1956 and the dropping of supplies in Malaysia during the Indonesian Confrontation of the mid-1960s.

A hundred C1s were built and more than forty C2s; the latter having a larger tail plane, more fuel and Hercules 106 engines. The C2 could carry up to fifty fully equipped troops or more than thirty paratroopers, or the same number of stretchered-casualties, or heavy freight, depending on its specific role at the time. Carrying a maximum payload, it had a range of 1,690 miles (2,720km) but by balancing its fuel load and freight this could be extended to 4,250 miles (6,840km).

Fourteen RAF squadrons were equipped with the Hastings before it was finally retired from service in 1968, by which time the Bristol Britannia had been introduced and the new American Lockheed C-130 Hercules was arriving in numbers. However, eight Hastings were retained and converted to the T5 standard as a multipurpose transport and radar training aircraft for the RAF's V-bomber crews, and these remained in service until 1977.

TG517 was the first airframe to have been converted as a T5, but it was originally the nineteenth C1 to have been built and first flew in 1948. It was initially delivered to No. 5 Maintenance Unit at RAF Kemble and then transferred to 47 Squadron for the Berlin Airlift. It later served with 53 Squadron and when the Hastings was retired from service as a transport aircraft, TG517 became a T5 and served with the RAF Bombing School and then the radar flight of No. 230 Operational Conversion Unit for the training of Vulcan aircrew. In its training capacity, three students could be trained at a time. TG517 is also known to have flown on fishery protection sorties during the so-called 'Cod War' of 1975–76. After completing its service with the RAF in June 1977, TG517 was flown into the former airfield of RAF Winthorpe, now the site of the Newark Air Museum, where it remains on display.

56

David Brown Light Diesel Aircraft Tractor

THE RAF REQUIRED large numbers of towing vehicles on its airfields and so a common sight in the post-war period was the David Brown tractor, like the one shown here.

Built onto a sturdy cast iron chassis, the tractor is 9ft 9in (3m) long and 5ft 7in (1.7m) wide. It weighed 4,368lb (1,981kg) and was initially powered by a David Brown 4-cylinder 2500cc overhead-valve petrol engine, delivering 37bhp, although the later versions, like this MkII, were built with a diesel engine.

The tractor was fitted with a 5-ton winch at the rear. A four-speed gearbox drove its rear wheels through a turbo transmitter torque converter, giving it a towing pull of 2.5 tons. Effectively, this meant the David Brown light tractor could pull a small or medium-sized aircraft, but it is also known to have towed larger transport aircraft on a hardened surface. In fact, the tractor was so versatile that it was used for almost anything; from towing bomb trolleys or other pieces of specialist ground equipment to giving ground crew a lift across the larger airfields.

David Brown also built aircraft tugs for the RAF and went on to become one of the biggest British tractor manufacturers in the post-war period. Its tractors were extensively used at airfields until the mid-1950s when they were finally phased out of service, although these MkII diesel engine versions seem to have been retained on some RAF airfields until the 1980s.

A few David Brown tractors have survived and this example is on display at the RAF Museum Hendon.

Country of Origin: UK
Date: c. 1950
Location: RAF Museum Hendon, London
(© RAF Museum)

3rd Edition
June, 1956

PILOT'S NOTES

CANBERRA
B.2

Prepared by Direction
of the
Minister of Supply

Promulgated by Command
of the
Air Council

J. R. C. Helmore

M. J. Dean

57

Pilot's Notes

PILOT'S NOTES WILL be familiar to many former RAF aircrew and the example shown here is for the Canberra B2. It is the 3rd Edition dated June 1956 and belonged to Flying Officer R. Feakes of 73 Squadron. The squadron had just moved to RAF Akrotiri in Cyprus (from Aden) and was in the process of converting to the Canberra B2 (from the de Havilland Venom) as part of the Middle East Air Force Strike Wing.

The Canberra had been developed by English Electric as the RAF's first jet-powered bomber, and the B2 was the first main production variant. It was capable of 450mph (724km/h) at 15,000ft (4,572m) and Mach 0.84 at high altitude (with Mach 1 being equal to the speed of sound), and could carry a bomb load of up to 10,000lb (4,536kg). The first aircraft was delivered in May 1951. It was the start of Bomber Command's overall plan to equip twenty-four squadrons. These squadrons were to be organised into wings of four squadrons at six bases (Binbrook, Coningsby, Hemswell, Marham, Scampton and Wittering) – a total of 240 aircraft. This plan would later be modified and as the Canberra force continued to expand, more squadrons were equipped overseas – for example, 73 Squadron in Cyprus.

The Pilot's Notes were issued to each pilot as complementary to Air Publications and assumed a thorough knowledge of the AP chapters relevant to the operation of the aircraft type; in this case the Canberra B2. These Pilot's Notes have been broken down into six parts. Part 1 is titled Descriptive and includes a description of the aircraft type:

Country of Origin:
UK
Date: 1951
Location: Private
Collection

The Canberra B.2 is a light bomber powered by two [Rolls-Royce] Avon Mk 1 engines, each of 6,500lb

Canberra PR9 of 39 Squadron. (Crown Copyright 1996)

static thrust. The cabin is pressurized and provides accommodation for a crew of three seated in ejection seats. There is an alternative position in the nose for the air bomber, but no provision is made for his ejection from this station. Bombs are carried in a bay in the belly of the fuselage, and provision is made for carrying a camera in the rear fuselage.

Also included in Part 1 are brief details of the fuel and oil systems, engine controls, main services (hydraulics, electrics, flying controls etc.), cockpit equipment, radio and radar equipment, and operational controls. Part 2 is the Limitations section while Part 3 is Handling, which includes: the management of systems; starting, taxying and take-off; handling in flight; circuit and landing procedure; and asymmetric flying. Part 4 is Emergency Handling, Part 5 is Operating Data and Part 6 is the Illustrations section.

The Canberra had excellent performance for its day and for much of the 1950s could fly higher than any other aircraft in the world. In 1957, for example, a B2 set a world record when WK163 recorded an altitude of 70,310ft (21,430m). The Canberra also set nineteen official point-to-point records including, in 1951, being the first jet aircraft to make a non-stop transatlantic flight.

Although some had seen the Canberra as a short-term stopgap for Bomber Command, it quickly proved to be a highly adaptable aircraft. It went on to be built in several variants and served with many air forces across the world. The B2, for example, was further developed into the B6, which had more fuel to give it greater range. A total of 773 Canberras were built for the RAF, by four different manufacturers (English Electric, Short Brothers, Handley Page and Avro), including 418 Canberra B2s, which up until 1975 served at one time or another with over forty RAF squadrons.

The Canberra was finally retired from RAF service in 2006. During its fifty-plus years it had operated at some point with sixty different squadrons and in many different parts of the world – notably in Germany, Cyprus, the Middle East and the Far East – including the Malayan Emergency of 1955–59 and the Suez Crisis of 1956. The Canberra had also operated in many different roles; high-altitude light bomber and a low-altitude intruder (both nuclear and conventional); high-altitude strategic reconnaissance aircraft (for example, during the Cold War and then later over Bosnia, Iraq and Afghanistan) and for low-level tactical reconnaissance duties; as a trainer; a specialist electronic warfare training aircraft; and even for target-towing. The list goes on.

58

MkIA Flying Helmet

THE INTRODUCTION OF the jet age meant the type of flying helmets previously worn would no longer offer sufficient protection to aircrew during flight. The combination of high-speed and high-altitude flight, and the introduction of the ejection seat, were all reasons why a new protective flying helmet was required, not only in the event of an emergency but also in routine flight when severe buffeting could be encountered at high speed.

The early ideas included the design of a protective outer shell, constructed from moulded and bonded laminations of nylon fabric, to be worn over an inner flying helmet containing the communications element and to which the oxygen mask was fitted.

These ideas led to the MkIA flying helmet, a basic protective helmet that was otherwise known to aircrew as the bone-dome, which was introduced during the early 1950s. It was leather-lined fibreglass with a non-adjustable webbing harness to give a comfortable fit over the inner cloth flying helmet and was initially designed to be used with the H-type oxygen mask, although it was also used with later designs. The MkIA was the first helmet to have a fixed anti-glare visor, of various tints, which slid on a track attached from the centre to the front of the helmet. The visor could be locked in a number of positions to make it more robust to air blast.

The helmet was initially issued in a silver-coloured shell, although it also later came in matt green or grey, and was worn by all aircrew flying front-line aircraft; everything from helicopters to supersonic fighters. However, using the combination of an inner and outer helmet was not without its problems, particularly when it came to stability on the head, and so the first one-piece protective helmet, the MkII, was introduced during the 1960s.

Country of Origin: UK

Date: Early 1950s

Location: RAF Scampton Heritage Centre, Lincolnshire (By kind permission of the Station Commander RAF Scampton)

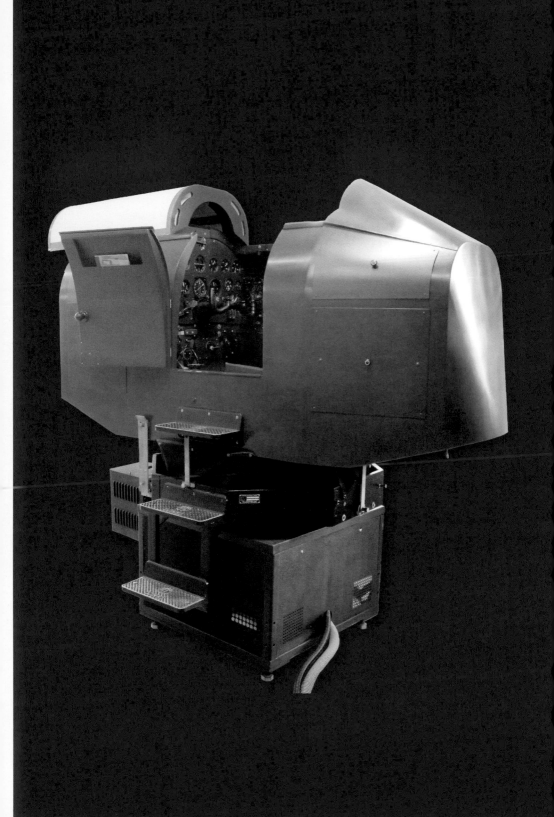

59

Link Trainer

Country of Origin:
USA
Date: 1952
Location:
Trenchard
Museum,
RAF Halton,
Buckinghamshire
(Trenchard
Museum by
kind permission
of the Station
Commander RAF
Halton)

PILOTS WHO TRAINED in the immediate aftermath of the Second World War will remember the Link Trainer, the RAF's first flight simulator, otherwise known as 'The Blue Box' or 'The Pilot Maker'.

Named after Edwin Albert Link, an American pioneer of aviation (amongst other things), the Link Trainer was first developed during the late 1920s. Link had developed a passion for flying during his boyhood years but the high cost of flying led to him building a device shaped like an aircraft fuselage, with short wooden wings and a cockpit, with controls that produced the motions of flying. It was mounted on a universal joint and used organ bellows, driven by an electric pump, to make it pitch and roll. To some, it might have resembled a toy aeroplane but Link's idea went into production during the 1930s.

At that stage the interest in Link's idea was not from the military but more from those running amusement rides for commercial purposes. But finally, the idea caught on. The United States Army Air Corps bought half a dozen during the mid-1930s and by the end of the Second World War some 10,000 had been built; they had become a standard piece of equipment at all flying training schools and it is estimated that half a million airmen had been taught to fly in the Link Trainer.

Flight simulation had arrived, although the Link Trainer was some way off what we know to be flight simulators today. Nonetheless, the early trainer was a moving platform that could simulate the pitch, roll and yaw of an aircraft. Although it did not resemble a specific aircraft type, or could resemble all phases of flight, it was a safe way of teaching new pilots how to fly using instruments and quickly proved to be a valuable step toward the complex aircraft equipment that a pupil would later experience. Its advantages were obvious. The Link Trainer meant pilots could be trained more efficiently in terms of cost and without the disastrous possibilities that could result from trial and error in flight.

The Link Trainer consists of two main components; the trainer itself and the instructor's station, which consisted of a repeated display of the main flight instruments, a large map table and a moving marker (known as a crab). The marker moved across the surface of the map table to plot the aircraft's track. The pupil pilot and instructor could communicate using headphones. Several models were developed up until the late 1950s, although they all retained the basics of the first design. The most prolific version was the ANT-18 (Army Navy Trainer Model 18), which was produced for the RAF with the model designation of D2. It was fitted with a removable opaque canopy, used to simulate blind flying, and was particularly useful for instrument and navigation training. Its design features included rotation through all three axes and it could simulate conditions such as pre-stall buffet and spinning.

Many of these trainers have survived worldwide, including several in the UK. The example shown in the main image is the original D4, which entered service with the RAF in 1952. It is one of three Link Trainers belonging to the Trenchard Museum at RAF Halton.

A 1942 model with its characteristic yellow tail section and wings. It is one of three examples of the Link Trainer belonging to the Trenchard Museum at RAF Halton. (Trenchard Museum)

60

No. 1 Service Dress Jacket
of Air Chief Marshal The Honourable
Sir Ralph Cochrane GBE KCB AFC

SHOWN HERE IS the No. 1 Service Dress jacket worn by Air Chief Marshal The Honourable Sir Ralph Cochrane GBE KCB AFC, the Vice-Chief of the Air Staff in 1952, which is on display at the RAF Scampton Heritage Centre.

Born in Scotland in 1895, the youngest son of Thomas Cochrane, 1st Baron Cochrane of Cults, Ralph Cochrane served with the RNAS piloting airships during the First World War, for which he was awarded the AFC, before transferring to the RAF in 1920. He was posted to HQ Middle East where he carried out experimental duties with 70 Squadron at Heliopolis in Greece, flying the Vickers Vimy biplane bomber, before serving as a flight commander with 45 Squadron, also equipped with the Vimy, at Almaza in Egypt. He then converted to the Vickers Vernon, the RAF's first dedicated troop-carrying aircraft, flying from Basra in Iraq, and, in 1923, took part in the RAF's first strategic airlift of nearly 500 troops to Kirkuk after Kurdish forces had overrun part of the town. After briefly returning to the UK to attend the RAF Staff College, he was posted overseas once more in 1929 – this time to command 8 Squadron at Khormaksar in Aden, flying the Fairey IIIF reconnaissance biplane.

Cochrane then returned home again to various staff appointments before attending the Imperial Defence College in 1935. He was now a wing commander and was next seconded to the New Zealand government to help establish the Royal New Zealand Air Force (RNZAF) as an independent service after two decades of struggle for parity with its army and navy counterparts. On 1 April 1937, and

Country of Origin: UK
Date: 1952
Location: RAF Scampton Heritage Centre, Lincolnshire (By kind permission of the Station Commander RAF Scampton)

Air Chief Marshal The Honourable Sir Ralph Cochrane.

now as a group captain, Cochrane was appointed Chief of the Air Staff of the RNZAF; a post he held for two years.

By the outbreak of the Second World War Cochrane had returned to the UK, first to command RAF Abingdon and then to take up a staff appointment at HQ No. 6 Group. He was then appointed as Air Officer Commanding (AOC) No. 7 (Operational Training) Group, part of Bomber Command, after which he became AOC No. 3 Group and then, in February 1943, he took command of No. 5 Group based in and around Lincolnshire.

No. 5 Group's activities have, perhaps, received wider acclaim than any other bomber group of the Second World War; not only because of its contribution to the strategic heavy bombing offensive against Nazi Germany but also because of its dramatic and specialised attacks, such as the Dams Raid in May 1943 and the sinking of the German battleship *Tirpitz* in November 1944. Cochrane was an advocate of precision bombing. As the AOC of No. 5 Group, he utilised 617 Squadron as a specialist squadron in the precision bombing and target-marking role.

With the war all but over, Cochrane was first knighted and then appointed AOC-in-C Transport Command; a position he held until 1947. During his time at the helm he did much to reduce the accident rate amongst transport crews by increasing the amount of training and raising awareness of how to prevent air accidents. For example, his command was the first in the RAF to introduce the specialisation for pilots on one type. This built experience levels across his command and so further reduced the risk of accidents, rather than a pilot finding himself being moved from one type to another as had often been the case before. This idea paid dividends during the Berlin Airlift when aircraft losses were relatively few.

By 1949, Cochrane was an air chief marshal and the following year was appointed Vice-Chief of the Air Staff to Sir John Slessor. Sir Ralph Cochrane retired from the RAF in November 1952, after which he held a number of senior company appointments, most notably as director of Rolls-Royce between 1956 and 1961. He died in 1977 at the age of 82.

61

Air Forces Memorial Runnymede

ON 17 OCTOBER 1953, the Air Forces Memorial at Runnymede in Surrey was unveiled by HM Queen Elizabeth II. It commemorates by name more than 20,000 British and Commonwealth air force servicemen and women who lost their lives during the Second World War and have no known graves.

From its beautiful location, high up on Cooper's Hill at Englefield Green near Windsor, and overlooking the River Thames and Runnymede Meadow where in 1215 the Magna Carta was sealed by King John, this Grade 2* listed memorial commands a spectacular view over west and central London. It was designed by Sir Edward Maufe, with sculpture by Vernon Hill. The engraved glass and painted ceilings were designed by John Hutton, with a poem written by Paul H. Scott engraved on the gallery window. The names of those commemorated are engraved into the stone walls of the memorial, by country and unit; they served in all commands and came from all parts of the Commonwealth.

Amongst the many notable names recorded are: First Officer Amy Johnson CBE (Panel 288), the legendary pioneering English aviatrix and the first female to fly solo from Britain to Australia who died in 1941 while serving with the Air Transport Auxiliary; Wing Commander Brendon Eamonn Fergus 'Paddy' Finucane DSO DFC and two Bars (Panel 64), the high-scoring RAF ace with at least twenty-six victories who at the age of 19 was one of The Few during the Battle of Britain and at the time of his death in 1942 was the youngest wing commander in the RAF at the age of 21; Wing Commander John Dering Nettleton VC (Panel 118), who received the highest award

Country of Origin: UK
Date: 1953
Location: Englefield Green, Surrey

for gallantry for leading a daring low-level daylight raid by a small force of Lancasters on a diesel engine factory at Augsburg in 1942 and was killed the following year; and Section Officer Noor Inayat Khan GC (Panel 243) of the Women's Auxiliary Air Force (see Object 47).

The memorial is well worth a visit. It is open to the public every day with the exception of Christmas Day and New Year's Day, although times vary throughout the year.

The Air Forces Memorial at Runnymede.

62

Gloster Meteor

THE GLOSTER METEOR was the RAF's first jet fighter and the Allies' only operational jet aircraft of the Second World War. It was later developed into several major variants, each incorporating new technological advances.

Powered by two new turbojet engines pioneered by Frank Whittle, the Meteor had first flown in 1943. The first production variant, the F1, boasted a top speed of around 415mph (668km/h) at sea level and commenced operations with 616 Squadron in July 1944, mostly being used to counter the large numbers of V-1 flying bombs appearing over south-east England. By the end of the year, the F1 was being replaced by the F3 (the F2 was cancelled). This latest version alleviated some of the shortcomings of the first production variant, and in early 1945 the first Meteors crossed the Channel to operate with the RAF's 2nd Tactical Air Force over north-west Europe.

After the war, the Meteor F4 became the main production variant. Powered by Rolls-Royce Derwent 5 engines, it was some 170mph (270km/h) faster than the F1. So fast was the Meteor at the time that the RAF re-formed the High Speed Flight in 1946, under the command of the wartime ace Group Captain Teddy Donaldson, in an attempt to break the world speed record. The flight was given two modified F4s with uprated Derwent engines and an aluminium cockpit hood (the normal Perspex hood was found to soften during very high-speed flight), and included some of the RAF's most notable pilots. Then, on 7 September 1946, and over five laps of a 2-mile (3km) course set up along the south coast of England between Littlehampton and Worthing, Donaldson set a new official world record of 616mph (991km/h).

Country of Origin:
UK
Date: 1954
Location: Newark Air Museum, Nottinghamshire (By kind permission of the Newark Air Museum)

Because of its success, the Meteor was in high demand with many aircraft being exported overseas. However, by the late 1940s the F4's performance was being matched or bettered by newer designs and so Gloster worked on producing a newer variant with improved engines. The result was the Meteor F8, a potent fighter, which formed the backbone of Fighter Command during the early part of the 1950s. Powered by two Derwent 8 turbojets, the F8 was capable of 600mph (965km/h) at 10,000ft (3,000m), had a rate of climb of 7,000ft per minute (35.6m/sec) and a service ceiling of 43,000ft (13,100m). It was armed with four 20mm British Hispano MkV cannons, although it could also carry up to sixteen rockets under its outer wings.

The Meteor's conventional straight-wing design would see it replaced as a fighter in the 1950s. However, it was still considered a worthy successor to the de Havilland Mosquito in the night fighter role and so adaptation of the Meteor as a night fighter was passed to Armstrong Whitworth. Based on the T7 two-seat trainer variant, the result was the Meteor NF11, which used the design features of earlier variants with an extended nose containing an air intercept radar, the AI Mk10, operated by the navigator in the rear seat. The 20mm cannons were

Meteor F8s of 616 Squadron pictured at an armament practice camp in Malta during the mid-1950s.

moved into the wings and outboard of the engines, and the addition of wing-mounted drop tanks, additional to the aircraft's ventral fuel tank, gave the aircraft greater range and endurance.

As radar technology improved, the NF12 was introduced into service from early 1954 with seven RAF squadrons. Then, later that year, came the NF14, the final night fighter variant, which was based on the NF12 but had an even longer nose to accommodate its new radar equipment and a larger bubble canopy to replace the earlier framed ones. A hundred NF14s were built and these remained in service with the RAF until 1961.

By the time production ended, nearly 4,000 Meteors had been built for air forces across the world; some of which remained in service until the 1980s. The aircraft shown here is WS739, a Meteor NF14, built in 1954 by the Armstrong Whitworth facility at Baginton. It entered service with 25 Squadron at RAF West Malling later that year. In 1957 the squadron moved to RAF Tangmere and the following year to RAF Waterbeach where, in 1959, the squadron replaced its NF14s with Gloster Javelins. WS739 has been at the Newark Air Museum since 1984.

63

English Electric P.1A

JUST TEN YEARS after the Meteor entered operational service with the RAF, WG760, the first of two English Electric P.1 single-seat research aircraft, made its maiden flight. It was 1954 and the P.1 was the experimental design of an aircraft that would soon become known as the Lightning; the first and only truly supersonic aircraft developed by Britain alone.

When English Electric first came up with the idea of producing a high-performance swept-wing jet fighter, there was a certain amount of scepticism amongst officials at the Ministry of Supply and at the Royal Aircraft Establishment. The primary concern seemed to be with the sweepback of the wing and the low position of the tail plane. Nevertheless, an experimental study was agreed, after which two English Electric P.1 prototypes were ordered, although an independent prototype, the SB5 (an aircraft whose wing sweepback could be changed and the tail plane raised or lowered) was also ordered from Short Brothers to test the concept.

As things were to turn out, both designs proved the concept viable. WG760 made its maiden flight at the Aeroplane and Armament Experimental Establishment, Boscombe Down on 4 August 1954 with the legendary test pilot and former RAF fighter ace Roland 'Bee' Beamont at the controls. Powered by two Armstrong-Siddeley Sapphire Sa5 engines, each developing 10,300lb thrust, it comfortably exceeded the speed of sound in level flight, achieving Mach 1.22; the second prototype went even faster, achieving Mach 1.53.

Later that year, WG760 moved to Warton to carry out more development work before moving back to Boscombe Down the following year. Further trials took place over the

Country of Origin: UK
Date: 1954
Location: RAF Museum Cosford, Staffordshire
(© RAF Museum)

next three years, including trials held at RAF Finningley and Bedford, although the aircraft twice lost its canopy in flight during 1956. But WG760 had proved the P.1 design worked. However, it was only ever going to be capable of Mach 1.53 due to directional stability limits, and so a second phase of prototypes were built that would enable the aircraft to eventually reach Mach 2 (twice the speed of sound). These were designated P.1Bs while the earlier prototypes, including WG760, were reclassified as P.1As. In 1958, the P.1B became the first British aircraft to fly at Mach 2.

WG760 was a vital part of the Lightning story. Once the Lightning had entered service, WG760 was withdrawn from flying in 1962 to become an instructional airframe at RAF Weeton with the serial number 7755M. In 1986 it was transferred to the Aerospace Museum at RAF Cosford and remains on display today.

64

Campaign and Long Service Medals

SHOWN HERE IS a fine group of medals to Sergeant Brian Francis. They represent both campaign service and exemplary conduct in the RAF over a career spanning thirty-five years.

Since its formation, the RAF has taken part in several campaigns across the world that have fallen short of full-scale war. For campaigns in Africa and India there were already medals in existence, but to recognise service in campaigns elsewhere, the General Service Medal (GSM) was instituted in 1923 for army and RAF personnel of all ranks (the Royal Navy had its own Naval General Service Medal). The GSM has always been issued with a clasp to mark the campaign it is awarded for. Additional service in a further campaign (or campaigns) is recognised by an additional clasp, or clasps, for the campaign(s) served. The medal is silver and named to the recipient.

Between the wars, the GSM was awarded to RAF personnel who saw service in any of the seven interwar campaigns: South Persia (1918–19); Kurdistan (1919 and 1923); Iraq (1919–20); North West Persia (1920); Southern Desert, Iraq (1928); Northern Kurdistan (1932); and Palestine (1936–39). After the Second World War the GSM was awarded for nine campaigns: South East Asia (1945–46); Bomb and Mine Clearance (1945–49); Palestine (1945–48); Malaya (1948–60); Canal Zone (1951–54); Cyprus (1955–59); Near East (1956); Arabian Peninsula (1957–60); and Brunei (1962).

In 1962, a new GSM replaced the earlier medal as it was to be awarded to all members of the armed forces, including the Royal Navy. Thirteen clasps were awarded: Borneo (1962–66); Radfan (1964); South Arabia

Country of Origin: UK
Date: 1955
Location: Francis Family
(By kind permission of Brian Francis)

(1964–67); Malay Peninsula (1964–66); South Vietnam (1962–64); Northern Ireland (1969–2007); Dhofar (1969–76); Lebanon (1983–84); Mine Clearance, Gulf of Suez (1984); Gulf (1986–89); Kuwait (1991); Northern Iraq & South Turkey (1991); and Air Operations Iraq (1991–2003). In 2015, a new GSM was introduced for minor campaigns dating from 2008. So far, five clasps indicating the geographic area of operation have been issued: Eastern Africa; Western Africa; Arabian Peninsula; Northern Africa; and Southern Asia. Separate medals have been awarded for other conflicts since the Second World War: Korea (1950–53); the South Atlantic (1982); the Gulf (1990–91); Sierra Leone (2000–02); Afghanistan (from 2001); and Iraq (2003–11). In addition to these, RAF personnel have also been eligible for various United Nations (UN) and North Atlantic Treaty Organisation (NATO) medals, awarded for their corresponding operations.

The Long Service and Good Conduct Medal (LSGCM) was instituted in 1919 and is awarded to non-commissioned officers and other ranks for exemplary service, initially over a period of eighteen years but since 1977 the qualifying period has been reduced to fifteen years. The medal is silver and is issued named. Since 1944, a Bar has been awarded for further unblemished service; again, this was initially a further eighteen years of service but was later reduced to fifteen. In 1947, officers became eligible for the award provided they had served at least twelve years of the qualifying period in the ranks and provided the conduct requirements for the award had been met.

Brian Francis (known to his colleagues as Ray) joined the RAF in 1951 at the age of 17 and served in the General Duties trade until he left the service in 1986. He was awarded the Africa General Service Medal (furthest left) in 1955 for serving at RAF Eastleigh, near Nairobi in Kenya, during the so-called Mau Mau rebellion, and, in 1972, the General Service Medal (centre) for service in Northern Ireland. In between, he was awarded the LSGCM (far right) in 1966 and then the clasp in 1981 after completing thirty years of service. He now lives in Lincoln.

65

Hawker Hunter

WITH ITS CLEAN lines and swept wing, the single-seat Hawker Hunter was the iconic jet fighter of its time. Developed as a replacement for the Meteor under Hawker Siddeley's chief designer, Sydney Camm, the Hunter was the company's first jet aircraft to enter service with the RAF, and went on to serve as an interceptor, a fighter-bomber and as a reconnaissance aircraft in numerous conflicts, with more than twenty air forces across the world.

Powered by a new single Rolls-Royce Avon turbojet, the transonic and highly manoeuvrable Hunter F1 entered service with the RAF in July 1954. Only the year before, the modified prototype, flown by Hawker Siddeley's chief test pilot and former war ace Neville Duke had broken the world air speed record for a jet-powered aircraft over Littlehampton, having reached 727.6mph (1,171km/h).

It was an exciting time, and rapid advances in engine technology and aerodynamic design quickly led to the development of more variants. Early problems with surging and stalling led to the F2 being powered by the Armstrong-Siddeley Sapphire, while a modified wing for the F4, which entered service in 1955, countered the earlier limitation in range. A Sapphire-powered modified aircraft became the F5, while the F6 was powered by an improved Avon 203 engine, giving the aircraft a top speed of 715mph (1,150km/h) at sea level, a rate of climb of more than 17,000ft/min (87m/s) and a service ceiling of nearly 50,000ft (15,240m).

Country of Origin: UK
Date: 1956
Location: RAF Museum Hendon, London
(© RAF Museum)

The Hunter F6 was built in greater numbers than any other variant with 379 built for the RAF. It had a combat range approaching 450 miles (720km) and was armed with four 30mm (1.18in) Aden cannons. Several of these aircraft were later modified to F6A standard with strengthened wings to enable greater loads to be carried.

During the years that followed the Hunter was involved in many overseas operations. First, during the Suez Crisis of 1956, Hunters were deployed to Cyprus from where they provided local air defence, as well as flying as fighter escorts for RAF Canberra bombers over Egypt. Then, in 1962, Hunters provided support for British ground forces during the Brunei Revolt, and during the Borneo Confrontation of the mid-1960s Hunters were deployed to Borneo and Malaya.

Not only did the Hunter prove to be an excellent combat aircraft, it also looked great in the air and so was used by two RAF display teams over a period of seven years; first by the Black Arrows of 111 Squadron (1956–60), which initially operated four aircraft and then nine, and achieved fame by setting the record of looping and barrel-rolling twenty-two aircraft in formation at the 1958 Farnborough Air Show, and then the Blue Diamonds of 92 Squadron (1960–63), which flew sixteen aircraft. By then, though, the Hunter's days as an interceptor were over, as it was gradually being replaced by the much faster and far more capable English Electric Lightning.

But the Hunter was too good an aircraft to be phased out of RAF service altogether and so many were modified for the close air support or reconnaissance roles, with its hard points under the wings allowing the carriage of rockets, missiles, bombs or drop tanks for extra fuel. The definitive close air support version was the Hunter FGA9, derived from the F6, of which 129 served with the RAF

Hunter FGA9 of 20 Squadron based at Tengah in Singapore.

for many years, while the tactical reconnaissance variant was the FR10. The FGA9 was also the variant on which most exports were based. To supplement the four 30mm cannons of the F6, its primary weapons were 3in (76mm) rockets, twelve of which could be carried under each wing, while an alternative weapon load included 1,000lb (453kg) bombs. Operating from Khormaksar in Aden, the RAF's FGA9s and FR10s were used extensively during the Radfan campaign of 1964 when they operated against insurgents attempting to overthrow the Federation of South Arabia; they remained in Aden until the UK withdrew its forces at the end of 1967.

The Hunter spent its final years with the RAF (and the Royal Navy) in the training role (with the two-seat T7 and T8 variants) and in various other supporting roles, before it was finally retired in the early 1990s after nearly forty years of service. By then, nearly 2,000 Hunters had been built in the many different variants and even when it was finally phased out of service with the RAF, the Hunter remained in service with other air forces and civil operators across the world.

Several Hunters have survived. The example shown on the previous page is XG154, a Hunter FGA9, which is on display at the RAF Museum Hendon. It was built in 1956 by Armstrong Whitworth at Coventry (having been subcontracted from Hawkers at Kingston) to the F6 standard and made its first flight from RAF Bitteswell, Leicestershire. It then moved to No. 19 Maintenance

Unit at RAF St Athan in Wales before being delivered to 66 Squadron at RAF Linton-on-Ouse. Early the following year the squadron moved to RAF Acklington and during the next couple of years was detached to the Middle East.

XG154 was modified to FGA9 standard in 1959 and joined 43 Squadron at RAF Leuchars in Scotland. The squadron soon moved to Nicosia in Cyprus to become the resident FGA (fighter ground-attack) squadron in the Near East Air Force. By 1963, XG154 was serving in Aden with 8 Squadron based at Khormaksar as part of the Tactical Wing. It was the opening phase of the Radfan campaign and for the next eight years XG154 remained in the region, serving at various times with each of the wing's three squadrons (8, 43 and 208 Squadrons), before returning to the UK in 1971. XG154 then served with No. 229 Operational Conversion Unit (the longest-serving Hunter operating unit) at RAF Chivenor in Devon, after which it was transferred to the Tactical Weapons Unit at RAF Brawdy in Wales, before being moved to St Athan in 1984 for long-term storage. After more than 5,500 flying hours this great aircraft's flying days were over. It was then allocated the ground instructional number 8863M and has been on display at Hendon since 1989.

66

Vickers Valiant

IN 1955 THE Vickers Valiant became the first of the RAF's three new V-bombers to enter service. Although more than a hundred were eventually built, XD818 is the only fully intact Valiant still in existence and it was this aircraft that, in 1957, dropped Britain's first live H-bomb over the Pacific Ocean.

America's use of an aircraft to deliver the first atomic bomb during the final days of the Second World War had taken air warfare to another level. In 1947 the Air Ministry issued the first specification for a new jet-powered bomber capable of carrying a 10,000lb (4,53kg) weapon load over a range of 3,500 nautical miles (6,482km) at a speed of 500 knots (925km/h) and with a delivery height of not less than 50,000ft (15,240m). Six aircraft companies were invited to submit tenders and as the designs were expected to be radical, an Advanced Bomber Group, consisting of structural engineers and aerodynamics experts, was set up at the Royal Aircraft Establishment at Farnborough to consider the proposals.

As things were to turn out, the proposals from Avro and Handley Page offered significant advantages over the other submissions, but the group did not want to commit to just one design should a major design flaw later emerge. And so, to reduce the overall risk to the programme, the group decided to continue with both designs. Vickers had also been working on a new design, the Type 660. It was a more conventional aircraft with a shoulder-mounted wing of a compound sweep configuration (where the inboard section of the wing was swept forwards) and with four Rolls-Royce Avon turbojets installed in pairs embedded within each wing root. Its design was considered low risk. It was based on proven aerodynamics rather than

Country of Origin: UK
Date: 1956
Location: RAF Museum Cosford, Staffordshire
(© RAF Museum)

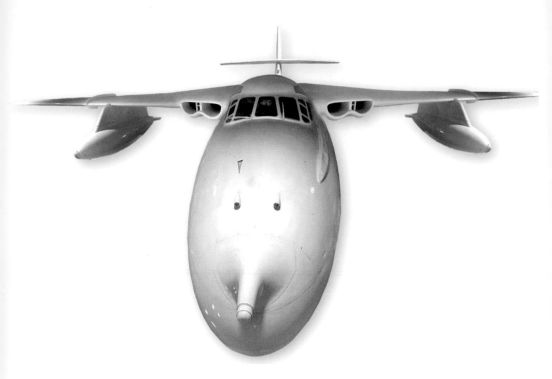

theory, and so Vickers was also instructed to proceed with development as an interim solution, pending further development of the Avro and Handley Page designs.

Although there was a time when it looked as if one design might have to be rejected, all three were to be accepted into service with the Vickers design becoming the Valiant, while the Handley Page and Avro designs became the Victor and Vulcan respectively.

The Valiant prototype first flew in 1951. Two years later the first production aircraft flew and in early 1955 the Valiant B1 entered service with the RAF. It was just over 108ft long (33m), 32ft tall (9.8m) and had a wingspan of just over 114ft (34.8m). Because its wing design had been compromised to accommodate the engines and landing gear, there was only limited space for fuel and so large external fuel tanks could be carried beneath each wing to extend the range. The crew of five were contained in a pressurised cockpit at the front of the aircraft. The two pilots were seated side by side on ejection seats on a raised level within the cockpit, while the three rear crew members (two navigators – one plotter and one radar bomber – and an electronics operator) were sat at stations

Valiants of 214
Squadron carrying
out in-flight refuelling
trials in 1958. (via
MRAF Sir Michael
Beetham)

at a lower level to the rear and would be required to bale out manually through the crew door in the event of an emergency.

The first squadron to receive the Valiant B1 was 138 Squadron, which re-formed at RAF Gaydon in Warwickshire in January 1955 for the strategic nuclear bombing role, and at the aircraft's peak of strength nine RAF squadrons were equipped with the type. The Valiant might have been less advanced than the other V-bombers but it was the only one of the three to drop live nuclear weapons. In 1956 a Valiant became the first RAF aircraft to drop a British atomic bomb during tests carried out at Maralinga in Australia (Operation Buffalo), and the following year XD818 dropped the first British hydrogen bomb (a thermo-nuclear fusion device) over the Pacific Ocean (Operation Grapple). The Valiant was also the first V-bomber to see action during the Suez Crisis in 1956, when aircraft operating from Malta dropped conventional bombs on targets in Egypt. It was then at the forefront of the RAF developing its air-to-air refuelling capability and some aircraft were also modified for radio counter-measures as well as for the photoreconnaissance role.

The rapid development of Soviet surface-to-air missiles led to a change in tactics as strategic bombing moved from high-level to low-level missions. But operating a large aircraft at low level was not without its problems, not least because of the increased stress on the airframe. By 1964 it was discovered that all Valiants were showing premature signs of fatigue and corrosion was found in the main wing spar attachments. Rather than embark on a costly rebuilding programme, the Valiant was retired from service in 1965, with its roles being absorbed by the Victor and Vulcan squadrons.

XD818, shown here, was built by Vickers-Armstrongs to B1 standard and first flew on 4 September 1956, after which it joined 49 Squadron at RAF Wittering. It was one of eight Valiants to be specially modified for Operation Grapple in the central Pacific, which included measures to protect the aircraft and crew, instrumentation for scientific operations and the addition of extra and special equipment for navigational and bombing requirements. On 15 May 1957, flown by Wing Commander Kenneth Hubbard (the squadron's commanding officer), XD818 dropped Britain's first live H-bomb – a Green Granite device within a Blue Danube ballistic case – off Malden Island, 400 miles to the south of Christmas Island. The drop was made from 45,000ft (13,716m), the air burst yielding 150 to 200 kilotons. Having then returned home to become a public attraction, XD818 twice returned to the Pacific the following year as part of the Grapple series of tests. By the end of 1958, the nuclear testing was over and so 49 Squadron reverted to its standard bombing role with XD818 being de-modified. In 1961 the squadron moved to RAF Marham with XD818 then being converted to the air refuelling tanker configuration before it was grounded with the other Valiants at the end of 1964 and retired from service in 1965.

XD818 remained at Marham until 1982 when it was dismantled and moved by road to the RAF Museum Hendon where it was reassembled and displayed until 2005. It was then dismantled again and moved to the RAF Museum Cosford to take up its home in the new National Cold War Exhibition building the following year. It is the only place where all three V-bombers can be seen together.

67

Rescue and Target Towing Launch

SHOWN HERE IS Rescue and Target Towing Launch No. 2757, which is on display at the RAF Museum Hendon.

The fact the RAF operated large numbers of marine vessels for nearly seventy years, or even had a Marine Branch, often goes unnoticed. The branch had, in fact, formed within days of the RAF's formation, with vessels established at bases where floatplanes and flying boats were operating. These vessels provided marine support for maritime operations in the same way that vehicles provided support for land-based aircraft. Marine Craft training schools were established for the training of RAF personnel and, gradually, more specialised vessels arrived in service, with most officers initially transferring from the Royal Navy.

In 1920 the new Marine Craft branch was issued with a directive stating that all units operating motor boats should have one vessel standing by, either under way or ready for immediate departure, to assist in the rescue of the crew of an aircraft should it ditch in the sea. Air–Sea Rescue (ASR) as we know it today had begun, and for the next forty years ASR cover was not just provided around the waters of the UK but was also provided in all theatres across the world, wherever the RAF was involved. During the Second World War, for example, a total of 13,619 Allied servicemen were rescued from the sea.

Country of Origin: UK

Date: 1956

Location: RAF Museum Hendon, London

(© RAF Museum)

The Marine Branch continued to support the maritime-equipped RAF squadrons until the last Sunderland flying boats were withdrawn from service. From 1959 the Marine Craft sections began to close as the primary means of ASR was passed to helicopter squadrons. But not all marine units were disbanded. Some were retained to carry out a

wide range of supporting roles for the RAF. These included target towing, gunnery range safety patrols, aircrew sea survival training, helicopter winching exercises, and assistance to Special Forces and other covert operations. Several units were also retained overseas (the last Marine Craft Unit was based at Gibraltar) until the Marine Branch was finally disbanded in 1986.

The launch shown here, 2757, was still in service when the Marine Branch disbanded. She was built by Vosper Thorneycroft in the mid-1950s and is 68ft (20.7m) long with a beam of 19ft (5.8m). With an aluminium superstructure, and powered by two 1450 hp 12-cylinder Rolls-Royce Sea Griffons, she was capable of 39 knots (56km/h) and had a maximum range of 530 nautical miles (740km). Fully laden with her crew of nine and with a maximum of 120 passengers her gross weight was 65 tons (66 tonnes).

2757 entered RAF service in 1956 and first served with No. 1100 Marine Craft Unit (MCU) at Alness, Cromarty Firth, in Scotland. Having then undergone modifications in 1965 she was moved the following year to No. 1105 MCU at Portrush, County Antrim, in Northern Ireland. Then, in 1971, she moved to RAF Mount Batten in Plymouth, Devon, from where, in November 1977, she made her final sea voyage to the Royal Victoria Dock in London. She was later moved by road to the RAF Museum Hendon, where 2757 remains on display today.

Part 5
The Cold War

68

Alert State and NBC/Air Raid State Board

ONE EXHIBIT ON display at the RAF Waddington Heritage Centre is the station's former Alert State and NBC/Air Raid State board. Waddington was one of the RAF's key strategic V-bomber bases during the height of the Cold War and so the importance of this status board cannot be overstated. By using a simple system of colours and abbreviations, station personnel could instantly determine the threat level at any one time.

It was not long after the North Atlantic Treaty was signed in 1949 that the newly formed NATO established a system of military alert measures in preparation for any attempt by the Soviet Union to mount a surprise attack from which the Allies would have little, if any, advanced warning. NATO constitutes a system of collective defence, whereby its member states agree to mutual defence in response to any attack by an external party, and so by having a military alert system in place it was believed that NATO forces could survive an attack and then to prepare counter action. The system put in place was designed to affect only military forces, implementable by military commanders and not dependent upon prior political negotiations and agreement. Essentially, it was a system that allowed NATO military commanders to declare, through the calling of alert states, that a situation was believed to exist; although the state could vary from nation to nation or even region to region.

How to display the alert states varied but the status board shown here gives the overall Alert State on the top row; working from MV (Military Vigilance) on the left, through a series of increasing alert states – SA (Simple Alert), RA (Reinforced Alert) and GA (General Alert). Furthest right,

Country of Origin: UK
Date: Mid-1950s
Location: RAF Waddington Heritage Centre, Lincolnshire (By kind permission of the Station Commander RAF Waddington)

the Orange (later considered to be Amber) and Scarlet (later Red) refers to the NATO Alarm Stage; Orange Alert being a precautionary stage and the higher Scarlet Alert indicating that an attack was imminent or was already under way. On the bottom row is the NBC (Nuclear, Biological and Chemical) and Air Raid state, working from Low through Medium to High with the white indicator showing all clear. Any escalation of a situation could clearly be shown on the board so that crucial information could be passed to everyone who needed to know – on the ground or in the air – but it was not necessarily the case that one condition would be followed by the next. The system had been designed to allow an instant jump from a relatively low state to one much higher. However, the higher the alert state then the amount of time that forces could be maintained at a high readiness state reduced.

In response to any possible attack against the UK, Bomber Command developed a state of increased preparation; ranging from Alert Condition 4 (the lowest) to Alert Condition 1 when the V-bombers were generated for war and dispersed to several UK airfields ready for their operational mission. These alert conditions were qualified by a series of readiness states for the aircraft and crews; ranging from Readiness State One-Five (fifteen minutes' readiness) to Readiness State Zero-Two, with the crew at two minutes cockpit readiness and at a holding point near the runway awaiting further instructions, from where they would be scrambled for their operational mission.

69

Avro Shackleton

DEVELOPED FROM THE Avro Lincoln, itself born from the highly successful Lancaster bomber, the Shackleton played an essential part in Britain's defence during the early Cold War years as the RAF's long-range maritime patrol and anti-submarine aircraft. It remained in the role for nearly twenty years and then went on to serve in small numbers as an airborne early warning aircraft, taking the Shackleton's total length of service with the RAF to a remarkable forty years.

The Shackleton had been designed with long-range maritime patrols in mind. Britain needed an aircraft that could guard against the increasing number of Soviet submarines that were likely to be operating in the North Atlantic. The first variant to enter service, the Shackleton MR1, was delivered to 120 Squadron at RAF Kinloss in Scotland during 1951 and by the end of the following year seven squadrons had been equipped with the type. However, the MR1 was only ever intended to be a short-term solution. Its shortcomings were put right in the MR2, which had a re-designed airframe and an upgraded ASV (Air-to-Surface Vessel) Mk13 radar, capable of detecting a destroyer-sized ship out to a range of 40 miles (64km) or a surfaced submarine at 20 miles (32km), with its radome being moved from the nose of the aircraft to a ventral position just aft of the bomb bay.

Production of the MR2 ended in 1954, after which came the MR3. Powered by four Rolls-Royce Griffons, with their large contra-rotating propellers, the MR3 was capable of 302mph (486km/h), a service ceiling of 19,200ft (5,852m) and a range of 3,660 miles (5,889km). Its many improvements included a lengthened fuselage, new wings with tip tanks to increase its fuel capacity, and a

Country of Origin: UK

Date: 1957

Location: Newark Air Museum, Nottinghamshire (By kind permission of the Newark Air Museum)

new tricycle undercarriage to replace the earlier tail-wheel configuration. Its capability was also upgraded to include three homing torpedoes, twelve sonobuoys and nine depth charges, including nuclear depth bombs to counter the new Soviet submarines operating deeper than before. The MR3 was also fitted with two 20mm cannons in the nose. To facilitate long flights of up to fifteen hours, a galley and sleeping quarters were provided for the crew, which, typically, would number ten: two pilots; two navigators; a flight engineer; an air electronics officer; and four air electronics operators.

The Shackleton MR3 entered service in 1957 with 220 Squadron at RAF St Mawgan in Cornwall. More than fifty had been ordered but cuts in Defence spending announced the previous year meant this figure was eventually reduced to just over thirty. Although the number of MR3s had been reduced, the aircraft did go through three phased modification programmes. The first of these was essentially an update to existing equipment while the second introduced electronic counter-measures (ECM) and improved communications. The third included a new navigation system and the addition of two Armstrong-Siddeley Viper turbojets, fitted at the rear of the outboard engine nacelles, to assist with the take-off due to the significant increase in weight of the MR3.

Shackleton of 205 Squadron based at Changi in Singapore. The squadron provided the RAF's maritime reconnaissance in the Far East throughout the 1960s.

The Shackleton was eventually replaced in the maritime patrol and anti-submarine roles by the Nimrod MR1, which was introduced into service from 1969. During its time with the RAF the Shackleton had also seen operational service overseas. First in 1955, when aircraft were used to transport British troops to Cyprus and again the following year when Shackletons were involved in the Suez Crisis, and then again during the Indo-Malaysia confrontation of the mid-1960s.

However, the Shackleton's days were not completely over as it was to be temporarily saved by the UK's need for an airborne early warning aircraft following the withdrawal from service of the Fleet Air Arm's Fairey Gannet. As an interim measure, the AN/APS-20 radar was installed into twelve modified Shackleton MR2s and the aircraft re-designated the AEW2. From 1972 the Shackleton AEW2 provided airborne early warning as part of the nation's air defence system. It was only ever intended to be in service for a short time until its intended replacement, the Nimrod AEW3, arrived. However, the subsequent cancellation of the Nimrod AEW aircraft in favour of the American Boeing E-3D Sentry meant the Shackleton continued in the airborne early warning role until 1991.

Shown on p. 232 is WR977, a Shackleton MR3, which was built at Woodford in 1957 and entered RAF service the following year with 220 Squadron (soon to be renumbered as 201 Squadron) at RAF St Mawgan in Cornwall. In 1959, WR977 was transferred across the airfield to 206 Squadron but returned to 201 Squadron in 1963. It then went through its Phase 3 modification (completed in 1966) after which it was again transferred across the airfield – this time to 42 Squadron. During the late 1960s, WR977 is also known to have served with 203 Squadron at RAF Ballykelly in Northern Ireland and then with 206 Squadron again, by then based at Kinloss, before it was transferred back to 203 Squadron after its move to RAF Luqa in Malta. WR977's flying days ended in 1971 and it was later transferred to the old RAF Winthorpe, now the site of the Newark Air Museum, where it has been on display since 1977 as a tribute to this wonderful aircraft.

70

Yellow Sun

SHOWN HERE IS Yellow Sun, Britain's first operational high-yield strategic nuclear weapon, which entered service in 1958 and was designed to be carried by the RAF's V-bombers, the Victor and Vulcan.

The political decision for the UK to proceed with an atomic bomb had been made as early as 1947. RAF personnel were involved in the development programme from the outset, but it was not until 1954 that the introduction of nuclear weapons into RAF service began when No. 1321 Flight was formed at RAF Wittering with the Valiant to integrate Blue Danube, the RAF's first nuclear weapon, into service. For political reasons, Blue Danube was being introduced into service at an early stage of its development, which nowadays might be considered premature, and so for the next two years the flight conducted a series of tests, many with concrete cores, to assess the performance of the bomb casing at various altitudes and speeds. Drops were made at the Atomic Weapons Research Establishment's Cold War Research and Development site at Orford Ness in Suffolk, where science and politics merged with environmental testing to simulate the conditions that nuclear weapons and their components might experience during trials and while in service use. Telemetry was used to check that everything was working as it should, particularly the new electronic circuitry, with the trajectory of the bomb tracked by kinetheodolites to determine its ballistic characteristics.

Country of Origin: UK
Date: 1958
Location: RAF Museum Cosford, Shropshire
(© RAF Museum)

The RAF's first testing of nuclear weapons was carried out in 1956. Called Operation Buffalo, these tests took place at Maralinga, South Australia, as part of Britain's main atomic bomb development programme. Buffalo consisted of four bursts; two of Blue Danube, including

an air drop by a Valiant that detonated at 500ft (152m) above the ground, and two of Red Beard, a smaller weapon but a significant improvement on Blue Danube. Because Red Beard could also be carried by aircraft such as the Canberra, it would replace Blue Danube in the early 1960s to become Britain's first tactical nuclear weapon.

Operation Buffalo was an important moment in the RAF's history and was followed by Operation Grapple, a series of megaton nuclear weapons tests carried out between 1956 and 1958 at Malden Island and Christmas Island in the central Pacific Ocean. The UK had become the third recognised possessor of thermonuclear weapons and by employing the radiation implosion technology used during Grapple, Yellow Sun became the country's first H-bomb.

First came Yellow Sun MkI, an interim solution until the MkII was ready to be introduced in 1961, with Yellow Sun referring to the outer casing while its warhead was either Green Grass for the MkI (with a yield of 400 kilotons) or Red Snow (a lighter Anglicised version of the American W28 warhead of around 1.1MT) for Yellow Sun MkII. With its tail fin fitted, Yellow Sun was 21ft (6.4m) long and 4ft (1.2m) in diameter. With the Green Grass warhead, it weighed 7,250lb (3,288kg) while the lighter Red Snow warhead meant that Yellow Sun MkII weighed just 1,700lb (771kg), and so ballast was added to maintain its overall weight and aerodynamic property.

Unlike other contemporary bombs of similar destructive power, Yellow Sun was not designed with a parachute to retard its fall. Instead, its design incorporated a blunt nose to induce drag and slow the fall of the weapon sufficiently to allow the bomber to make its escape. The blunt nose

Britain's first operational high-yield strategic nuclear weapon called Yellow Sun was designed to be carried by the RAF's V-bombers, including Vulcans. Shown here are three Vulcans from RAF Waddington flying in formation. (Crown Copyright 1957)

also ensured that Yellow Sun did not encounter problems with transonic/supersonic shock waves that had previously plagued Blue Danube.

As the V-Force was forced into operating at low level, delivery of Yellow Sun MkII would typically involve a low-level ingress to the target area and then for the bomber to pull up to a release height of around 20,000ft (6,096m). During this high-risk manoeuvre the aircraft and crew would be exposed to any enemy surface-to-air missile defences, and so as soon as the weapon had been released the aircraft would then either quickly return to low level to make its escape or continue climbing to as high a level as possible, depending on the threat at the time.

Yellow Sun was only ever designed as an emergency weapon, meaning that little or no consideration had been given to its long-term stockpiling. However, Yellow Sun MkII, of which, it is believed, around 150 were built, remained the RAF's primary air drop strategic weapon until the late 1960s and was not fully replaced until the early 1970s.

71

Bloodhound
Surface-to-Air Missile

A KEY PART of the UK's air defence system during the Cold War was the Bloodhound surface-to-air missile. It was brought into service during the late 1950s to protect the RAF's strategic V-Force bases against attack from Soviet high-flying bombers and remained in large-scale service for more than thirty years.

Britain's defence during the height of the Cold War was based on a mix of manned fighters and surface-to-air missiles; the concept being the RAF's supersonic Lightning would provide the first line of defence out over the North Sea while the Bloodhound squadrons would attack any enemy bombers that had managed to penetrate the outer line of defence. And so, from the end of 1958, several RAF fighter squadrons were re-equipped with the Bloodhound and missile sites established near to the V-bomber bases in eastern England: at Breighton and Carnaby in Yorkshire; Dunholme Lodge in Lincolnshire; Marham and Watton in Norfolk; Rattlesden in Suffolk; Woolfox Lodge in Rutland; Warboys in Huntingdonshire; and Misson in Nottinghamshire.

From the mid-1960s, the improved Bloodhound MkII replaced the MkIs. Longer than the earlier missile, the Bloodhound MkII had two Bristol Siddeley Thor ram jets plus four Gosling solid-fuel rocket boosters, which boosted the missile to a speed above Mach 2 and up to an altitude of 59,000ft (17,984m), giving it a range of around 100 miles (160km). With its boosters fitted, the MkII was 27ft 9in (8.5m) long and had a span of just over 9ft (2.8m), although its body diameter was less than 2ft (0.6m). Its weight at launch was 5,200lb (2,359kg).

Country of Origin: UK
Date: 1958
Location: RAF Museum Hendon, London
(© RAF Museum)

The Bloodhound's computer steered the two central stub wings and adjusted the fuel flow to the ram jets, while a Ferranti semi-active homing radar provided guidance. The warhead was high-explosive continuous steel rod fragmentation and was detonated using a proximity fuse.

When responsibility for the UK's nuclear deterrent passed to the Royal Navy in 1970, the RAF's Bloodhounds were either withdrawn from service or transferred to RAF Germany for airfield defence. However, just a few years later, Bloodhound was reintroduced back home following a revised appraisal of the threat to the UK at the time, resulting in 85 Squadron at West Raynham in Norfolk being re-equipped with the Bloodhound MkII. And when airfield defence in Germany was taken over by the RAF Regiment with its Rapier surface-to-air missiles, the remaining Bloodhounds returned to the UK and four additional sites were established at Barkston Heath (Lincolnshire), Bawdsey and Wattisham in Suffolk, and Wyton (Cambridgeshire).

Bloodhound remained in service until the end of the Cold War, after which the sites were removed. Although the missile never had to be fired in anger, it had always proved very good during tests. Several examples can be found in the UK. The Bloodhound shown here stands at the main entrance to the RAF Museum Hendon. It is in the markings of 85 Squadron, which operated the Bloodhound MkII at West Raynham from 1975 until 1991.

72

St Clement Danes, the Central Church of the RAF

SITUATED IN THE City of Westminster in the heart of central London, outside the Royal Courts of Justice on the Strand, is the Anglican church of St Clement Danes, the Central Church of the RAF.

Clement was Bishop of Rome at the end of the first century and legend has it that he was martyred during the persecution of Christians under Emperor Trajan by being tied to an anchor and thrown into the sea. Although the original church on the site was reputedly founded in the ninth century by the Danes, the church as we know it today was completed in 1682 by Sir Christopher Wren.

However, the church was virtually destroyed during the Second World War when a direct hit from a German incendiary bomb on the night of 10 May 1941 left it in a derelict state. Only the outer walls and the tower were left standing but after the war a proposal to the Diocese of London suggested that the RAF be allowed to restore and rebuild the church as its own. And so it was that St Clement Danes, destroyed by the actions of one air force, was given into the care of another. An appeal was launched that attracted support not only from within the RAF but from other air forces across the world. The architect appointed, Anthony Lloyd, closely followed Wren's previous design and in 1958 St Clement Danes was re-consecrated as the Central Church of the Royal Air Force.

The church's role today is to be a place of regular worship and to be a living memorial to those who have died whilst serving in the RAF. Inside the church there are several attractions of historical importance to be seen, including: the Coat of Arms of Viscount Trenchard, the

Country of Origin: UK
Date: 1958
Location: The Strand, London (By kind permission of St Clement Danes)

founder of the RAF; a rosette of Commonwealth air force badges; a memorial to Polish squadrons who flew with the RAF during the Second World War; the pulpit, designed by Grinling Gibbons, which was stored for safe keeping in St Paul's Cathedral during the London Blitz; a lectern gifted by the Royal Australian Air Force; a memorial book containing 16,000 names of United States air force personnel who died during the Second World War whilst based in the UK; almost 900 squadron and unit badges made of Welsh slate set into the floor of the church; the Victory Tapestry in memory of London in her finest hour, designed and worked by Janet Barrow; and several books of remembrance in which are recorded the names of over 150,000 men and women who have died whilst serving in the RAF.

Outside the church stand the statues of two of the RAF's greatest wartime leaders, Hugh Dowding, who had helped save the nation during the Battle of Britain, and Arthur Harris who had paved the way for victory. The church is open daily (except bank holidays) for visitors.

73

Uniform of the Princess Mary's Royal Air Force Nursing Service

SHOWN HERE IS the uniform of Squadron Officer Gladys Pilgrim of the Princess Mary's Royal Air Force Nursing Service (PMRAFNS), the nursing branch of the RAF.

Established in 1918 to meet the needs of the new RAF, the nursing branch was initially called the RAF Temporary Nursing Service. In 1921 it became part of the permanent organisation and then two years later picked up the 'Royal' prefix to become the PMRAFNS after HRH Princess Mary agreed to become its Patron.

The nursing service owes its early success to the dynamic personality and energy of its first matron-in-chief, Dame Joanna Cruickshank, now regarded as its true founding member. It was she who encouraged the sisters to endure the personal hardships encountered through those difficult early years. Until the Second World War the PMRAFNS was only open to unmarried women or childless widows, and had a rank system of its own based on the qualifications and expertise of the individual. The rank started as staff nurse and worked up through sister, senior sister, matron, principal matron and chief principal matron to the highest rank of matron-in-chief (equivalent to air commodore). From June 1943, those in the PMRAFNS were granted emergency commissions and wore the rank insignia corresponding to their equivalent RAF officer rank; for example, the rank of squadron officer was equivalent to squadron leader. The PMRAFNS had now grown in strength to 1,126 sisters staffing thirty-one

Country of Origin: UK
Date: 1958
Location: Trenchard Museum, RAF Halton, Buckinghamshire (By kind permission of the Station Commander RAF Halton)

RAF hospitals and seventy-one sick quarters on RAF stations. Its peak of activity was following D-Day in 1944 when 300,000 casualty evacuations were carried out; the most ever in the history of the service. After the war, the PMs (Princess Marys) as they had become known wore the same officer badges of rank as their RAF colleagues, but continued to use their professional titles (sister, matron etc.) when in the clinical environment.

The PMRAFNS was a women-only service until 1980 when men were also allowed to join. In 1985 the PMs became part of the Tri-Service Defence Nursing Services, which is now under the overall umbrella of the Defence Medical Services that encompasses the entire medical, dental, nursing, health professionals, paramedical and support personnel for the armed forces. It totals around 9,100 personnel (6,900 regulars and 2,200 reserves) working alongside civil servants and other supporting units to provide healthcare to all forces personnel in military bases, at sea and in areas of conflict. Today the PMRAFNS is committed to providing a skilled, knowledgeable, and able nursing workforce to deliver high-quality care, whilst being responsive to the dynamic nature of RAF nursing in peacetime and on operations.

Miss Gladys Pilgrim joined the PMRAFNS in September 1938, initially serving as a staff nurse and then as a sister during the Second World War. She was promoted to squadron officer in 1950 and finally left the service at the end of 1958 after twenty years of service. The medal ribbons on her uniform show her wartime service, with the ribbon furthest left depicting the award of the Royal Red Cross for exceptional services in military nursing.

Her uniform is now on display at the Trenchard Museum at RAF Halton, which was home to one of two RAF Hospitals opened after the First World War. The hospital then consisted of huts but a more permanent structure was built and opened in 1927 by HRH Princess Mary, after whom the hospital was named. During the Second World War the

hospital was expanded to take 700 beds and by the end of hostilities had treated some 20,000 casualties from operational theatres all over the world. The Princess Mary's Hospital at Halton gained international recognition for its development and innovation in medical science and surgical techniques. During the First Gulf War of 1991 more than half of the hospital's personnel were deployed to various parts of the Mediterranean and Middle East. In 1996, several RAF hospitals were closed under the post-Cold War Defence Costs Studies, including the hospital at Halton, leaving the hospital at RAF Akrotiri in Cyprus to assume the distinguished title of The Princess Mary's Hospital (TPMH) as a Tri-Service hospital.

RAF medics have continued to operate all over the world, in this case in Sierra Leone. (Crown Copyright 2013)

74

Thor Intermediate-Range Ballistic Missile

FOR A SHORT while in its long history the RAF entered the age of the ballistic missile. Until then its nuclear weapons capability was based on free-fall bombs delivered by V-bombers, but it had become increasingly apparent that if the UK wanted to remain a major post-war power and, more importantly, have an independent nuclear deterrent, then the procurement of a ballistic missile was essential. It would never become accepted doctrine to replace bombers with missiles but there were obvious advantages and disadvantages with each system, and so it was decided that the RAF's V-Force and ballistic missiles would share responsibility for the nation's nuclear deterrent.

As the V-bombers were entering service during the latter half of the 1950s, the Air Ministry issued a series of operational requirements calling for a new weapon with a megaton warhead to improve Bomber Command's strategic nuclear capability. The British government's preferred option was to procure Blue Streak, a British-built intermediate-range ballistic missile (IRBM), but, as things were to turn out, Blue Streak was later cancelled. However, an agreement had been reached with the US government for the supply of sixty Douglas PGM-17/SM-75 Thor IRBMs as an interim solution.

Thor was 65ft (19.8m) long and 8ft (2.4m) in diameter. Its all-up weight was 110,000lb (49,895kg), of which 90 per cent was fuel. The Rocketdyne liquid propellant rocket motor burned for just under three minutes, boosting the missile to around 14,400ft per second (4,400m/s) and taking it to an altitude up to 280 miles (450km), giving Thor a range of around 1,725 miles (2,776km). The total flight time was typically around eighteen minutes, with the

Country of Origin: USA
Date: 1959
Location: RAF Museum Cosford, Shropshire
(© RAF Museum)

missile using an autopilot and inertial navigation system to accurately control its flight path. At the point when the motor stopped burning, the nose cone containing the warhead separated from the missile's body; the height and speed of this occurring depended on the range to the target. Finally, the single W49 warhead, weighing just 2,200lb (1,000kg), produced a yield equivalent to 1.44 megatons of TNT.

The first RAF squadron prepared to receive its missiles was 77 Squadron, which re-formed at Feltwell, Norfolk in September 1958. Its task was to work with the Americans to establish training techniques and operating procedures. The launch crews – made up of a Launch Control Officer (usually a flight lieutenant) plus various ground technicians and an American Authentication Officer (typically a captain in the US air force) – were trained in America and on 16 April 1959 at Vandenberg Air Force Base the RAF launched its first missile, as captured here in this spectacular image.

The missiles were to be operated under the dual-key system, where the UK controlled the missiles but the US controlled the warheads and with targeting a matter of joint operational policy. 77 Squadron received its first missile in 1959 (flown to the UK in an American Douglas C-124 Globemaster), signalling the start of a programme that would see twenty RAF squadrons, each with three missiles, declared operational during the year. The squadrons were spread across eight counties in the eastern part of England – grouped around four main sites at Feltwell, Hemswell (Lincolnshire), Driffield (East Riding of Yorkshire) and North Luffenham (Rutland) – with between forty-five and fifty missiles permanently maintained at fifteen minutes' readiness to launch. At this readiness state the missiles lay horizontal in their shelters but it allowed enough time for them to be erected, fuelled and launched. Without fuel and liquid oxygen, the missiles could maintain this readiness state without any problem but once fuelled the missile would either need to be fired within less than twenty-four hours or de-fuelled and put back on standby; an operation that took six hours to complete.

In 1962, a confrontation between the United States and the Soviet Union concerning the deployment of Soviet ballistic missiles to Cuba, took the world to the brink of nuclear war. For the RAF's Thor squadrons the escalation made no significant difference to their normal readiness state, but it did mean that more missiles were prepared and two launch crews were made available on base at any one time. All but one of the sixty missiles were brought up to fifteen minutes' readiness; the only missile not prepared was one used for training purposes, although the order would later be given to prepare this missile as well. Eventually, after days of negotiations between the world's two superpowers, and following some uncomfortable incidents in the waters off Cuba, the threat of all-out nuclear confrontation was averted.

The thirteen-day Cuban Missile Crisis of October 1962 marked the darkest days of the Cold War. Military doctrine at the time was one of massive retaliation and although the crisis had shown the real value of Thor, it had also shown the disadvantage and potentially disastrous consequences of such a system. On the plus side the missiles had been prepared ready for launch through simple communications and without any obvious visible signs to the public. But, of course, the Thor sites were at fixed and known locations, and therefore would have been obvious targets themselves. Furthermore, the missiles could not have been recalled or immobilised if they had been launched.

Thor was only ever intended to be an interim measure for the UK and was scheduled to be withdrawn from service at the end of 1964, but it did not survive long after the Cuban Missile Crisis. Within months of the crisis being over the missiles were withdrawn from the UK and returned to America. Although short-lived, Thor had satisfied a political rather than a military requirement and was an important and effective part of the national deterrent, but its departure from the UK was as low-key as its arrival.

The RAF's last surviving Thor missile can be seen as part of the National Cold War Exhibition at the RAF Museum Cosford. (© RAF Museum)

75

Jet Provost

KNOWN SIMPLY AND affectionately by those who flew it as the 'JP', the Jet Provost basic jet trainer served the RAF for well over thirty years.

Initially developed by Hunting Percival from its earlier piston-engine Percival Provost basic trainer, the Jet Provost prototype first flew in 1954. The following year the first pre-production T1 made its maiden flight, after which three T1s were delivered to the Central Flying School to begin service trials to determine the JP's value as a basic trainer, and to start developing a training syllabus for the RAF. From the early trials came improvements to the design and this led to the T2, which first flew in 1955, although only a handful of this variant were built for development purposes. Two years later the RAF ordered its first forty of the production aircraft, designated the T3, which featured a more powerful Armstrong-Siddeley Viper 102 engine, a re-designed airframe and ejection seats. Finally, in 1959, the Jet Provost entered service with the RAF.

The JP was carefully designed with *ab initio* students – i.e., with no previous flying experience – in mind. It featured side-by-side seating in the cockpit, with both positions duplicated in terms of flight controls and instrumentation making it extremely well suited for the instructor and pupil. Its aerodynamic design features focussed on good handling characteristics rather than speed, and ease of recovery from potentially dangerous situations such as stalling and spinning. The aircraft's ability to operate at higher altitudes than earlier trainers necessitated the requirement for an oxygen system in the cockpit, although the early production variants were unpressurised.

Country of Origin:
UK
Date: 1959
Location:
RAF Cranwell,
Lincolnshire

Changes in company name led to the later JPs being built by the British Aircraft Corporation. By 1962 around 200 T3s had been delivered to the RAF across several different flying training units: No. 1 Flying Training School (FTS) at RAF Linton-on-Ouse; 2 FTS at RAF Syerston; 3 FTS at RAF Leeming; 6 FTS at RAF Acklington; 7 FTS at RAF Church Fenton; the Central Flying School at RAF Little Rissington; and the RAF College Cranwell. The later T4 variant, of which around 200 were built, was fitted with the more powerful Viper ASV and first flew in 1960, while the T5, powered by the Viper 201, had cockpit pressurisation and first flew in 1967.

The T5 entered RAF service in 1970, more than a decade after the T3 had first entered service, and like the earlier marks proved to be an excellent trainer. Capable of a top speed of 440mph (708km/h) at 25,000ft (7,620m), it was also an excellent aircraft for teaching aerobatics. More than a hundred were built for the RAF, serving throughout the 1970s and 1980s with the various Flying Training Schools and the Central Flying School. Most of these were later fitted with improved avionics to become the T5A, while some were fitted with tip-tanks and used for navigator training as the T5B. The Jet Provost was also exported as a jet trainer (as the T51, T52 and T55, essentially export versions of the T3, T4 and T5 respectively) and a ground-attack version was developed from the T5 to become the BAC Strikemaster, again for the export market.

Jet Provost T3s
over Cranwell.

After more than thirty glorious years with the RAF, the Jet Provost was finally withdrawn from service in the early 1990s to be replaced by the Short Tucano, a turbo-prop aircraft, as the RAF's new basic trainer. However, the JP has remained a popular aircraft amongst private owners and enthusiasts, with many having survived to this day.

The Jet Provost shown on the previous page is XW353, a T5A. It started life as a T5 and was first delivered to RAF Cranwell in January 1971. It flew 1,660 hours in the flying training role before being converted to the T5A standard some four years later. In February 1976, it moved to RAF Leeming and eight years later to RAF Scampton before returning to Cranwell in October 1990 where it was finally retired from flying training after 6,243 flying hours, and having consumed over 97 per cent of its fatigue life. XW353 has stood as the station gate guardian at RAF Cranwell since 1991.

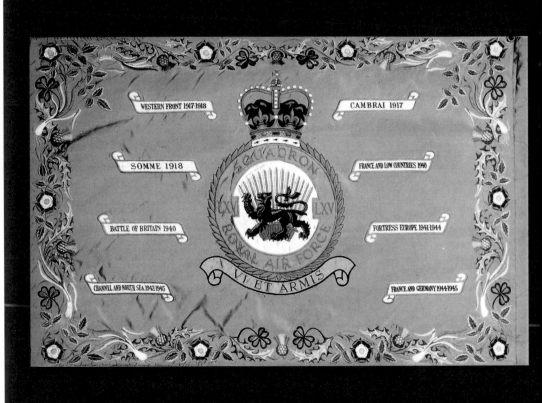

76

Squadron Standard

IN THE SAME way that a Regimental Colour has historical importance for the army, a Squadron Standard carries the same historical importance for the RAF. It is the ceremonial flag of the squadron and is generally only paraded on special occasions, such as on formal parades and dinners. The example shown here is that of 65 Squadron, which was presented to the squadron at RAF Duxford in 1960 and then later laid-up at the RAF College Cranwell after the squadron had been disbanded for the last time.

Squadron Standards date back to 1 April 1943 when first instituted by HM King George VI to mark the twenty-fifth anniversary of the RAF. The basic requirement for a squadron to receive a Standard is the completion of twenty-five years of service, although a Standard might also be granted to a squadron which had earned the Sovereign's appreciation for especially outstanding operations.

The Standard measures 4ft (1.2m) by 2ft 8in (0.8m) and is made of RAF light-blue silk, fringed and tasselled in gold and blue. It has a border of roses, thistles, shamrocks and leeks – devices of the countries of the UK – and a central motif of the approved squadron badge. The Standard also includes any official Battle Honours to which the squadron is entitled; these being depicted in scrolls and selected by the squadron, to a maximum of eight, and forwarded along with the formal request for a Standard to the Sovereign for approval. The limit of eight Battle Honours seems to have been dictated as a purely aesthetic consideration of space and balance on the Standard. The Standard is mounted on an 8ft 1in (2.4m) staff, surmounted by a gold eagle with outstretched wings.

Country of Origin: UK
Date: 1960
Location: RAF College Cranwell, Lincolnshire (Crown Copyright by kind permission of the Commandant RAF College Cranwell)

The presentation of the Standard usually follows a set formal pattern, including the dedication ceremony. The Standard shown here was presented to 65 Squadron by Marshal of the Royal Air Force Sir William Dickson at a formal ceremony held at RAF Duxford on 6 July 1960. At the time the squadron was equipped with the Hunter F6 and had been a fighter squadron since its formation in 1916, having first flown Sopwith Camels (amongst other types) during the First World War. Like so many other fighter squadrons, 65 had been disbanded after the war but reformed again in 1934 in response to an unsettled Europe. During the Second World War, it flew Spitfires, most notably during the Battle of Britain when 65 Squadron was based at RAF Hornchurch. The squadron then disbanded for a second time in 1961, only to reform again three years later as a Bloodhound surface-to-air missile squadron.

65 Squadron disbanded for the third and last time in 1970, after which its Standard was laid up at the RAF College Cranwell on 17 July 1974 where it has remained ever since. The squadron badge is described as fifteen swords in pile, the hilts in base, with a lion passant in front. The motto is translated as 'By force of arms'. The eight Battle Honours are clearly shown; three from the First World War and five from the Second World War.

77

Hawker P.1127

THE AIRCRAFT SHOWN here on display at the Science Museum in London is the first prototype of the Hawker P.1127 (XP831), an experimental aircraft to prove the practicability of a new method of flight – vertical flight. The concept was a breakthrough in jet-powered aviation and led directly to an iconic aircraft that served the RAF for more than forty years – the Harrier, otherwise known to the British public as the Jump Jet.

The idea behind the P.1127 was to use the thrust of a jet engine in a downwards direction to enable an aircraft to take off and land vertically. Various ideas were tried, including the use of a separate downwards-thrust engine in addition to the aircraft's main engine used for forward flight. However, most ideas were either too complex to build or too difficult to fly and, in the end, the relatively simple idea of using a single powerful jet engine with four rotating nozzles was adopted. In simple terms, the idea was for the vectored thrust of the engine to support the aircraft in flight, like four stable 'legs', during take-off and landing. It might have seemed a relatively simple idea but, of course, it would be much harder to perfect.

Because of Defence cuts during the late 1950s, initial development of the P.1127 was only possible because Hawker had managed to secure commercial funding for the project to continue. It was a good job it did. The Ministry of Supply eventually contracted two prototypes, the first of which, XP831, was delivered for testing in July 1960.

Country of Origin: UK
Date: 1960
Location: Science Museum, London
(© Science Museum)

The engine designated for XP831 was the Bristol Engine Company's Pegasus vectored-thrust engine. The first tethered flight took place at Dunsfold on 21 October 1960 with Hawker's chief test pilot, Bill Bedford, a former RAF

pilot and instructor at the Empire Test Pilots' School, at the controls. It was the start of the P.1127's crucial hover test and development programme, specifically to refine the aircraft's control system, during which the aircraft flew free and achieved its first hover.

The second prototype, XP836, joined the programme the following year and between the two prototypes the gap between vertical take-off and forward flight continued to close. This was finally achieved in September 1961 and it was not long before the P.1127 had perfected the transition from hovering to conventional forward flight, and then from forward flight back to the hover.

Four more P.1127s were ordered, the third of which was designed with a taller fin and an anhedral tail plane, and the final prototype had a swept wing. Throughout those early years, the Pegasus was continuously improved and so the last prototype was fitted with the more powerful Pegasus 5. It was not long before the idea of operating the P.1127 from an aircraft carrier was trialled and the first vertical landing on a carrier, HMS *Ark Royal*, was performed by XP831 in 1963.

The dangers of operating the P.1127 were obvious. Each of the first three prototypes had incidents and crashed; fortunately, without the loss of life. The second and third crashed during development while XP831 crashed at the Paris Air Show in 1963; the cause later determined as dirt

A Harrier GR9 of
1 Squadron lands
at RAF Cottesmore
following a ceremony
to mark the retirement
of this famous aircraft
after more than forty
years of service.
(Crown Copyright
2010)

in the air feed lines of the nozzle control motor, causing the nozzles to stick. However, XP831 was repaired and soon returned to the development programme.

While the P.1127 had been the experimental aircraft, the Hawker Siddeley Kestrel, which incorporated the improved design features of the last two P.1127 prototypes, and was also powered by the improved Pegasus 5 engine, was to become the development aircraft. The Kestrel first flew in March 1964. By then there was plenty of international interest, particularly from the United States (which went on to develop the aircraft for the US Marine Corps as the AV-8), but the idea of developing a supersonic version of the aircraft, designated the P.1154, was cancelled in 1965. However, later that year, the RAF ordered six pre-production P.1127 (RAF) aircraft; the first of which flew in August 1966. Then, early the following year, an order was placed for sixty production aircraft, now called the Harrier.

The first RAF squadron to be equipped with the Harrier GR1 was 1 Squadron, which began its conversion at RAF Wittering in 1969. Two more squadrons converted to the Harrier the following year, both in Germany at RAF Wildenrath. It was the height of the Cold War and so, in 1977, both squadrons were moved to RAF Gütersloh to be closer to the East German border. Those serving with the Harrier squadrons in Germany soon became used to spending endless days under camouflage in heavily wooded areas during countless NATO exercises. The squadrons were also regularly on exercise in Norway and the Harrier was also deployed to the former British colony of Belize, where there was tension over a Guatemalan claim to Belizean territory.

During its long RAF service the Harrier was used for close air support, reconnaissance and in other conventional ground-attack roles. In 1982 it went to war during the Falklands conflict. Operating from a carrier alongside the Royal Navy's Sea Harriers, the Harrier GR3s of 1 Squadron were used to attack Argentine positions and to provide close air support for British forces on the ground.

After its success in the Falklands, the early Harriers were replaced by a second-generation aircraft known as the Harrier II; a joint US-UK development between McDonnell Douglas and British Aerospace as an Anglicised version of the American AV-8A. This latest version entered RAF service in the late 1980s as the Harrier GR5, subsequently upgraded to the GR7 and then the GR9, and saw service in Bosnia, Iraq and Afghanistan. However, budgetary pressures led to the Harrier being retired in 2011 after more than forty years of unblemished service. It was, and remains, a controversial decision as it left the UK with no fixed-wing carrier-capable aircraft until the new Lockheed Martin F-35 Lightning II enters service.

Not only was the Harrier an extremely flexible and capable aircraft for the RAF, it was always a favourite amongst the British public, with its appearance at air shows thrilling generations over many years.

78

Westland Whirlwind HAR10

THE INTRODUCTION OF the helicopter into military service opened up the possibility of a wide range of new capabilities, one of which was search and rescue (SAR). But although the helicopter had been used for rescue duties in the Far East during the latter period of the Second World War, there appears to have been little appetite within the RAF for the helicopter in the immediate aftermath of war. It was a period when the focus seemed to be on bringing new jet aircraft into service and so it was not until the Bristol Sycamore entered service in the early 1950s that its crews helped pioneer techniques for maritime helicopter operations, including air–sea rescue.

While the Sycamore could rescue one or two aircrew out to a range of about 50 miles (80km), for example from a downed fighter just off the coast, it was not capable of carrying several people (five or six) over twice the distance, and so it was to the new Westland Whirlwind that the RAF turned to meet this requirement. With two pilots and a crewman to operate a winch, the Whirlwind was far better placed to perform air–sea rescues than the rope ladder and safety lines previously used.

Although its range when operating from land would always be a limitation, the helicopter's advantages had been obvious from the outset. It could travel quicker than a motor launch and then hover and winch survivors to safety – something that a fixed-wing aircraft could not do.

Country of Origin: UK
Date: 1961
Location: RAF Museum Hendon, London
(© RAF Museum)

Over the next few years, the Whirlwind began replacing fixed-wing aircraft and supplementing marine craft in the SAR role. The RAF's first dedicated air–sea rescue variant was the Whirlwind HAR2 (the HAR1 being a Royal Navy variant), which entered service with 22 Squadron in early

1955. The HAR4 followed and by the end of the 1950s Coastal Command had taken over all responsibility for search and rescue. Then came the Whirlwind HAR10, a helicopter that was to become the backbone of the RAF's SAR force. Its gas turbine engine was lighter and more powerful than the piston engine it had replaced and offered improved performance and reliability.

The first unit to receive the Whirlwind HAR10 was 225 Squadron based at RAF Odiham in Hampshire, which became operational with the type in 1961. It was the start of a long and distinguished period of service lasting twenty years. Sixty-seven HAR10s were built for the RAF and during its operational life the helicopter served in Europe, the Mediterranean and the Far East. The last squadron to be equipped with the type was 84 Squadron in Cyprus, which operated the HAR10 until March 1982.

After the Whirlwind came the Wessex HAR2 and later the Sea King HAR3, both dedicated SAR variants and developments of American Sikorsky helicopters built under licence by Westland; the latter entering RAF service during the late 1970s to replace the Whirlwind HAR10. When the RAF's Marine Branch disbanded in 1986, its helicopter element became the Search and Rescue Force and for the next thirty years provided SAR cover around the UK and at RAF bases overseas. The ability to save lives has always been a wonderful motivator for those involved

Whirlwind HAR10 during a winching exercise. (RAF Museum)

and amongst their ranks as a trained SAR pilot in recent years has been HRH The Duke of Cambridge.

The Whirlwind HAR10 shown on the previous page is XP299. Built by Westlands at Yeovil, Somerset in early 1961, it was the first of the Gnome turbine-engine examples and the first HAR10 produced for the RAF. Its first flight was at Yeovil on 28 March 1961. Being the first production aircraft it then underwent lengthy and extensive service trials, and was even exhibited at the Farnborough Air Show in 1964 and then at Paris the following year. Having then been fully modified and furbished as an HAR10, XP299 was delivered to the Helicopter Wing of the Central Flying School at RAF Tern Hill, Shropshire in 1966. The following year it was transferred to RAF Odiham and allocated to 230 Squadron, and was then temporarily loaned to the Queen's Flight at RAF Benson, Oxfordshire to replace a crashed Whirlwind from the flight, although it was never cleared to fly members of the Royal Family. XP299's travels continued as it then moved to Cyprus on transfer back to 230 Squadron. The squadron was now nominally based at RAF Wittering but was operating a detachment in Cyprus for peacekeeping duties.

In 1971, XP299 returned to the UK and was transferred to 22 Squadron, headquartered at RAF Finningley, Yorkshire, for the search and rescue role. During its time carrying out SAR duties, it is known to have operated from RAF St Mawgan, Cornwall and later with the squadron's A Flight at RAF Chivenor, Devon, where it covered the south-west coastline of England and the Bristol Channel. XP299's flying days came to an end on 8 December 1981. It was by then the squadron's last operational Whirlwind and was flown from Chivenor to RAF Cosford in Shropshire where XP299 was presented for display at the Aerospace Museum. Allocated the maintenance serial number 8726M, it was first displayed in Queen's Flight colours and later in the SAR paint scheme of yellow. Then, in 1998, it was one of a number of aircraft donated by the Ministry of Defence to the RAF Museum Hendon. XP299/8726M made its final journey to its new home by road and has been on display at Hendon since 2003.

79

English Electric Lightning

THE LIGHTNING ENTERED service in 1960 and its unrivalled performance meant that it remained the RAF's primary interceptor for more than twenty years. Shown here is XN776, a Lightning F2A in the markings of 92 Squadron, which is now on display at the National Museum of Flight in Scotland.

The Lightning was designed and developed by English Electric (soon to be absorbed by the newly formed British Aircraft Corporation) as the only all-British Mach 2 fighter. With its highly swept wing, two immensely powerful Rolls-Royce Avons (configured in a unique stack-staggered arrangement within the fuselage), an airborne radar and air-to-air missiles, the Lightning F1 was a complex fighter for its day, and so its introduction into service was never going to be straightforward.

Nineteen F1s were built, the first of which was delivered to 74 Squadron at RAF Coltishall in Norfolk in early 1960, but the problems of serviceability and an initial lack of spares meant that it was to be a slow and, at times, frustrating start for the pilots. This, however, lasted weeks rather than months and the improved Lightning F1A (of which twenty-eight were built) soon followed. With better avionics and the provision for an air-to-air refuelling probe, two more squadrons were formed with the type during 1961. Within two years the even better F2 had entered service with two more squadrons, as had the T4 and T5 trainer variants (with two seats side-by-side) with the Lightning Conversion Squadron (later renamed No. 226 Operational Conversion Unit). Then came the Lightning F3, of which seventy were built, with more powerful engines and a later generation of air-to-air missiles. It

Country of Origin: UK

Date: 1962

Location: National Museum of Flight, East Fortune Airfield, East Lothian, Scotland (© National Museums Scotland)

was a significant improvement on the earlier types but it was the F6 variant (thirty-nine were built), an improved and longer-range version of the F3, that was to be the most capable of all.

Powered by two Rolls-Royce Avon 301R after-burning turbojets, the Lightning F6 had a phenomenal rate of climb of 20,000ft/m (100m/s), was capable of Mach 2 (1,300mph/2,100km/h) at 36,000ft (10,973m) and had a maximum operating altitude of 54,000ft (16,000m), from where it could then zoom another 15,000ft or so. It was armed with two 30mm (1.18in) Aden cannons and its hard points under the fuselage allowed it to carry two air-to-air missiles; either two Firestreak (a first-generation passive rear-aspect infrared homing missile) or two Red Top (a later limited all-aspect infrared homing missile). The F6's design also featured a modified wing, to improve efficiency and subsonic performance, and the addition of over-wing fuel tanks (each of 260 gallons) and a larger ventral fuel tank to increase its maximum range out to 850 miles (1,370km/h).

When Fighter Command was disbanded in 1968 (on the formation of Strike Command), there were six Lightning squadrons based in the UK. There were also Lightning squadrons overseas; one in Singapore, one in Cyprus and two squadrons serving with RAF Germany in the low-level

Cockpit of XN776.
(National Museums
Scotland)

air defence role. The Lightning was also used by RAF squadron aerobatic display teams and served in the Middle East with the Royal Saudi Air Force and the Kuwait Air Force. A total of 337 Lightnings were built.

The Lightning had been designed as a relatively short-range fighter during the height of the Cold War, with its principal task being to defend the RAF's V-Force airfields against attack; just for long enough to allow the nuclear-armed bombers to get airborne. The Lightning was, therefore, always a fuel-critical aircraft and with an increasing threat from more capable bombers of the Warsaw Pact, Britain's air defence was supplemented by the arrival of the American-built McDonnell Douglas F4 Phantom, until the Lightning was finally retired from service in 1988 to be replaced by the Tornado F3.

Several Lightnings have survived, although very few are early types like XN776 shown here. It was built to F2 standard and first flew in October 1962, after which it was delivered to 19 Squadron at RAF Leconfield in Yorkshire. In 1965, the squadron moved to RAF Gütersloh in Germany to be close to the East German border. In early 1969, it was flown back to Warton for conversion to the F2A standard, which incorporated some of the improved aerodynamic features of the F6 and an enlarged ventral tank, arriving back at Gütersloh a few months later to return to its front-line duties with 19 Squadron. XN776 remained with the squadron until January 1977 when it was transferred across the airfield to 92 Squadron, just as the squadron was in the process of converting to the Phantom, and so it flew its last operational flight just two months later, after nearly 3,300 flying hours. XN776 then returned to the UK to its new home at RAF Leuchars in Scotland where it was used for ground duties. It has since remained in Scotland and is now on display at the National Museum of Flight, located at the former RAF airfield of East Fortune in East Lothian.

80

Blue Steel

WITH TECHNOLOGICAL ADVANCES and the further development of enemy surface-to-air missiles, it was becoming prohibitively dangerous for the RAF's V-bomber crews to attack targets with free-fall nuclear weapons. What the V-Force needed was an air-launched, high-speed stand-off missile, to keep its bombers out of range of Soviet ground-based defences. The result was Blue Steel, which entered service in 1963.

Built by Avro, Blue Steel's design had been rather drawn out. The specification required the missile to carry a large nuclear warhead at a speed of up to Mach 3 over a range of at least 50 miles (80km) but designers had initially lacked crucial information, including the size and weight of the proposed warhead. And so, operational trials of the new weapon did not start until 1960, around the time that the new weapon should have been entering service.

Blue Steel was designed to be carried beneath the Victor and Vulcan bombers. It was, essentially, a small pilotless aircraft with clipped delta wings and small canard fore planes, 35ft (10.7m) in length, 4ft (1.2m) in diameter and with a wingspan of 13ft (4m). Powered by an Armstrong-Siddeley Stentor Mk101 rocket engine, burning a combination of hydrogen peroxide and kerosene, Blue Steel carried the British thermonuclear warhead Red Snow at Mach 3 up to an operational ceiling of 70,000ft (21,336km) and over a maximum range of 150 miles (240km). It used a new inertial guidance system and manoeuvrable flight control surfaces to arrive over the target area, after which its engine then cut so that it was left to free-fall before the warhead detonated above the ground (known as an air burst) within 100 yards (less than 100m) of its intended target.

Country of Origin: UK
Date: 1963
Location: Newark Air Museum, Nottinghamshire (By kind permission of the Newark Air Museum)

By the time Blue Steel entered operational service with the RAF, many of its advantages had already been overtaken by advances in Soviet technology. In response, the V-Force was forced to modify its tactics from operating at high altitude to having to ingress towards a target at low level. This meant Blue Steel had to be modified so that it could be launched from as low as 1,000ft (305m) – something it had not originally been designed to do. This, in effect, severely limited its capability as a stand-off nuclear weapon and so led to the development of an extended-range version, known as Blue Steel 2.

Blue Steel 2 was intended to have a range of up to 600 nautical miles (1,111km), but the idea was abandoned when the British government opted to procure the American Douglas GAM-87A Skybolt air-launched ballistic missile instead. However, when the decision to buy Skybolt was also cancelled, the value of Blue Steel was revisited. But it was decided there was to be no value in procuring more of the current Blue Steels, nor would Blue Steel 2 give value for money, and so the in-service Blue Steel remained the country's primary strategic nuclear weapon until 1970, when responsibility for the nation's nuclear deterrent was handed over to the Royal Navy with its Polaris-equipped submarines.

81

TSR2

OF ALL THE projects to have been cancelled in the RAF's long history, there can surely be none more controversial than the cancellation of the TSR2 (Tactical Strike and Reconnaissance, Mach 2) programme. Despite its huge potential, and the fact that this magnificent aircraft was years ahead of its time, the TSR2 was never developed beyond the prototype stage.

The introduction of increasingly sophisticated Soviet radar-guided surface-to-air missiles meant that aircraft flying at subsonic speed, even at very high altitude, could no longer be considered safe. What the RAF needed now was an aircraft to replace the Canberra but the new aircraft would not only have to be able to fly at Mach 2 at high altitude, it would also need to be supersonic at low level, i.e. below 1,000ft (305m). Furthermore, it would need to be able to fly in all weather conditions and deliver its tactical nuclear or conventional weapons on a target up to 1,000 nautical miles (1,850km) away. Finally, it was also required to carry out photoreconnaissance missions at high speed, from various altitudes in daytime or at night, and have a short take-off run so that it could operate from a prepared airstrip of no more than 1,000 yards (914m).

It was, without doubt, an immense challenge for industry given the technology at the time. There then followed some years of industrial, political, and inter-service debate but eventually it was decided that the aircraft to meet the requirement was the TSR2, and so an initial order was placed for nine prototypes.

Built by the newly created British Aircraft Corporation, the TSR2 incorporated elements of designs from English Electric and Vickers-Armstrongs, and its technical advances made it the best performing and most advanced

Country of Origin: UK
Date: 1964
Location: RAF Museum Cosford, Shropshire
(© RAF Museum)

aircraft of its day. It was 89ft (27.1m) long and had a wingspan of just over 37ft (11.3m), and powered by two Bristol Olympus B.01.22R turbojets, the TSR2 was capable of exceeding Mach 2.

Flown by 'Bee' Beamont, the first prototype (XR219) made its maiden flight from Boscombe Down on 27 September 1964. By the end of March 1965, the aircraft had completed twenty-four test flights and the second prototype (XR220) was now ready to join the programme. However, just a week later, and on the same day that the second prototype was due to make its maiden flight, the project was cancelled, the reason being the political opposition to the nature of the programme and its rising costs.

The TSR2 was, without doubt, a world-beating aircraft and a technological triumph for Britain, but it had been cancelled in favour of the American General Dynamics F-111 swing-wing bomber as a cheaper option. Ironically, though, this programme would also later be cancelled, effectively leaving the RAF with a capability gap that would take many years to fill. More than fifty years on the debates continue but, without doubt, the cancellation of TSR2 was not only a devastating blow to industry, it was, above all, a devastating blow to the RAF.

Shown here is the second prototype, XR220, which had been due to fly in 1964 but its first flight had been delayed because of design and production difficulties. By March 1965 the initial ground engine test programme had been completed and it was being prepared for its first flight on 6 April when the news broke that the project was cancelled. XR220 was then grounded permanently. It was later used for noise tests for the Concorde programme at Boscombe Down and in 1967 was transferred to the Ministry of Defence for preservation. Having been stored at RAF Henlow for eight years, XR220 was transferred to RAF Cosford in 1975 where it is now on display at the RAF Museum.

82

S6 Respirator

DEVELOPED DURING THE late 1950s at Porton Down, the S6 Respirator was introduced into service in 1966 to replace the earlier Lightweight Respirator. It was an enormous leap in technology for the British gas mask industry and for the next twenty years the S6 was the standard respirator worn by all branches of the British armed forces.

The S6 was made by two manufacturers – Avon and the Leyland and Birmingham Rubber Company. It is made of thick but soft and extremely durable black rubber, and allows an excellent field of vision using large eyepieces, while offering the wearer improved levels of protection with its air seal around the inside of the face piece to improve the fit. A small tap inside the respirator allows the equalisation of pressure inside the seal when operating under different climatic conditions.

The S6 came in different sizes, with an elasticated six-point cloth head harness for adjustment when being worn. Two variants existed: one for a right-handed shooter and the other for a left. The filter canister (shown with a red ring around it because this one was used for training purposes) was NATO compliant, meaning the filter thread was of a standard diameter and pitch so that any filter utilising the same thread could be used. When not being worn, the respirator was carried in a nylon haversack to make it more resistant to chemical agents. The haversack also contained a spare canister, atropine, autoject pens, a puffer bottle of Fuller's earth and pads.

The S6 respirator is shown here being worn with the NBC (Nuclear Biological Chemical) protection suit, as worn by British armed forces during the height of the Cold War. Also shown being worn is the associated webbing,

Country of Origin: UK
Date: 1966
Location: RAF Waddington Heritage Centre, Lincolnshire (By kind permission of the Station Commander RAF Waddington)

which has a pouch for a water bottle holder (on the lower right of the picture) and the respirator haversack (left). The NBC suit was designed to provide protection against direct contact with, and contamination by, radioactive, biological or chemical substances. It was designed to be quickly donned over normal service clothing and worn for extended periods, up to several days, to allow the wearer to function while under the threat of, or actually under, nuclear, biological or chemical attack. The olive green, charcoal-lined suit consisted of a smock with various pockets (depending on the mark) and Velcro adjusting tabs on the waist and cuff, an attached hood with elasticated opening, and trousers with pockets. To make sure that no part of the skin was exposed, NBC protective rubber gloves were worn, as were tied NBC protective over-boots when working outside to prevent the carrying of any contamination into protected buildings via the soles.

As well as equipping the British armed forces, the S6 respirator was used by numerous other military, paramilitary and police forces worldwide. It had a service life of twenty years, although the life of the canister was half this. The S6 was eventually replaced by the S10, which was also in service for twenty years until it was gradually phased out to be replaced by the more modern General Service Respirator (GSR), which today provides UK forces with enhanced levels of protection in very demanding and challenging conditions.

83

Nimrod

INTRODUCED INTO SERVICE in 1969, the Nimrod maritime patrol aircraft was at the forefront of the UK's defences during the Cold War years.

Developed from the de Havilland Comet, the world's first jet airliner, the Nimrod MR1 was designed and developed by Hawker Siddeley to replace the ageing Avro Shackleton as the RAF's first jet-powered aircraft for the anti-submarine warfare (ASW) role. The first Nimrod MR1 entered service with the RAF in October 1969. It was the first of forty-six airframes ordered to equip five squadrons; four to be permanently based in the UK and one initially in Malta. From the mid-1970s, thirty-five aircraft were upgraded to the MR2 standard. The most significant changes were the replacement of the old ASV Mk21 radar with the new EMI Searchwater radar, an improved electronic suite, a new acoustic processor capable of handling more modern sonobuoys and the installation of electronic support measures (ESM) in new pods on the wingtips.

Powered by four Rolls-Royce Spey turbofans, the Nimrod was capable of 575mph (923km/h), although its cruising speed when on task was more in the region of 490mph (788km/h), and a maximum altitude around 44,000ft (13,411m). Two under-wing hard points allowed the fitting of pylon stations for the carriage of a variety of weapons, such as air-to-surface missiles, including the AGM-65 Maverick, the most widely produced tactical precision-guided missile in the western world, and AGM-84 Harpoon, an all-weather over-the-horizon anti-ship missile. The Nimrod's design also featured a sizeable bomb bay in which an impressive array of weapons, sensors and specialist equipment could be carried. Over

Country of Origin:
UK
Date: 1971
Location:
Yorkshire
Air Museum,
Elvington, North
Yorkshire
(© Neill Watson
via the Yorkshire
Air Museum)

the years its stores included depth charges (including nuclear), mines and torpedoes, in addition to its 150 or so sonobuoys used for ASW. It could also carry multiple air-deployed dinghies and droppable survival packs for use during rescue missions.

Nimrod R1s of 51 Squadron. (Crown Copyright 2004)

The Nimrod's crew typically consisted of twelve: two pilots and a flight engineer on the flight deck; two navigators (one being the tactical navigator when on task); an air electronics officer; and six weapon systems operators, typically two to operate as a sonobuoy sensor team and four electronic warfare (EW) specialists to manage the aircraft's on-board active and passive EW systems. A larger crew could be carried, depending on the mission.

The Nimrod's range and endurance enabled the aircraft to stay airborne for around ten hours, enabling it to comfortably operate to the north of Iceland or up to 2,500 miles (4,000km) out into the Atlantic. In addition to ASW, the MR2 had two other main roles – anti-surface unit warfare and search and rescue. During the Falklands conflict of 1982 provision was made for in-flight refuelling, enabling the aircraft to operate even further afield, while other additions included provision for the aircraft to be armed with AIM-9 Sidewinder air-to-air missiles for self-defence. Later, during operations in the Gulf theatre, some MR2s were fitted with new electronic counter measures and improved communications.

During its heyday, there were five Nimrod squadrons in the UK; three based at RAF Kinloss in Scotland and one squadron plus the operational conversion unit at RAF St Mawgan in Cornwall. However, the restructuring of Britain's armed forces in 1990 at the end of the Cold War, called Options for Change, reduced the Nimrod force by one squadron.

The Nimrod MR2 remained in service until 2010 when it was due to be replaced by its successor, the Nimrod MRA4 (an extensively rebuilt MR2). However, due to a combination of considerable delays, increased costs and Defence savings measures, development of the MRA4 was finally abandoned under the 2010 Strategic Defence and Security Review. It was the end of the Nimrod after a remarkable forty years of being at the forefront of the nation's maritime operations, and the controversial decision to cancel the MRA4 had left the UK without a dedicated maritime patrol aircraft.

In addition to the MR2s, two further Nimrod variants were developed. The first, the Nimrod AEW3, was an airborne early warning aircraft under development during the late 1970s and early 1980s but was subsequently cancelled in favour of the Boeing E-3D Sentry. The second was the Nimrod R1, which was far more successful. Three airframes were adapted to become a highly sophisticated aircraft that was used until 2011 for reconnaissance and electronic intelligence gathering.

The Nimrod shown on p. 276 is XV250. It was built at Woodford as a standard MR1 and first flew on 21 January 1971 before being delivered to RAF Kinloss the following month. A year later it was transferred to 203 Squadron at RAF Luqa in Malta but XV250 returned to Kinloss in 1975 before returning to Woodford for conversion to the MR2 standard. Its first flight as a MR2 was in June 1983, after which XV250 returned to Kinloss the following month. Except for periods at RAF St Mawgan during the 1980s, XV250 remained at Kinloss until withdrawn from service on 31 March 2010. The aircraft then made its last flight to Elvington on 13 April 2010 where it remains in ground operational condition and is on display as part of the Yorkshire Air Museum.

VC10 refuelling
Typhoons with a
Tornado GR4
alongside. (Crown
Copyright 2004)

84

Air-to-Air Refuelling Probe

PICTURED HERE IS an air-to-air refuelling (AAR) probe fitted to a Handley Page Victor K2 refuelling aircraft. To have an AAR capability is a major asset to any air force. It enables aircraft to be deployed very quickly over large distances or to stay on an operational patrol longer, or to carry larger weapon loads further into enemy territory. Quite simply, AAR has changed the way that air warfare is conducted.

For the RAF, the development of an AAR capability began in 1958. The concept of in-flight refuelling was not new. Its origins date back to the RAF's early days when the idea of transferring fuel between aircraft to increase time in the air had first been explored. More recently, in 1953, a hose drum unit (HDU) had been fitted to a Canberra by Flight Refuelling Limited as a trial to see what potential the aircraft had as a tanker. Yet it was the RAF's first V-bomber, the Vickers Valiant, that was to be first used as a dedicated air-to-air refuelling aircraft, with 214 Squadron at RAF Marham in Norfolk chosen to be the trials and development unit.

The squadron's Valiant B1s were modified to the B(K)1 by fitting a Mk16 HDU mounted on the bomb-mounting hard points in the rear of the aircraft's bomb bay and a 4,500lb (2,041kg) fuel tank in the front. This meant the aircraft's bomb doors had to be opened while carrying out in-flight refuelling. The Valiant could transfer 45,000lb (20,411kg) of fuel at a rate of 4,000lb (1,814kg) per minute. To receive fuel, an in-flight refuelling probe was fitted to the front of the Valiant's navigation and bombing system scanner bay, connecting it internally to the aircraft's fuel system to extend the range of the aircraft.

By early 1959 the Valiants were successfully transferring fuel to each other, initially by day and then at night. It

Country of Origin: UK
Date: 1972
Location: Yorkshire Air Museum, Elvington, North Yorkshire
(© Neill Watson via the Yorkshire Air Museum)

was then a matter of determining how far the RAF's operational capability could be extended, and so a series of long-range flights were carried out; the most notable being on 9 July 1959 when a Valiant flew non-stop from Marham to Cape Town, South Africa, in eleven hours and fifty minutes. The aircraft completed two refuelling brackets with other squadron aircraft pre-positioned in Libya and Nigeria, and the 6,060 miles (9,753km) from overhead London to landing at Cape Town was timed at a record-breaking eleven hours and twenty-eight minutes.

More long-range flights followed and in May 1960 a Valiant of 214 Squadron flew non-stop from Marham to Changi in Singapore. Then, the following year, a Vulcan of 101 Squadron, supported by nine Valiants of 214 Squadron, flew non-stop from RAF Scampton to RAAF Richmond in Australia. This latest record-breaking flight of 11,500 miles (18,507km) was flown in twenty hours and three minutes.

When the Valiant was prematurely withdrawn from service, the RAF was left without a dedicated tanker. In a rush to get aircraft into service as quickly as possible, six Victor B1As were hastily converted to B(K)1A standard. During 1965, a two-point refuelling system of a hose and drogue was fitted under each wing of aircraft belonging to 55 Squadron at Marham, while work continued developing a definitive three-point variant that would be capable of refuelling bombers as well as fighters. The result was twenty-five more Victors fitted with an additional two fuel tanks in the bomb bay and a centreline hose. These were designated Victor K1s and K1As (eleven were formerly B1s and the rest had been B1As). And when the V-Force began operating at low level, an environment not suitable for the Victor, combined with the fact the RAF was in the process of passing responsibility for the UK's nuclear deterrent to the Royal Navy, the Victor B2s were declared surplus to requirements. Twenty-four airframes were converted to the K2 standard to become dedicated tankers.

The first modified airframe made its maiden flight as a K2 in 1972. With a crew of five and powered by four Rolls-Royce Conways, it had a maximum speed of Mach 0.92 at 40,000ft (12,192m), an operational ceiling of 59,000ft (17,983m), a range of 3,500 miles (5,633m) and could carry 91,000lb (41,000kg) of fuel. During 1982 the Victor played a significant part in the Falklands conflict with the

K2s flying more than 600 AAR sorties from Ascension Island (more than 3,000 hours of flying time) in support of the Vulcans, Nimrods, Hercules and Harriers. Victors also flew in the Gulf War of 1991 when they were used to refuel RAF Tornados as well as other Allied aircraft.

The Victor was finally withdrawn from its tanker role in 1993. Of the RAF's three V-bombers, the Victor had served the longest. Since then, a few different aircraft types have provided the RAF with an AAR capability. These include the Lockheed Tristar (K1 and KC1) and the Vickers VC10 (K3 and K4). The RAF's latest AAR aircraft is the twin-engine Voyager, a dual air transport/AAR variant of the Airbus A330, with the K2 being the two-point tanker (with two pods) and the K3 being three-point. The fact that only one Voyager is required to refuel four combat aircraft, such as the Typhoon or Tornado GR4, for a typical deployment across the Atlantic, while still carrying 11,000lb (5,000kg) of freight/passengers, shows just how far AAR has come in the past sixty years.

The Victor shown here is XL231, the prototype K2 refuelling tanker. It was built in 1961 at Handley Page's facility at Radlett in Hertfordshire and started life as a standard B2 conventional bomber serving with 139 Squadron at RAF Wittering before it was converted to carry Blue Steel to become part of the Wittering Wing in 1964. Then, in January 1972, XL231 was converted again, this time to become the prototype K2 tanker. For the next five years, it took part in numerous refuelling trials, mostly from Woodford and Boscombe Down, before it returned to front-line duties with 57 Squadron at RAF Marham. XL231 saw operational service during the Falklands conflict of 1982 and when the squadron disbanded four years later it was transferred across the airfield to 55 Squadron. XL231 again saw operational service during 1990–91, this time in the Gulf as part of Operations Desert Shield and Desert Storm, and it was then the aircraft was given its nose art and nicknamed 'Lusty Linda'. Finally, after more than thirty years of service, its last flight was in November 1993 when it flew into retirement at Elvington, where it has since been on display at the Yorkshire Air Museum.

Part 6
Recent Times

85

FV101 Scorpion

SHOWN HERE IS a FV101 Scorpion light armoured vehicle of 34 Squadron RAF Regiment. It represents the ground fighting force of the RAF that today provides a range of force protection effects underpinned by its air-minded ground fighting capabilities.

The RAF Regiment was formed during the Second World War to provide light anti-aircraft and ground defence for RAF airfields at home and overseas. After the war it became involved in many campaigns and skirmishes, such as in Malaya and the Aden Protectorate. Closer to home, during what was the Cold War, the 1970s saw the introduction of the Rapier surface-to-air missile for RAF Regiment squadrons based in Germany and tasked with the protection of airfields, whilst highly mobile, flexible, and well-equipped field squadrons provided ground defence. And it was during this period that the Combat Vehicle Reconnaissance (Tracked) family of armoured vehicles was introduced into service.

Manufactured by Alvis, the CVR(T)s were designed to share common automotive components and suspension. They were first introduced into the British Army and one of these vehicles was the light armoured FV101 Scorpion. It weighed around 8 tons and was initially powered by a Jaguar J60 4.2-litre engine, giving it a top speed of 50mph (80km/h). Armed with the low-velocity 76mm gun, it could fire high-explosive, smoke and canister rounds, at a rate of six rounds per minute, with an effective range out to 2,400 yards (2,200m). Another member of the family was the FV107 Scimitar, which was very similar to the Scorpion but boasted a 30mm high-velocity cannon instead of the 76mm gun.

Left: A member of the RAF Regiment surveys the terrain whilst on patrol with a Panther Protected Command Vehicle outside Camp Bastion in Afghanistan. (Crown Copyright 2010)

Country of Origin: UK
Date: 1981
Location: RAF Leeming, North Yorkshire (By kind permission of the Station Commander RAF Leeming)

The RAF Regiment took delivery of its first Scorpion in 1981. More than 180 would eventually serve at RAF airfields in the UK, Germany and Cyprus. The Scorpion's 76mm gun made it ideal for airfield defence, particularly when firing the relatively short-range canister rounds as they minimised the risk to aircraft and infrastructure.

Over 3,000 CVR(T)s were produced for the British Army, RAF Regiment, and the export market, and were used for reconnaissance or as a light armoured vehicle until they were finally retired from service in 1994.

The Scorpion shown here served with 34 Squadron RAF Regiment in Cyprus during the 1980s. Formed in 1951 as a light anti-aircraft unit, 34 Squadron first operated overseas during the Suez Crisis. Thereafter based in Cyprus, the squadron underwent a re-role during the 1970s to become a field squadron, initially equipped with Land Rovers, mortars and machine guns before taking delivery of the Scorpion-range of light armoured vehicles in 1982. After its involvement in the First Gulf War of 1991, during which the squadron provided ground defence for RAF forward operating bases in Bahrain and Saudi Arabia, 34 Squadron reverted to being a field squadron and returned to the UK. It has been based at RAF Leeming in North Yorkshire ever since. Amongst its many operational commitments in recent years, the squadron's personnel have been deployed to the Balkans, the Gulf, Iraq and Afghanistan.

86

Air Officer's Hat

SOME MIGHT SAY that 'a hat is a hat is a hat' but, of course, each hat has its own story to tell. This example is an air officer's lightweight No. 1 Service Dress hat of the early 1980s. It was made by Bates, the specialist hatters of Jermyn Street in London, and belonged to Marshal of the Royal Air Force Sir Michael Beetham GCB CBE DFC AFC, the RAF's longest-serving chief of the air staff since Lord Trenchard had formed the service more than sixty years before.

Sir Michael was one of the RAF's great post-Second World War leaders, with a career spanning the years from the piston-engine Lancaster through the dawn of the jet age and ultimately to the modern era in the shape of the Tornado.

Summarising such a long and distinguished career is never easy, but the young 18-year-old Beetham joined the RAF as a pilot in 1941 and was awarded the DFC whilst serving with Bomber Command at the age of 21. Remaining in the post-war RAF, several flying and staff appointments followed before he joined the V-Force in 1958 to command 214 Squadron, a Valiant squadron, at RAF Marham in Norfolk. It was during this tour that he became a pioneer of air-to-air refuelling and was at the forefront of developing the RAF's long-range strategic bombing capability, for which he was awarded the AFC; the highlight being in 1959 when he carried out the first non-stop flight from the UK to South Africa. Beetham then served at the heart of Bomber Command's affairs during a time when the RAF's V-Force maintained the UK's national deterrent, the most critical time being the Cuban Missile Crisis in 1962. He was then given command of Khormaksar, the RAF's biggest overseas station, operating

Country of Origin: UK
Date: 1982
Location: Beetham Family (By kind permission of the Beetham family)

Marshal of the Royal Air Force Sir Michael Beetham escorting the Queen Mother at the unveiling of the memorial to Arthur Harris outside the RAF's church of St Clement Danes, 31 May 1992. (via Sir Michael Beetham)

ten different aircraft types, and the largest staging post between the UK and Singapore; his arrival coinciding with the start of a terrorist campaign against British forces in Aden. More senior appointments followed, notably as Commander 2nd Allied Tactical Air Force and Commander-in-Chief RAF Germany, but the highest accolade came in 1977 when Beetham was appointed Chief of the Air Staff.

Beetham had taken over as CAS at a difficult time. His first year was mostly spent dealing with issues such as low pay and low morale in the service, which had come about following a series of successive Defence cuts. Then, in April 1982, and just as Beetham was preparing to hand over to his successor, Argentina invaded the Falkland Islands.

The decision by Argentina's junta to invade the Falklands in the belief that Britain would not respond with military force, proved to be a grave error of judgement. And in the same way that Argentina's invasion of the Falkland Islands had taken the British by surprise, Britain's response, under the leadership of the Prime Minister Margaret Thatcher, was probably not what the Argentinians had expected. As CAS, Beetham was heavily involved in the decision to send a naval task force to the South Atlantic to take back the islands by force. It was the start of Operation Corporate and the Falklands conflict that followed proved to be a swift and decisive victory; albeit at a cost to British forces with 255 killed and more than 700 wounded.

With the Falklands conflict over, Beetham handed over as CAS and was appointed marshal of the Royal Air Force. His career had started and ended with conflict on the world stage. Encapsulated in one individual is the story of rapid advance and revolutionary impact of air power on military operations and the wider world. Sir Michael Beetham died in 2015 at the age of 92.

87

Vulcan XM607

STANDING PROUDLY AS the guardian of RAF Waddington, alongside the main A15 approaching the southern part of Lincoln, is Vulcan XM607, which in 1982 carried out what was the longest-range air attack in the history of air warfare.

Until the Falklands conflict the story of this famous aircraft was little or no different to any other Vulcan. Built as a standard B2 it was delivered to the RAF in 1963 and for the next eighteen years served with different squadrons at various V-Force bases. By 1982 it was on the books of 44 Squadron at Waddington and facing retirement but then came Argentina's invasion of the Falkland Islands. XM607 was about to take its place in aviation history.

With Argentine forces digging-in on the Falklands and the British Task Force heading south, the use of the Vulcan for long-range bombing missions was one of several offensive options being explored by the RAF and so three aircraft, including XM607, were deployed to Ascension Island in case they were required. But deploying the Vulcans was not as simple as it might sound. Its operational days were almost at an end and so the aircraft no longer had an air-to-air refuelling capability. Given the distance between Ascension Island and the Falklands, or mainland Argentina for that matter, any long-range missions would be beyond its operational range. This meant the refuelling system had to be reactivated and the crews trained so that, if required, the Vulcans would be able to refuel from Victor tankers. Furthermore, the three Vulcans had to be converted back to their pre-nuclear weapon days to allow each aircraft to carry a conventional bomb load of 21,000lb (9,525kg) bombs.

Left: XM607 stands proudly as the gate guardian of RAF Waddington in Lincolnshire. (Crown Copyright via RAF Waddington)

Country of Origin: UK
Date: 1963
Location: RAF Waddington, Lincolnshire (Crown Copyright by kind permission of the Station Commander RAF Waddington)

As the British Task Force sailed deep into the South Atlantic the air threat it faced included the possibility of Argentine combat aircraft operating from the airfield at Stanley, the islands' capital on East Falkland. The runway was just over 4,000ft (1,219m) long, which made it suitably long enough for Argentine fighters as well as transport aircraft bringing in supplies to the occupying forces. Discussions on how to deny the runway to the enemy concluded that just one Vulcan operating from Ascension Island, but supported by several Victor tankers for air-to-air refuelling, could carry out a bombing attack on the airfield at Stanley. Finally, after assessing the best way to attack the airfield, it was decided to bomb at an angle of thirty degrees off the direction of the runway rather than to try and bomb along its length. This method, it was considered, would be more likely to result in success, as the probability of getting one bomb, or even two, to crater the runway was assessed to be 75 per cent or better.

On the evening of 30 April 1982, two Vulcans took off from Ascension Island under Operation Black Buck. Accompanied by eleven Victor refuelling tankers, the plan was for one of the Vulcans to continue all the way to the Falklands to bomb the airfield at Stanley, while the second acted as an airborne spare. It was not long after take-off when the crew of the lead Vulcan discovered a problem with their aircraft and so the second, XM607, captained by Flight Lieutenant Martin Withers, continued. During the long transit south, the Vulcan took on fuel five times and once within 300 miles (483km) of the target Withers took the aircraft down to low level to approach Stanley beneath the cover of the Argentine early warning radars on the islands. Then, at just 50 miles (80km) from the airfield, he pulled up to the attack height of 10,000ft (3,048m).

At 4.46 a.m. (Stanley time) on 1 May the crew of XM607 carried out their attack against the runway at Stanley. Having released their bombs, Withers turned hard to the north and began to climb for the long transit back. After the final rendezvous with a Victor tanker off the coast of Brazil, XM607 landed back at Ascension after a round-trip of nearly 8,000 miles (12,875km). It was a record-breaking mission that had lasted nearly sixteen hours.

The attack on the airfield at Stanley had taken the Argentinians completely by surprise. Of the twenty-one bombs dropped by XM607, one had hit the runway at its mid-point while the rest caused damage to the airfield's installations and aircraft on the ground. Three nights later Black Buck 2 took place, using the same aircraft but a different crew. It was almost identical in detail to the first and resulted in the western end of the airfield being cratered, preventing any possible extension of the runway for high-performance combat aircraft. In all there were seven Black Buck missions, with XM607 also flying Black Buck 7 against Argentine positions around Stanley on 12 June, just two days before the battle for the Falklands was over.

After returning to Waddington, XM607 was retired from service at the end of 1982 having played a major part in demonstrating the far-reaching capability of the RAF.

88

AIM-9L Sidewinder

DEVELOPED BY THE United States as early as the 1950s (although its concept dates back even further to the end of the Second World War), the AIM-9 Sidewinder was the RAF's main short-range, heat-seeking air-to-air missile fitted to most of its combat aircraft from the mid-1970s.

The workings of an air-to-air missile are complicated but essentially the AIM-9 (AIM standing for air intercept missile) is split into four main sections; an infrared (IR) guidance section, a target detector, a high-explosive warhead, and a rocket motor. At the very front of the missile is the IR seeker. Its head is cooled to ensure that it tracks the source of heat, while the rest of the front section contains the electronics and mechanical components that enable the missile to function and guide towards the target. Behind the guidance assembly is the target detector, which ultimately sends a signal to detonate the expanding-rod blast fragmentary warhead once the missile is in lethal range (later models were configured with an annular-blast fragmentation warhead). The rear portion of the missile, the motor, is a solid-fuel rocket that accelerates the missile to a speed of Mach 2+.

Country of Origin: USA

Date: c. 1982

Location: Newark Air Museum, Nottinghamshire (By kind permission of the Newark Air Museum)

Once launched the Sidewinder is a truly fire-and-forget missile, meaning it requires no further information from the launch aircraft. Its first reported combat success was in the Taiwan Strait in 1958 when an AIM-9B (an early version of the Sidewinder) was fired by a F-86 Sabre of the air force of the Republic of China (Taiwan) against a Mig-17 of the People's Republic of China.

The Sidewinder had been designed with upgrades in mind, making it relatively easy and cheap to improve over the years. Although the US Air Force and US Navy pursued their own versions, the Sidewinder continued to evolve throughout the 1960s through a series of upgrades. These included more sensitive seekers, better cooling, and improvements to the propulsion, fusing and warheads, and by the time air combat broke out over North Vietnam, the Sidewinder had become the standard short-range air-to-air missile carried by most American combat aircraft.

The Sidewinder's success led to the RAF buying the AIM-9G (a development of the US Navy's AIM-9D) during the 1970s for its own combat aircraft. At that stage, the Sidewinder was a rear-aspect-only missile, meaning that the attacking fighter had to be in the stern sector of an opponent for the IR seeker to detect the heat source from its jet engine. But soon came the next major advance in the missile's development with the AIM-9L (known as the 9-Lima), the first all-round aspect Sidewinder and distinguishable from earlier variants by its double-delta forward canard configuration.

Armed with the AIM-9L, a fighter could now attack an opponent from any aspect, including head-on. This dramatically changed air-to-air combat tactics, and so the UK opted to replace its AIM-9Gs with the AIM-9L as its primary short-range air-to-air missile. From the early 1980s, most of the RAF's main combat aircraft were modified to carry the AIM-9L. These included all the main variants of the Phantom, Harrier (plus the Royal Navy's Sea Harrier), Jaguar, Buccaneer, and Tornado. Even the Hawk jet trainer could be armed with the AIM-9L for short-range air defence.

The AIM-9L is just over 9ft (2.85m) long and has a span of 2ft (0.63m). Its total weight is 188lb (85.3kg), of which 20lb (9.5kg) is the warhead. Its operational range could vary enormously, depending on all sorts of factors; such as the target's height and speed, the fighter's height and speed, the aspect, and just how much all the previous factors are changing, to list just a few. And, of course, there may be other heat sources to take into consideration, for example the sun! Air combat can be a very dynamic environment. Typically, though, its range could be anything from less than a mile (1km) out to 5 miles (8km), or even further given the right set of conditions.

The Falklands conflict of 1982 saw the first large-scale use of the Sidewinder with eighteen Argentine aircraft shot down by Sea Harriers of the Royal Navy. The AIM-9L

AIM-9L Sidewinder (with yellow 'noddy cap') fitted on the wing pylon of a Harrier GR7, also armed with a 1,000lb Paveway II laser-guided bomb. (Crown Copyright 1999)

was finally phased out of service around the turn of the century to be replaced by ASRAAM (Advanced Short-Range Air-to-Air Missile), which was introduced into RAF service from 1998.

Well over 100,000 Sidewinders have been built for the United States and a reported twenty-seven other nations across the world, making it the most widely used air-to-air missile amongst the western nations. It even remains in service with some air forces today, sixty years after it was first developed. With an estimated 270 successes, the Sidewinder is one of the oldest, least expensive, and most successful missiles of all time.

89

Control Tower

Country of Origin:
UK
Date: c. 1942
Location:
Yorkshire
Air Museum,
Elvington, North
Yorkshire
(By kind
permission of the
Yorkshire Air
Museum)

CONSIDERING THE LARGE number of airfields used by the RAF throughout its history, particularly during the Second World War, very few have survived. The majority have long disappeared but fortunately the sites of some can still be visited today. Largely run by volunteers, organisations across the country preserve the legacy of these former airfields and their people, relying on fundraising and public donations to keep the memories alive. One such site is the former wartime bomber airfield of RAF Elvington, now home to the Yorkshire Air Museum, where the original control tower stands proudly amongst other wartime buildings at the heart of the museum.

Elvington was originally a grass airfield but was brought up to the standard of most Bomber Command bases during 1942. Three hardened runways and thirty-six aircraft dispersals were constructed, all connected by a hardened perimeter track, with each dispersal hard enough to accommodate a fully laden bomber. As a sub-station of nearby RAF Pocklington, and grouped with RAF Melbourne, the three airfields formed No. 42 Base, part of No. 4 Group Bomber Command. For eighteen months Elvington was home to the four-engine Handley Page Halifax bombers of 77 Squadron but in May 1944 the squadron moved out to make way for two French squadrons – 346 (Guyenne) and 347 (Tunisie) Squadrons – both equipped with the Halifax and the only Free French squadrons to serve with Bomber Command.

As soon as the war was over the squadrons left for France. Elvington then became part of Maintenance Command until the early 1950s when it was earmarked for the Americans as part of the US Strategic Air Command's expansion programme. The main runway was extended to become one of the longest in the country, but the idea never came to fruition. The airfield was then left vacant until the 1960s when it was given a new lease of life by the Blackburn Aircraft Company at Brough, which used the runway at Elvington for test flying its Buccaneer. The runway was then used for practice circuits and landings by RAF flying training schools based in Yorkshire until 1992 when RAF Elvington closed.

Part of the former airfield is now the site of the Yorkshire Air Museum. One of the first buildings to have been restored by the museum's volunteers was the original control tower. Today it accurately represents how it looked more than seventy years ago during the Second World War. Downstairs, the radio room and other areas show the equipment used to communicate with the bombers, while upstairs is where operations were overseen by a controller and associated staff, with boards showing aircraft status – in flight, missing or overdue. In addition to the control tower and other original wartime buildings, the museum has more than sixty historic aircraft and vehicles, as well as exhibitions, a memorial garden, a shop and a restaurant. It is a great day out!

90

Prisoner of War Jacket

AT FIRST SIGHT it might not be obvious what a yellow jacket bearing the letters 'PW' might be. But this prisoner of war jacket represents the RAF's involvement in the First Gulf War of 1991, as it was worn throughout his captivity by Flight Lieutenant John Nichol, a Tornado GR1 navigator who was shot down over Iraq.

Iraq's invasion of Kuwait in August 1990 brought an immediate international response and UN condemnation. To counter the renewed threat to the region, a coalition of more than thirty nations, led by the United States, launched Operation Desert Shield to move forces into the area to protect Saudi Arabia. During the following months, diplomatic efforts tried to persuade Iraq to withdraw from Kuwait but despite pressure from the international community, Iraq refused to do so. In the meantime, the Allies had continued to pile military forces into the region. The UN deadline for Iraq to withdraw came and went, without a diplomatic resolution, and so the Allies were authorised to use military force.

During the early hours of 17 January 1991 (local time) the first Allied air strikes took place. It was the start of Operation Desert Storm, aimed to cripple the Iraqi air defence command and control system. Taking part in these first Allied attacks were RAF Tornado GR1s. Flying long-range missions from bases in the Gulf, and supported by air-to-air refuelling tankers, their task was to hit Iraqi airfields deep behind enemy lines. One of these was ZD791, an aircraft belonging to XV Squadron, flown by Flight Lieutenant John Peters and Flight Lieutenant John Nichol. Operating from the airfield at Muharraq in Bahrain, their target was the Iraqi airfield of Ar Rumalah

Country of Origin: Iraq

Date: 1991

Location: Nichol Family (By kind permission of John Nichol)

John Nichol (top) with other Tornado aircrew following their release from captivity after the First Gulf War of 1991. (via John Nichol)

South West, but during their run-in to attack they were shot down by a surface-to-air missile.

Nichol later described the experience like being hit by an express train. One moment they had been skimming just above the ground at 600mph (965km/h), then bang – they were falling like a leaf. With the Tornado on fire, Peters and Nichol had no option other than to eject, and just seconds later they were on the ground, in the desert and all alone. Deep inside enemy territory, they were never going to be able to get far and both were soon captured by Iraqi troops from the airfield they had just been attacking.

Only those who have been captured and held prisoner by a regime such as Saddam Hussein's Iraq at that time can know what it feels like during those initial uncertain moments of captivity. Whether they would live or die would remain to be seen, but the punishment started from the outset. Their captors wanted to know certain information and they seemed determined to try to get it. Over the following days, the interrogation continued in many forms, before Peters and Nichol were paraded on national television for all to see. With an AK47 assault rifle pointed at their heads, the two RAF officers, both under duress, were individually forced in front of the camera. The effects of the Gulf War were now there for everyone at home to see, provoking worldwide condemnation and leaving one of the enduring images of the war.

Having been forced in front of the cameras, Peters and Nichol were thrown chained and blindfolded back into their cells. There then followed a period when they merely existed as prisoners of war. They were being held at Abu Ghraib, a prison complex to the west of Baghdad, and the next seven weeks were punctured by isolation, fear, boredom and beatings. Then suddenly it was all over. The conflict had come to an end and they were to be allowed to go home. Within days, Peters and Nichol were reunited with their families and friends. Their ordeal was over but the memories will never go away.

The RAF was at the forefront of the UK's contribution to Desert Shield and Desert Storm, with more than 7,000 personnel directly involved from bases in the Gulf and with more than 6,000 sorties flown – the largest number mounted by any nation except the United States. Not only were the Tornado GR1s heavily involved, air operations were also flown by Tornado GR1As (a reconnaissance variant), Buccaneers, Jaguars, Tornado F3s and Nimrods, all supported by air-to-air refuelling tankers, transport aircraft and helicopters.

The Tornado GR1s had flown more than 1,500 sorties, during which weapons such as the ALARM (air-launched anti-radiation missile) was used for the first time in action with great success. However, success had come at a cost. Six GR1s were lost in action with the loss of five lives but in relation to what had been achieved, these losses were remarkably low.

John Nichol left the RAF in 1996 after fifteen years of service. He has since become a broadcaster, journalist, author and motivational speaker. The jacket shown here was on loan to the Imperial War Museum where it was on display for a number of years, but is now back with Nichol at his family home.

91

The National Memorial to the Few

THIS QUITE STUNNING image, captured by Tom Dolezal and titled 'Sunrise', is of the National Memorial to the Few at Capel-le-Ferne in Kent, atop the famous White Cliffs and overlooking the English Channel towards France.

The memorial is dedicated to the memory of the men who fought during the Battle of Britain. It was the vision of Wing Commander Geoffrey Page DSO DFC & Bar, who had served as a 20-year-old Hurricane pilot during the battle and, in August 1940, had been shot down and baled out into the sea suffering from terrible burns. After lengthy treatment at the Queen Victoria Hospital by a team of plastic surgeons led by Archie McIndoe, Page went on to become a wing leader and after the war became a founding member of the Guinea Pig Club. Years later, and having realised there was no memorial to his comrades who had flown with Fighter Command during the Battle of Britain, Page was determined that The Few should be remembered. The Battle of Britain Memorial Trust was established and fundraising began, with Page's dream eventually realised on 9 July 1993 when HM Queen Elizabeth The Queen Mother opened the National Memorial to the Few at Capel-le-Ferne.

The seated airman looking out to sea across the English Channel is quite moving through its simplicity. Surrounded by the badges of the Allied squadrons and other units that took part in the Battle of Britain, it was designed by Harry Gray. The site of the memorial was chosen because of its association with both world wars – first as a mooring station for airships during 1914–18 and then as a site for a gun battery during the Second World

Country of Origin:
UK
Date: 1993
Location:
Capel-le-Ferne,
Folkestone, Kent
(© Tom Dolezal by
kind permission
of the Battle of
Britain Memorial
Trust)

War. It is also situated in the part of the country where most of the heavy aerial fighting during the summer of 1940 had taken place. This area between Dover and Folkestone was known to The Few as 'Hellfire Corner'.

Geoffrey Page died in August 2000, shortly after attending the Memorial Day marking the sixtieth anniversary of the Battle of Britain. In his memory, the starboard wing of the Wing Building, a dedicated education resource for schools, is now named the Geoffrey Page Centre. The National Memorial to the Few is a truly marvellous and quite stunning memorial, with Memorial Day at Capel-le-Ferne always a special day.

The National Memorial to the Few at Capel-le-Ferne in Kent is a truly marvellous and quite stunning memorial.

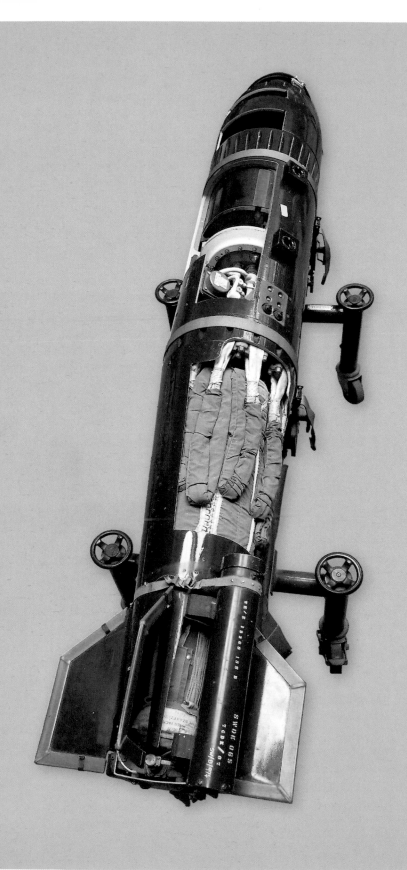

92

WE177

SHOWN HERE IS WE177, the last nuclear bomb in service with the RAF and the last tactical nuclear weapon deployed by the UK. It was finally withdrawn in 1998 after thirty years of service with the RAF.

The origins of WE177 date back to the early 1960s when the American decision to cancel its Skybolt air-launched ballistic missile left the UK with an enormous problem. The RAF was to have received Skybolt for its V-bombers, and this would have been the basis of the UK's nuclear deterrent, but with the programme cancelled it was decided the US would provide the UK with Polaris missiles for its Royal Navy submarines instead.

The political decision to opt for Polaris and hand responsibility for the UK's strategic nuclear deterrent to the Royal Navy was not without its critics within the RAF, particularly because the decision implied the credibility of Bomber Command's deterrent would decline until 1970 when Polaris was due to become operational. This left a capability gap that would last several years, and so the decision was made to provide the RAF's strategic bombers with a suitable nuclear weapon that could be delivered at low level, as an interim solution until Polaris was up and running.

The interim solution was WE177, a range of British tactical and strategic nuclear bombs adapted from the original version of the weapon (a boosted fission weapon designated WE177A) to produce a high-yield interim strategic weapon.

With its tail fin, WE177A was just over 9ft (2.8m) long and weighed just over 600lb (280kg). There were two further versions. The adapted version, a thermonuclear weapon designated WE177B, required a longer and heavier

Country of Origin:
UK
Date: 1966
Location:
Boscombe Down
Aviation Collection,
Old Sarum Airfield
Museum, Wiltshire
(By kind
permission of
the Boscombe
Down Aviation
Collection)

bomb casing to the original, while a further development of the weapon, designated WE177C, used a new warhead in a B-casing and was then ballasted to have identical weight and ballistics as the WE177B. Otherwise, the external measurements of the B and C versions were the same as the WE177A, although they both weighed more than half as much again as the A.

The first version to be fully deployed was the WE177B, which was delivered to the RAF in 1966. This was followed three years later by the WE177A, first delivered to the Royal Navy and then, in 1971, to the RAF, after there had been delays in the production of its warhead. All three types of WE177 – the A, B and C – could be delivered by fixed-wing strike aircraft and all could be parachute retarded. In the case of the WE177A in its anti-submarine mode, it could be operated as a depth charge by the RAF's Nimrod and Royal Navy helicopters.

More than 300 WE177s are believed to have been built and throughout its time with the RAF it could be carried by several different aircraft types, including the Canberra, Victor, Vulcan, Buccaneer, Jaguar and Tornado, using a variety of delivery methods.

Shown here is a sectioned WE177A, one of only two inert examples of its kind that was used for instructional purposes. It is externally identical to the operational round but did not contain any fissile materials, explosives or other hazardous components. This rare example is part of the Boscombe Down Aviation Collection and is on display at the Old Sarum Airfield Museum.

93

Chinook

A WORKHORSE OF the RAF for the past thirty-plus years has been the very capable and extremely versatile Chinook helicopter. Based on the American Boeing CH-47, the RAF's Chinooks have operated in many diverse environments – ranging from the arctic to the jungle to the desert – where they have provided heavy-lift support and transport for all parts of the British armed forces.

The Chinook can carry more than fifty troops or up to 10 tons of freight. Since its introduction into RAF service in 1980, its many theatres of operations have included the Falklands, the Gulf, the Balkans, Sierra Leone and, most recently, Iraq and Afghanistan.

The operations in Iraq and Afghanistan saw some of the largest deployments of British forces since the Second World War. In 2003 the RAF formed part of the UK's military contingency preparations in relation to Iraq. As part of Operation Telic (the name under which all the UK's operations were to be conducted), the initial air component numbered around 100 aircraft and twenty-seven support helicopters, operating from air bases throughout the region. In all, some 7,000 RAF personnel, including mobilised reservists, were deployed to support the operation. After the invasion of Iraq in March 2003, until the end of the main mission in 2009, a roulement system was put in place – Telic II, Telic III etc., with the last being Telic XIII – although the last British forces did not leave until 2011 when the UK's military operation in Iraq officially ended.

Country of Origin:
USA
Date: 1980
Location: RAF
Odiham, Hampshire
(Crown Copyright
2014)

Meanwhile, RAF personnel were also involved in Operation Herrick, the name given to all British operations in Afghanistan under its contribution to the UN-authorised and NATO-led International Security

A Chinook firing flares over Afghanistan. (Crown Copyright 2015)

Assistance Force. Conducted from 2002 until the end of combat operations in 2014 (Herrick XX), the conflict in Afghanistan was a costly one, with official government figures showing the loss of more than 450 British military personnel. It was arguably this conflict above all others that saw the British public take the Chinook (and its crews) to their hearts for its emergency response role in support of British troops on the ground.

The Chinook crew normally consists of two pilots and two crewmen, although these can be supplemented by other specialists depending on the task. There have been several RAF variants of this magnificent helicopter, the first being the Chinook HC1 (Helicopter Cargo 1) and the latest being the HC6, with upgrades including an increase in range and endurance, updated avionics including a new cockpit display system (allowing a full low-level night capability when operated with night vision goggles) and mission management system, and a new digital automatic flight control system.

The Chinook can be armed with two M134 six-barrelled mini-guns, one in each front side window, and an M60D machine gun on the ramp. It is also well equipped with defensive aids and has a radar-warning receiver, an ultra-violet and Doppler missile approach warning system, infrared jammers and chaff and flare dispensers.

Since its introduction into service, more than fifty Chinooks have been built for the RAF. Three squadrons are currently based at RAF Odiham in Hampshire. The Chinook has, without doubt, been a great servant of the RAF and no book about the RAF's 100 years would be complete without its inclusion.

94

Combat Body Armour

TWO OPERATIONS DOMINATED the early part of the twenty-first century: Iraq and Afghanistan. During these operations, RAF personnel were first introduced to a specialist piece of protective equipment known as combat body armour (CBA), something that was previously more familiar to those in the army.

Although a relatively new piece of equipment as far as most RAF personnel were concerned, the issuing of CBA was not new in concept. The British Army had been wearing flak jackets in Northern Ireland for many years and then during the 1990s – for example during the First Gulf War and for operations in the former Yugoslavia – lightweight CBA had been more widely introduced after it had been realised that anything up to two-thirds of casualties on the battlefield were caused by low-velocity fragments.

Simply put, CBA is designed to provide personnel with ballistic protection without causing too much discomfort or preventing them from performing their primary duty. During the early stages of operations in Iraq, CBA was often borrowed or passed around between individuals as there was not enough to go around, but harsh lessons learned soon led to more equipment being procured and advances being made in its design. For example, the protective plates that had been designed to absorb the energy of high-velocity rounds or shrapnel were considered too small, and so this led to the introduction of the Osprey armour system in 2006, which was subsequently issued to personnel serving in Afghanistan.

The combat body armour shown is the waistcoat-style cover, in desert shade two-colour DPM (destructive pattern material), as worn in Iraq during the early years of Operation Telic. With its protective plates it weighs nearly 4.7kg (10lb).

Country of Origin: UK
Date: 2003
Location: Historical Training Facility, RAF Leeming, North Yorkshire (By kind permission of the Station Commander RAF Leeming)

THE RAF IN 100 OBJECTS

95

Royal Air Forces Association Remembrance Garden

KNOWN SIMPLY TO those in the service as RAFA, the Royal Air Forces Association is a membership organisation and registered charity that provides welfare support to the RAF Family, which includes all serving and ex-serving personnel and their dependants. To be eligible for welfare support, for either themselves or those who depend upon them, service personnel need to have served a minimum of just one day in the RAF.

The origins of RAFA go back to 1929 when the idea of forming a single organisation dedicated to the welfare of serving and ex-serving personnel was first discussed. By the following year a provisional committee had been set up. It was then called the Comrades of the Royal Air Force Association with the first meeting taking place in London. Air Ministry support soon followed and the Air Council then recognised the organisation with Lord Trenchard accepting the Presidency. In 1936, HM King George VI gave his patronage and the association has been honoured with royal patronage ever since. Then, after merging with the Women's Royal Air Force Old Comrades Association during the Second World War, the organisation's name was changed to the Royal Air Forces Association.

Country of Origin:
UK
Date: 2009
Location:
National Memorial
Arboretum,
Alrewas,
Staffordshire

After the war, RAFA's numbers grew rapidly at around 10,000 a month. By 1947 membership had peaked at 200,000 members with 565 branches throughout the UK (administered over nine separate areas, each with its own headquarters) as well as overseas. Since then, RAFA has adapted to an ever-changing society and its welfare

needs. At the turn of the century it underwent a complete reorganisation and relocated its Central Headquarters to Leicestershire, in the heart of the country, and amalgamated its areas into five.

In recent years RAFA has provided much needed support to those who served in the Second World War as well as giving assistance to veterans who served in Korea, the Middle East, the Falklands and most recently in Iraq and Afghanistan. RAFA continues to operate a network of 422 branches worldwide and has a membership of over 63,500. More than eighty years after it first began, RAFA is still making a huge difference to the lives of former service personnel and their families. Its work is funded by the generosity of its members and through vital donations from the public as well as from business. Whether it is to help an injured member of the service get back on their feet, or a young child missing their parent away on operations overseas, or a veteran needing someone to talk to, RAFA is always there to help all generations of RAF service personnel and their families. They do it exceedingly well.

The Royal Air Forces Association Remembrance Garden is a marvellous tribute to this wonderful organisation. It is located near the Armed Forces Memorial at the National Memorial Arboretum in Alrewas, Staffordshire. Opened in 2009 the garden is dedicated to all those who selflessly devoted their lives to their country, regardless of the length of service.

RAFA's Remembrance Garden at the National Memorial Arboretum at Alrewas in Staffordshire is a marvellous tribute to this wonderful organisation.

96

158 Squadron Memorial

SQUADRON MEMORIALS PLAY a huge part in helping to preserve the history of the RAF and the legacy of its people, but few, if any, capture the loss and emotiveness of war better than the 158 Squadron Memorial at Lissett in the East Riding of Yorkshire. Designed by Peter Naylor, this award-winning design presents an outstanding and moving tribute to those who lost their lives with the squadron during the Second World War.

RAF Lissett opened in 1943 as an airfield of No. 4 Group Bomber Command. 158 Squadron was to be its only resident unit, operating the four-engine Halifax bomber until the end of the war, after which the land reverted to agriculture. Today, part of the former airfield is a wind farm and this wonderful memorial shows just how an energy company, a land owner and a squadron association have all worked together, with a common aim, to educate people about the existence of the airfield and the role 158 Squadron played during the Second World War.

The design of the memorial was the result of a competition. Funded by Novera Energy as part of the site's development under the slogan 'Propellers Back at Lissett', local artists were asked to submit their entries; the winning design being that of Peter Naylor from Beverley.

Naylor's design consists of a seven-man bomber crew, 8ft (2.4m) tall and crafted in 0.6in (15mm) weathering steel and raised on a small knoll, walking towards the viewer and heading east on yet another mission. The figures are in silhouette – revealing their flying jackets, boots and parachutes – and so, when viewed from the other side, they appear to be returning to the airfield. Only their faces are cut out in the steel to show the mix of emotions running through the young men. The 851 names of those killed and

Country of Origin: UK

Date: 2009

Location: Lissett, East Riding of Yorkshire

(© Peter Naylor)

the words 'And for all who served with 158 Squadron' are etched into the bodies so that the memorial also stands for those who survived the war but, in most cases, have now passed on. The names are placed randomly, not alphabetically nor in columns, to reflect the haphazard nature of death. The top of the knoll contains the seven-link chain emblem of 158 Squadron, and the name block at the start of the path leading up to the memorial shows the squadron motto 'Strength in Unity'.

The memorial can be seen on Gransmoor Road at Lissett, overlooking the former wartime airfield. It took a year to complete and was unveiled on 16 May 2009 by Air Marshal Sir John Curtiss KCB KBE, who had served with 158 Squadron during the Second World War.

Peter Naylor is well known for producing a wide variety of work in various media. In 2010 his design of the 158 Squadron Memorial won the Marsh Award for Excellence in Public Sculpture, the UK's most prestigious award for public sculpture.

97

Bomber Command Memorial

ON 28 JUNE 2012, the Lancaster of the Battle of Britain Memorial Flight flew low over Green Park in London to release thousands of poppies in tribute to 55,573 who lost their lives while serving with RAF Bomber Command during the Second World War. It was the official unveiling of the Bomber Command Memorial and marked the end of a journey that had started more than four years before.

In 2008 the Bomber Command Association, led by its President, Marshal of the Royal Air Force Sir Michael Beetham, joined forces with the Heritage Foundation, which had commissioned more than a hundred memorials and plaques to famous Britons, to provide a permanent national memorial for those who had lost their lives while serving with Bomber Command during the Second World War. To discuss the proposal, the first meeting was held at the RAF Club in London, after which the campaign soon gathered strong support from the leaders of all three main political parties. The idea also gained huge public support following an appeal for funding to build the memorial. As well as substantial donations by many individuals, donations came from the public all over the world, including contributions from many wartime veterans of Bomber Command.

The result was the magnificent RAF Bomber Command Memorial in Green Park, designed by architect Liam O'Connor and built using Portland stone. At the heart of the memorial is the 9ft-high (2.7m) bronze sculpture of a Bomber Command crew, designed by the sculptor Philip Jackson to look as though the crew have just returned from a bombing mission and left their aircraft. Within the memorial the space is open to the sky, designed to allow

Country of Origin: UK
Date: 2012
Location: Green Park, London

light to fall directly onto the sculptures of the aircrew. The scale of the sculpture means that visitors can always see the profile of the sculpture against the sky above them, day and night.

The memorial was unveiled by HM Queen Elizabeth II in front of 6,000 dignitaries, veterans, and family members, after which the Lancaster scattered the poppies. The RAF Benevolent Fund is proud and privileged to be the official guardian of the memorial, but with no government funding it relies on the kind generosity of its supporters to help with its upkeep.

Every year millions visit Green Park to enjoy its forty-plus acres of mature trees and grassland next to Buckingham Palace, and this long overdue memorial will serve as a lasting reminder of the huge sacrifice made by those who served with Bomber Command during the Second World War.

98

Red One's Bone Dome

THE WORLD-FAMOUS RAF Aerobatic Team, the Red Arrows, one of the world's premier aerobatic display teams, need little or no introduction. Shown here to represent their outstanding contribution to the RAF for more than fifty years is Red One's bone dome, impressively captured by the team's photographer.

The team has come a long way since 1964 when the RAF decided to amalgamate its display teams into one. The new team was given the name Red Arrows. Its name was partly taken from a previous RAF display team, the record-breaking Black Arrows, which had formed in 1956 with the Hawker Hunter and had achieved a world-record feat by looping twenty-two aircraft in formation at Farnborough in 1958; a record that remains unbroken to this day. The colour red was a tribute to another RAF display team, the Red Pelicans, four Jet Provosts from the Central Flying School (the pelican being the mascot for CFS), while the aircraft chosen for the new team, the Folland Gnat, had previously been used by the Yellowjacks display team.

At the time the Red Arrows was formed, the team was based at RAF Fairford in Gloucestershire. Flying a formation of seven aircraft, its first official display was a media event held at nearby RAF Little Rissington on 6 May 1965, while the first public display was at RAF Biggin Hill nine days later. By the end of its first display season the team had performed an appropriate number of shows – sixty-five.

In 1968 the team increased to nine aircraft. The Red Arrows were by this point based at RAF Kemble in Gloucestershire, and by the start of the 1980 display season they had performed well over 1,200 displays. The ageing Gnat was then replaced by the RAF's new jet trainer, the

Country of Origin: UK
Date: 2016
Location: RAF Scampton, Lincolnshire (Crown Copyright by kind permission of the RAF Aerobatic Team Red Arrows and the Station Commander RAF Scampton)

The Red Arrows. (Crown Copyright 2008)

BAE Systems Hawk, and three years later the team moved to RAF Scampton in Lincolnshire, which, apart from five years at the end of the 1990s when the team moved to RAF Cranwell, has been home to the Red Arrows ever since.

Over the years, the Red Arrows have been seen at some of the UK's highest-profile public events, such as the opening ceremony of the London Olympics in 2012, watched by an estimated global television audience of one billion people, and at other major sporting and national events; for example, at the Queen's Golden and Diamond Jubilees. By the time the team celebrated its fiftieth anniversary the Red Arrows had completed more than 4,500 displays, including many overseas as part of official tours.

The team celebrated their fiftieth display season in 2015. A new paint scheme was revealed, incorporating the union flag to emphasise the Red Arrows' role as national ambassadors for the UK and to promote the best of British, as well as assisting in recruiting to the armed forces.

The Red Arrows have now flown more than 4,700 displays in fifty-six countries worldwide. The displays – of which there are three different types depending on the weather conditions – are seen by millions of people every summer. These displays are the result of nearly eight months of intensive training each year, supported by a large team of engineers and support staff. All nine pilots have fast-jet backgrounds and have previously served on front-line squadrons, and once they have completed their three years with the Red Arrows they return to their RAF duties.

Red One's bone dome, shown here, belongs to the 2016 team leader, Squadron Leader David Montenegro; a former Hawk instructor and Tornado F3 pilot. The visor cover clearly shows his rank and name, and position in the team's classic Diamond Nine trademark formation. Like other team leaders before him, Montenegro had previously completed a tour with the team earlier in his career, which had culminated in his role of Red Six, the team's Synchro Leader.

Much has changed since the Reds first formed, often because of Defence cutbacks. Thankfully for the British public, though, and the RAF for that matter, the Red Arrows have always managed to survive. They represent the speed, agility, and precision of the RAF and remain the public face of the service. And they do it exceptionally well!

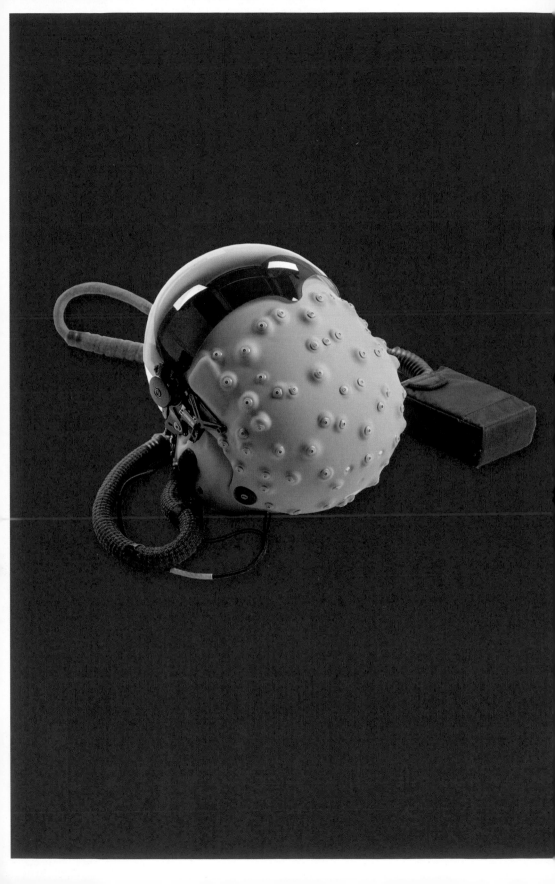

99

Typhoon Helmet Mounted Symbology System

Country of Origin:
UK
Date: The Present
and the Future
Location: RAF
Coningsby,
Lincolnshire
(Crown Copyright
by kind permission
of the Station
Commander RAF
Coningsby)

THE HELMET MOUNTED Symbology System (HMSS) shown here, otherwise known as Striker, provides today's fighter pilot with exceptional tracking technology integrated with a visor-projected system and is worn by pilots flying the RAF's latest combat aircraft, the single-seat Typhoon FGR4 – a highly capable and extremely agile multi-role combat aircraft.

Developed by the UK, Germany, Italy and Spain, the Eurofighter Typhoon entered service with the RAF in 2003. The first tranche of fifty-three aircraft were air-to-air capable only and at that stage, 17(R) Squadron, which had been given the responsibility of evaluating the new aircraft and its integration into operational service, was operating from Warton in Lancashire; alongside the BAE Systems factory where the new aircraft were being assembled. Two years later the first Typhoon squadron formed at RAF Coningsby in Lincolnshire, and two years after that the Typhoon F2 took over responsibility for the UK's air defence. By 2008, the aircraft had an air-to-ground capability as the Typhoon GR4 (the T3 was a two-seat trainer variant). By then, the second tranche of deliveries (sixty-seven aircraft) had begun, while Tranche 3 (forty more aircraft) will eventually replace the Tranche 1 aircraft due to be phased out of service, leaving the RAF with 107 Typhoons in service until 2030.

Powered by two Eurojet EJ200 engines, the Typhoon has a maximum speed of Mach 1.8 and an operating height up to 55,000ft (16,765m). Its array of weaponry enables the Typhoon to carry out a multitude of missions, ranging from the relatively benign policing of airspace to high intensity combat, and includes: advanced medium-range

air-to-air missile (AMRAAM); advanced short-range air-to-air missile (ASRAAM); Meteor (an active radar-guided beyond-visual-range air-to-air missile); Paveway IV (an advanced and highly accurate weapon using the latest Inertial Navigation and Global Positioning System technology); Storm Shadow (a long-range, stand-off, air-launched missile); and Brimstone (an advanced rocket-propelled, radar-guided weapon that can seek and destroy armoured targets at long range).

The RAF's latest combat aircraft, the Typhoon FGR4. (Crown Copyright 2016)

Being such a highly technical aircraft, the Typhoon pilot is superbly equipped for all aspects of air operations and can perform many functions by different methods; for example, using the hands-on throttle-and-stick system or by voice command. The HMSS, otherwise known as the Head Equipment Assembly (HEA), provides an excellent example of just how technically advanced the flying helmet has become. The image here clearly shows the Light Emitting Diodes (LEDs – i.e., the bumps), which are part of the Head Tracking System. Tracker Sensor Units in the aircraft cockpit detect infrared light from these LEDs and this head position tracking is important as it tells the aircraft systems where the pilot is looking, so that targets can be acquired accurately. The HEA has a custom-fit protective liner (CFPL) with a laser-scanning device used to measure the head profile of each pilot, so that each pilot has a specific CFPL that is not interchangeable with others.

The flying helmet is no longer a device for simply providing protection, suppressing noise and holding the oxygen mask and communications components, it must now provide the pilot with so much else. And all this while keeping comfort in mind and the overall weight of the helmet down, which includes ensuring the weight is distributed correctly, to reduce the neck loads, particularly important when the pilot is performing high-g manoeuvres.

With display technologies continuing to evolve, BAE Systems has already built on the success of Striker that has been successfully deployed on the Typhoon force by unveiling its next generation Striker II Helmet Mounted Display (HMD); a fully digital solution that provides the combat pilot with exceptional night vision and high-precision target tracking and engagement technology, as well as superior situational awareness and mission effectiveness. Who knows what will come next?

100

Reaper MQ9A Remotely Piloted Air System

Left: A RAF Reaper pictured at Kandahar airfield prior to a mission over Afghanistan. (Crown Copyright 2010)

Country of Origin: USA
Date: 2007
Location: RAF Waddington, Lincolnshire (Crown Copyright by kind permission of the Station Commander RAF Waddington)

AND SO WE come to the last object of the book – the Reaper MQ9A Remotely Piloted Air System (RPAS). It is an object that not only shows just how far the RAF has come in its first 100 years but also shows how the use of unmanned aerial vehicles and remotely piloted air systems have grown in importance. They have, quite simply, changed the thinking behind the use of air power; now and for the future.

The Reaper is an all-weather medium-to-high altitude long endurance (MALE) remotely piloted aircraft designed for the ISR role (Intelligence, Surveillance, and Reconnaissance). It is 36ft long (11m) and has a wingspan of 66ft (20.1m). Powered by a Honeywell TPE 331-10 turbo-prop engine, it has a maximum speed of 250 knots (462km/h) – although it cruises at around 100 knots (185km/h) – and a maximum altitude of 50,000ft (15,240m), although, again, its operating altitude is typically half that. Its range and endurance is remarkable, with anything up to 3,682 miles (5,925km) or twenty-four hours airborne possible.

The Reaper's impressive array of surveillance sensors makes it an increasingly vital system alongside traditional manned platforms and provides real-time video imagery to commanders on the ground. Furthermore, because Reaper is pilot-commanded, it offers commanders the opportunity to deal with fleeting targets that pop-up in the battlespace and so it can also be used to carry out ground attack missions if required, such as by providing forces on the ground with close air support. There are six hard points under the wings to allow a mix of weaponry, depending on its mission, up to a maximum payload of

4,200lb (1,905kg); a typical example being 2 x GBU-12 500lb laser-guided bombs and 4 x AGM-114 Hellfire air-to-surface missiles. A colour camera in the nose provides a forward view to assist in-flight control and for take-off and landing, while an infrared sensor, a colour/monochrome daylight electro-optical TV and an image-intensified TV provide the main imagery. The Reaper also has a laser rangefinder/designator, to precisely designate targets for laser-guided munitions, and a synthetic aperture radar, which will enable JDAM (Joint Direct Attack Munitions) and GMTI (Ground Moving Target Indicator) to provide its all-weather capability. The Reaper can also provide geographic location information to commanders on the ground, or to other systems capable of employing GPS (Global Positioning System) guided weapons.

Although the Reaper is a remotely piloted system, the rules of engagement for weapon release are no different than those used for manned combat aircraft, with any engagement usually authorised by a Forward Air Controller or Joint Terminal Attack Controller who will have been observing the target on the ground or from a Land Force headquarters.

Procured by the Ministry of Defence as an urgent operational requirement, the Reaper was first introduced into operational service in 2007 in support of coalition forces in Afghanistan. Ten UK Reapers flew some 50,000 hours over Afghanistan, gathering vital intelligence in support of Afghan, UK and International Security Assistance Force troops on the ground. Launched from an airfield in-theatre, the operational mission was flown from a ground control station by a pilot and a sensor operator of 39 Squadron, aided by a non-aircrew Mission Coordinator, based at Creech Air Force Base in the United States. This was achieved by using an advanced secure satellite communications system to operate the aircraft over the horizon. Then, once the operational mission was over, control of the Reaper was handed back to an in-theatre crew for landing.

39 Squadron continues to train and operate alongside its American counterparts as part of the Combined Joint Predator Task Force. During 2013 the RAF began operating the Reaper from the UK, with 13 Squadron at RAF Waddington becoming the RAF's first UK-based

Reaper squadron. Although the two Reaper squadrons both have RAF number plates, they are established with personnel from across the armed forces and supported by contractors.

For transportation, the Reaper system can be disassembled into its main components and loaded onto a transport aircraft for rapid deployment anywhere in the world. Since the withdrawal from Afghanistan, it has been deployed to the Middle East in support of ongoing operations against the so-called Islamic State. The Reaper and other such platforms will no doubt continue to play an important part in support of the UK's Defence policy as the RAF enters its next 100 years.

Acknowledgements

A book such as this would not be possible without the help of so many people, many of whom are former RAF colleagues. Firstly, I would like to thank Air Vice-Marshal Nigel Baldwin for agreeing to write the Foreword and for his kind words. Secondly, as for the 100 objects, please note this book is not, nor is it intended to be, an official RAF history, nor does it represent the views of any of those serving today. I have, nonetheless, been privileged to gain access to many RAF stations and other organisations during the past couple of years and so I would like to thank all who have made this possible, although many of the serving personnel will have now moved elsewhere. Here goes. From the Ministry of Defence – Squadron Leader Ian Moore (DDC Strategy Brand Manager, SO2); Air Historical Branch (RAF) – Graham Day (AHB 5); HQ Air Command – Air Vice-Marshal Jonathan Chaffey (RAF Chaplain-in-Chief) and Jay Myers (Air Command Media & Communications); RAF College Cranwell – Air Commodore Dawn McCafferty (Commandant Air Cadets), Group Captain Catherine Coton (GC Recruiting & Selection), Squadron Leader Steve Peters (OC Aptitude, HQ R&S), Flight Lieutenant Alex Ritchie (SO3 Aptitude), Liz Bamford (PA to GC R&S), Hazel Crozier (Curator, College Hall), Tim Pierce (RAFC Library), Denise Parker-Housby (Media & Comms, HQ Air Cadets) and Amy Zwaan (Media & Comms Web Journalist, HQ Air Cadets); RAF Coningsby – Group Captain Jez Attridge (Station Commander), Wing Commander Mark Tillyard (OC Eng & Logs Wg), Squadron Leader Wilf Martin (OC Fwd Eng Sqn), Flight Lieutenant Andy King (OC Survival Equipment Flight), Flying Officer Dean Thomas (Station Adjutant), Senior Aircraftman Chris Ellis (Photographic Section), Jim Robinson (Media & Comms) and Yvonne Masters (Dep Media & Comms Officer); RAF Halton – Group Captain Adrian Burns (Station Commander), Wing Commander Ray Morley (OC Ops Plans

Wing), Min Larkin (Archivist Trenchard Museum), Francis Hanford (Trenchard Museum) and Trixie Brabner (Halton House); RAF Leeming – Squadron Leader Alfie Hall (XO 607 Sqn RAuxAF) and Lynn Dunne (MCO); RAF Linton-on-Ouse – Group Captain Ian Laing (Station Commander), Wing Commander Alan Mawby (Curator, Memorial Room), Flt Lt Mike Lumsden (MCO) and Dick Arthurs (Assistant Curator, Memorial Room); RAF Scampton – Wing Commander Mike Harrop (Station Commander), Wing Commander Martin Higgins (OC RAFAT), Andrew Morton (PRM – Red Arrows), Jo Pearson (PRO – Red Arrows), Tom Evans (Scampton Heritage Centre) and Mark Wood (Heritage Centre – Air Cadets); RAF Waddington – Group Captain Rich Barrow (Station Commander), Wing Commander Colin Owen (OC Base Support Wing), Chief Tech Craig Smith (Waddington Heritage Centre), Lindsey Askin (Media & Comms) and Chris Dean (Waddington Heritage Centre); RAF Club – Wing Commander Michael Gilbert (Chairman Art Committee), Matthew Kent (Executive Assistant) and Dan Soliman (Human Resources Assistant); RAF Historical Society – Wing Commander Colin Cummings and Wing Commander Jeff Jefford; RAF Museum – Peter Elliott (Head of Archives), Derek O'Brien (Collection Sales and Brand Licensing Executive), Vinit Mehat (Merchandising Manager), Frances Galvan (Head of Retail), Bryan Legate (Assistant Curator), Christine Kemp (Accounts Assistant) and Belinda Day (Reading Room); Battle of Britain Bunker – Chris Wren; Boscombe Down Aviation Collection – David Woollatt (Marketing Director); Imperial War Museum – Lisa Olrichs (Image Sales) and Neera (Image Sales); National Museum of Scotland – Maggie Wilson (Picture Librarian, NMS Enterprises Ltd); National Memorial to the Few – Malcolm Triggs (Go4 Marketing & Public Relations Ltd) and Tom Dolezal; Newark Air Museum – Martin Smith (Curator); Science Museum – Sophia Brothers (Image Executive), Jasmine Rodgers (Image Executive) and Justin Hobson (Image Licensing Executive); Shuttleworth Collection – Ciara Harper and Malcolm English; St Clement Danes Church – Sharon Hardwick (Church Manager) and Phillippe Daveney (Church Clerk); Tiger Moth Club – Stuart McKay (Secretary) and David Porter; Wickenby Memorial Collection – Anne Law (Curator);

and the Yorkshire Air Museum – Ian Reed (Director), Ian Richardson (Communications Manager) and Neill Watson. Families and Individuals – MRAF Sir Michael Beetham (Air Officer Hat), AVM David Brook & the Brook family (Army Book 425), Kenneth Boardman (Image of Army Book 425), Richard Black (Air Force Cross), Cecilia Cooper-Colby (Image of Air Force Cross), Peter Giles & the Giles family (Metal Standing Cross), Deborah Mitchelson (Leather Gauntlet), Les Bartlett (Flying Scarf), John Nichol (PoW Jacket, Gulf War) and Peter Naylor (158 Squadron Memorial, Lissett). If I have misspelt a name or forgotten anyone then I can only apologise. Please also note that the location of each object is correct at the time of writing, although it may have since changed.

The book also relied on so many high-quality images. Many of these are Crown Copyright and are reproduced under the Open Government Licence (v3.0) or have been provided by stations with the kind permission of the Station Commanders. Others have been provided, or permitted to be used, without charge. In this latter category, I am particularly grateful to the following: Les Bartlett; the Battle of Britain Memorial Trust; Richard Black; the Boscombe Down Aviation Centre; AVM David Brook; AVM Jonathan Chaffey; Lincolnshire Aviation Heritage Centre; RAF Linton-on-Ouse Memorial Room; the National Memorial to the Few; Peter Naylor; Newark Air Museum; David Porter; RAF Club; RAF Scampton Heritage Centre; Shuttleworth Collection; St Clement Danes; Trenchard Museum RAF Halton; RAF Waddington Heritage Centre; and the Yorkshire Air Museum. Other images, unless stated, have been kindly provided by the Air Historical Branch (RAF). Where necessary, these images have been credited or acknowledged accordingly.

Finally, I would like to say a personal thank you to those at The History Press, initially Michael Leventhal and then Chrissy McMorris for the publication that you see today.

Index

To save space, the individual marks of aircraft types are not shown in the index below. In the case of an individual being mentioned more than once and where the rank has differed, the most senior rank is shown. The abbreviations used for the ranks are those used today and, to minimise space used, post-nominals are not shown.

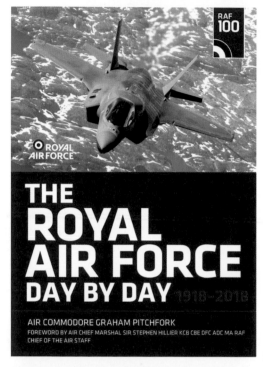

978 0 7509 7973 3

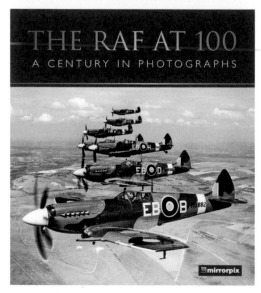

978 0 7509 8250 4

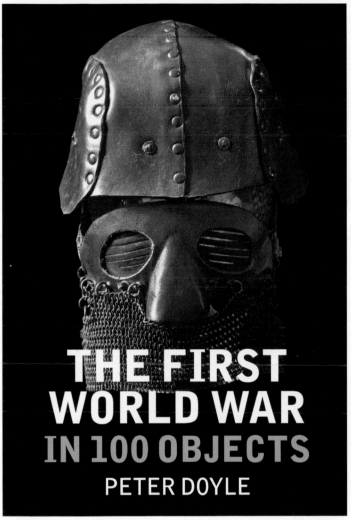

**THE FIRST
WORLD WAR
IN 100 OBJECTS**

PETER DOYLE

978 0 7509 6848 5

The destination for history
www·thehistorypress·co·uk